THE DINÉ READER

The Diné Reader

An Anthology of Navajo Literature

EDITED BY Esther G. Belin, Jeff Berglund,
Connie A. Jacobs, AND Anthony K. Webster

FOREWORD BY Sherwin Bitsui

WITH CONTRIBUTIONS BY
Jennifer Nez Denetdale AND Michael Thompson

THE UNIVERSITY OF
ARIZONA PRESS
TUCSON

The University of Arizona Press
www.uapress.arizona.edu

ISBN-13: 978-0-8165-4099-0 (paper)

Cover design by Leigh McDonald
Cover art: *With Glowing Words* by Shonto Begay
Designed and typeset by Leigh McDonald in Times New Roman 10/14 and Archetype [display]

All royalty proceeds from the book will be donated to causes that further educational endeavors to nurture future Diné writers.

The inclusion of some images in this book was made possible in part by support from the University of Texas at Austin and Anthony K. Webster.

Library of Congress Cataloging-in-Publication Data
Names: Belin, Esther G., editor. | Berglund, Jeff, editor. | Jacobs, Connie A., 1944– editor. | Webster, Anthony K., 1969– editor. | Bitsui, Sherwin, 1975– writer of foreword.
Title: The Diné reader : an anthology of Navajo literature / edited by Esther G. Belin, Jeff Berglund, Connie A. Jacobs, Anthony K. Webster foreword by Sherwin Bitsui ; with contributions by Jennifer Nez Denetdale, Michael Thompson.
Description: Tucson : University of Arizona Press, 2021. | Includes bibliographical references.
Identifiers: LCCN 2020036088 | ISBN 9780816540990 (paperback)
Subjects: LCSH: American literature—Indian authors. | Navajo literature.
Classification: LCC PS508.I5 D56 2021 | DDC 897/.26—dc23
LC record available at https://lccn.loc.gov/2020036088

Printed in the United States of America
♾This paper meets the requirements of ANSI/NISO Z39.48-1992 (Permanence of Paper).

I walk in the beauty that
binds my umbilicus
to early white dawn beginnings
to mid-season blue daylight
to evening twilight thoughts
to reflective dark, quiet remnants

I walk in the beauty that
holds creation
like an on-going shoe game
like Coyote scattering stars

—ESTHER G. BELIN

CONTENTS

FOREWORD

I OFTEN SPEAK TO NON-NAVAJO AUDIENCES that are little informed about Navajo history and culture. Some of these audience members may have gained some idea of Navajo culture by studying brief chapters in academic textbooks or online literature. They may also have heard about how our language, Diné bizaad, was used as code to help the United States and its allies defeat the Japanese in World War II. They may also have some understanding of us through our award-winning and much-sought-after textiles and silver and turquoise jewelry. More often, non-Navajo and non-Native people mention they've learned about Navajo culture through books by detective mystery writer Tony Hillerman (a non-Navajo). Hillerman's stories frequently include Navajo characters and criminal situations that arise in the Four Corners area near or on Dinétah. I'm always stunned by such misunderstanding; how regularly Navajo people are misrepresented and wrongly portrayed in the world. It's also baffling how such books can mislead audiences to assume that a Navajo person authored those works. During these exchanges, I offer names of many of the Navajo authors included in this anthology. These are the voices they should be reading if they want to understand the worldview and story of our people.

On the other hand, I've met young Navajo college students attending universities throughout the United States who are surprised to discover that Navajos have been writing books for decades—Blackhorse Mitchell's *Miracle Hill* was published decades ago, in 1967. The students, excited about stories and poems that reflect their own experiences, ask for the names of Navajo authors and their book titles with hopes of finding them in their local bookstores and libraries. Such works invoke memories of their families, reservation life, and cultural concerns. They also capture the red rock panoramas of their homeland, where stories and everyday life are perpetually intertwined. Each book contains an entire world and gives voice to Navajo thought and worldview with the utmost care and respect for language and ancestral knowledge.

Navajo poets and writers often refer to Diné bizaad as the source for their written work. Navajo Nation Poet Laureate Laura Tohe writes, "Diné bizaad is medicine for healing, was used as a secret code during World War II by the Navajo Code Talkers, and has blessed me in writing poetry, stories, essays, and now writing librettos for operas. It has grounded me to Navajo spirituality and community."

Whether Diné bizaad was forcibly repressed at boarding schools, or because a generation of traumatized parents were convinced not to teach their children, these writers rediscover it in their written work. The layers of each line, image, or word carry not only personal story but the entirety of a people's history and worldview. These stories restore memory and reconnect a people, some of whom have moved beyond the sacred mountains to work and live in distant cities. These stories are doorways opening inward, back into the world that is always home.

This anthology will aid in making known to readers the incredible diversity Navajo literature offers. These poems and stories are as vast and dynamic as the land on which they were imagined and created. The editors of this anthology have presented the works in a format that honors culture. They have provided interviews with the authors and resources for teachers to aid in the teaching of these works, elucidating the cultural context to bring greater depth to the reader's understanding. Elizabeth Woody, in her interview, gracefully sums up the thesis of this collection: "I write from the core belief the word of our ancestors still reverberates in our present. It is a whisper in the grasses moving in all directions." With the publication of this book, the whisper has grown louder and cannot be ignored any longer. The songs and memories of our ancestors continue to reverberate in these contemporary stories and poems; they bridge worlds and restore beauty within all things.

—*Sherwin Bitsui*

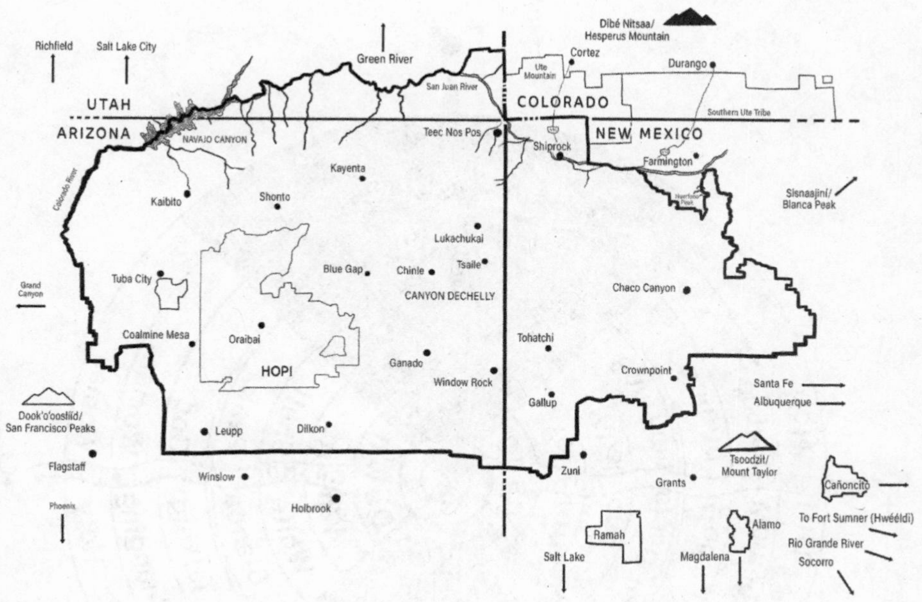

Map of the Navajo Nation and Dinétah. Credit: Sierra Edd

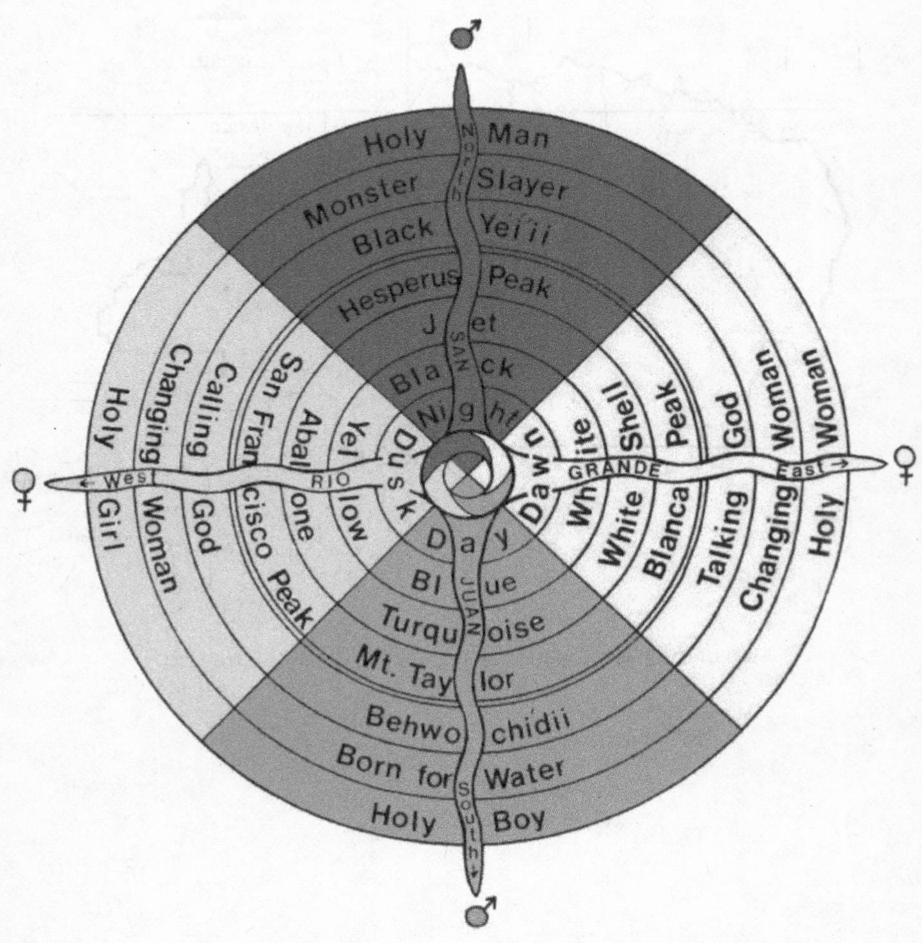

Diné Directional Knowledge and Symbolic Associations
(reprinted with permission of Harold Carey Jr.).

THE DINÉ READER

INTRODUCTION

Dear Reader,

This book is for you—the spirit and strength of Diné storytelling has always been the heart of this project. The poetry and prose of this book emerged into being by way of prayers from our ancestors—shimásani doo shicheii, doo—all The People who continue to be present, in our presence among us. These writers are from among The People—they reflect The People—the glittering presence of water, moisture, the breath of who we are and how we live in what is called the twenty-first century of existence.

Time immemorial, jiní. Time immemorial is where these stories transpired—carrying constellation chill and sparkle, drama and tragedy, hope and laughter. As you read these writings, accept them as an offering, bundles of stories and songs to lighten your journey. They are an offering of reunification, like the return of a child from boarding school. They are a surviving remnant, a time capsule gently crafted together. They are a roadmap, documenting, and redefining, home.

You are now invited to read, to learn from the sacred and powerful creative force of words, and, more specifically, the woven presence of Diné bizaad. You are invited to celebrate the legacy of The People.

Esther G. Belin

≑

The development of written stories among The People directly correlates to The People's history with Western, formal versions of education. After the Diné were freed from the physical imprisonment of Bosque Redondo, they were subject to the imprisonment of language and thought by means of government-operated schools. Yet, through the medium of poetry, many young Diné were able to release their thoughts, reflecting The People's worldview using the English language. Diné continue to use poetry and prose to write, document, release, and revitalize their stories. Found within the earliest published book of Diné poems, *The Colored Land: A Navajo Indian Book*, is an array of poetry and prose interspersed with illustrations, photographs, and general facts about The People. Published in 1937 and edited by Rose K. Brandt, the supervisor of elementary education, Office of Indian Affairs, the book's introduction describes how "making a poem was a joyful enterprise for the group of Navajo children whose joint authorship gave us these charming verses so manifestly Navajo in feeling and expression." And although there are many unanswered questions about the project itself and the unethical context in which the Diné children were being educated at boarding schools, either by force or coercion, these poems give voice to the enduring persistence of core Diné values and their presence filtered through the medium of English. Consider this poem, "Unity":

First
I'm on my horse,
We move,
Galloping, galloping
Together we move,
Now
I'm part of my horse.

Whether an oversight or intentional omission, the authors are not given credit; they are identified only as "a group of Navajo children at Tohatchi, New Mexico," and the illustrations are attributed to "sixth grade children at the Santa Fe school." The Tohatchi boarding school, established in 1904, was among the first boarding schools on the reservation. When reading the poems by these students, readers catch a glimpse of their take on school; in this seemingly simple poem of symbolism and imagery, their voices penetrate—clear and free:

IF

If I were a pony,
A spotted pinto pony,
A racing, running pony,
I would run away from school,
And I'd gallop on the mesa
And I'd eat on the mesa,
And I'd sleep on the mesa,
And I'd never think of school.

Little did these early writers know that their writing would begin the legacy of written Diné literature and poetics. All of the voices in *The Diné Reader: An Anthology of Navajo Literature* are symbolically united in a refusal to forget the powerful, creative intelligence of the unnamed child poets who began the rich and unforgettable legacy of a written Diné literature.

Later, in the 1960s, the Bureau of Indian Affairs (BIA) schools, through their creative writing project, encouraged writing by young Diné students as a way to teach them English. One BIA school of significance is the Institute of American Indian Arts (IAIA) in Santa Fe, New Mexico. IAIA opened in 1962 as a high school on the campus of the Santa Fe Indian School. Just three years later, in 1965, twenty-four students published their work in the BIA-sponsored publication, *Anthology of Poetry and Verse Written by Students in Creative Writing Classes and Clubs During the First Three Years of Operation (1962–1965)*. Seven of the twenty-four authors were Navajo; they included Emerson Charles Long, Dave MartinNez, Blackhorse Mitchell, Alberta Nofchissey, Calvin O'John, Tommy Smith, and Harry Walters. In that same year, the IAIA students produced a handmade book in a limited edition of one hundred copies, titled *Four*, created as a collaboration between the printmaking studio and the creative writing program. Diné writers included in the project were Dave MartinNez, Blackhorse Mitchell, Alberta Nofchissey, and Tommy Smith. Blackhorse Mitchell also was acknowledged under designers, editors, and printers in the book. The title of one of Mitchell's featured poems in *Four*, "Miracle Hill," became the title of his autobiography, *Miracle Hill: The Story of a Navaho Boy*, which was eventually published by the University of Oklahoma Press in 1967. Mitchell's *Miracle Hill*, the first book published by a Diné writer, debuted a full year before N. Scott Momaday (Kiowa) published his Pulitzer Prize–winning novel, *House Made of Dawn*, which, interestingly, makes reference to Navajo poetic and cultural traditions. In 1975, IAIA became a two-year college and continued growing into a four-year college; recently, in 2013, it began offering MFA degrees in creative writing. Fourteen of the thirty authors in this book have studied at or graduated from the IAIA. Additionally, the IAIA's student-run print and online venues regularly publish student work, including the work of the many alumni in this book.

In the context of the BIA schools, the annual journal *Arrow* was born. From 1968 to 1974, *Arrow* served as a venue for many young Native American writers, including Diné. Some published poetry included Diné vocabulary such as mą'ii (coyote) and shicheii (my grandfather). Poems published in the *Arrow* often addressed contemporary issues facing Diné, such as siblings at war in Vietnam or the poverty on Diné bikéyah. Three writers in this anthology—Grey Cohoe, Gloria Emerson, and Nia Francisco—were published in the *Arrow*. In 1970, seventeen-year-old Henry Tinhorn's *Handful of Sand* was published by the Language Arts Department of the Intermountain Indian School in Brigham City, Utah. While *Handful* marked a first as single-authored publication and a departure from other class projects, Intermountain, with its own printing press, had an extensive record of creating outlets for writing by Diné students. From 1950 to 1974, Intermountain enrolled Navajo students exclusively, before opening to other tribal enrollment from 1975 to 1984, when the school closed. The school's newspaper, *Smoke Signals,* was first published in 1951 and always featured dozens of stories authored by Navajo students; in 1966 the first issue of the annual literary magazine *Náátsʼíilid* (the Diné word for rainbow) was published with this guiding vision: "It is the intent of the magazine to capture the beauty, grandeur, and wealth of life and learning, as the rainbow captures the spectrum of color of the sky."

Gloria Emerson also published poetry in several volumes of the overtly political *The Indian Historian* (1967–79), out of San Francisco; and Cohoe's story included here was widely circulated and republished in numerous anthologies, including Natachee Scott Momaday's 1971 *American Indian Writers*. During the second half of the 1970s, Diné continued to write and publish their poetry. As English-language Diné writing became more visible, Nia Francisco published a poem in both Diné bizaad and English in a 1977 volume of the journal *College English*. Then, in 1978, Luci Tapahonso published her first short story, "The Snake Man."

These authors are part of the public record of early Diné written literature, but one must consider how many undocumented, unknown voices—like the child authors of Tohatchi—have been forgotten or unrecognized. During his research, editor Anthony K. Webster met Shonnie Allen, who self-published, in 1972, a volume of poetry titled *Yei*. Unfortunately, before Allen could share his book with Webster in 2000, he passed away. This story about Allen is representative of all the unknown Diné poets and writers who must have existed—those who may have thought of their writing as having little value, those whose work never made it past personal diaries, journals, family gatherings, or English classes. Regardless, the editors of *The Diné Reader* acknowledge that these unknown writers are part of this written Diné literary tradition, and it is our hope that this anthology will inspire the discovery and recognition of other earlier, previously undiscovered, authors.

This early creative output and public recognition paralleled and was supported directly and indirectly by what many have characterized as an American Indian literary renaissance that commenced in 1968 with N. Scott Momaday winning the Pulitzer Prize. Civil rights–era activism, specifically the Red Power movement's work, and shifting cultural sensibilities about diverse voices meant that publishers, academics, and the reading public more generally were interested in the perspectives of Native writers. Writers such as Simon Ortiz, Leslie Marmon Silko, James Welch, Paula Gunn Allen, Joy Harjo, Louise Erdrich, Gerald Vizenor, Maurice Kenny, Duane Niatum, and Joseph Bruchac, among others, led the way by providing mentorship and support, in many instances, and helped to establish among readers and academics an expectation of literary innovation and excellence. Work begun by Paula Gunn Allen and Robert W. Ackley of Navajo Community College initiated the founding of the Association for the Study of American Indian Literatures in 1971. The first gathering of Native American writers was at the Modern Language Association annual meetings in 1972, and a landmark 1977 National Endowment for the Humanities–sponsored seminar was held in Flagstaff, Arizona, at Northern

Arizona University. This seminar recognized the scholarly merits of studying and reading Native literature and enlisted participants to develop academic resources and interpretative approaches with intention and deliberation.

In the next decade, even more writing by Diné authors was published. In 1980 *The South Corner of Time: Hopi, Navajo, Papago, Yaqui Tribal Literature*, a collection of prose and poetry by Native authors of the Southwest, was edited by Larry Evers and published by the University of Arizona Press. Among the Diné authors included were Irene Nakai Hamilton, Agnes Tso, and, again, Nia Francisco. The next year, Laura Tohe published her first work, "Willow Man's Children," in Rudolfo Anaya and Simon J. Ortiz's anthology, *Ceremony of Brotherhood*. In 1982, Rock Point Community School published a collection of narratives, poems, and images titled *Between Sacred Mountains*. Among the contributors to that book was Rex Lee Jim, now also well known for serving as Navajo Nation vice president for four years. In 1988, Irvin Morris published his very first work, "The Homecoming," in *MAAZO Magazine*. Throughout the 1980s, individually authored books by Diné writers were appearing more frequently. In 1982, Luci Tapahonso published her first book, *Seasonal Woman*. In 1986, Laura Tohe published *Making Friends with Water*, her first book; Luci Tapahonso published her second, *A Breeze Swept Through* in 1987; followed in 1988 by Nia Francisco's first book, *Blue Horses for Navajo Women*, Elizabeth Woody's *Hand into Stone*, and, in 1989, Rex Lee Jim's first book, written entirely in Navajo, *Áhí Ni' Nikisheegiizh*. In 1985, *Stone Soup*, the literary magazine written and illustrated by children, first began publishing stories by young Navajo writers, and the March/April 1989 edition featured a special Navajo issue. The issue included stories, poems, photographs, and color art from eighteen Navajo children, all of whom were named and attributed as authors or artists.

In 1990, Tiana Bighorse published *Bighorse the Warrior*, her third book; of all her works, it has without a doubt garnered the most literary interest among broad and diverse audiences. This life history is the result of a collaboration between Tiana Bighorse and Noël Bennett (who is non-Diné) that began in 1968, when Bennett moved to the reservation to learn about weaving from Tiana Bighorse, who was a well-known weaver. *Bighorse the Warrior* is the author's record of her father Gus Bighorse's (b. 1846) eyewitness account of the Long Walk and his reflections on how The People were impacted in subsequent decades.

Bennett was instrumental in maintaining the unique voices of Bighorse and her father "to preserve the storyteller's essence in this culturally rich manuscript" by refuting editorial regularization of English grammar. The result is a stunning, unique work of great historical and cultural significance, extending the work first begun in 1971 by the Navajo Community College Press publication, *Navajo Stories of the Long Walk Period.* The impact of *Bighorse* on literary production and its reception cannot be denied, as other Diné writers continue to privilege uniquely Diné styles of using English. In 2004, for example, Blackhorse Mitchell rereleased his 1967 memoir, *Miracle Hill,* and asserted authorial control over elements that his teacher-editor, basically attempting to create a more "grammatically correct" text, had changed for him. A key feature of the original 1967 version of *Miracle Hill* was an introduction by the teacher-editor that apologized for Mitchell's use of his particular Diné-styled English. Such an apology diminished Mitchell's use of his Diné English and his creativity as an author. This early effort to eliminate or marginalize Diné-styled English reveals more of the intent behind teaching Diné students to write a particular kind of English. The objective was never to reveal or encourage The People's artistry but rather to erase memory and accept the forced federal policies, religious dogma, and other "assimilationist" tactics. Mitchell has removed the teacher-editor's problematic introduction from the 2004 reissue; in doing so, he has reversed his teacher-editor's erasure of the clear and very evident manifestation of The People's encounter, resistance, and artistry of language.

The first publication of editor Esther Belin appeared in 1991, written while she was an undergraduate at University of California, Berkeley. In the summer of 1990, Belin had an internship with an Asian American media arts center in L.A.'s Little Tokyo district. During that time, she synthesized commonalities of her urban Indian experience with the different waves of Asian American immigrants, in particular Japanese Americans who had been interned during World War II. The resulting poem was published in an anthology of Asian American media arts. Several years later, Paula Gunn Allen included Belin's story, "Indigenous Irony," in her anthology, *Song of the Turtle: American Indian Literature 1974–1994*.

Alyse Neundorf, a poet and linguist, published poetry in both Diné and English during the 1990s (in, for example, *Red Mesa Review*, published at the University of New Mexico–Gallup). Shonto Begay, who had previously illustrated books, published his first children's book, *Ma'ii and Cousin Horned Toad: A Traditional Navajo Story*, in 1992, followed by his *Navajo Visions and Voices Across the Mesa* in 1995, from which several works have been excerpted for this book. In 1993, the Navajo Community College Press published *Storm*

Patterns, a collection of poetry featuring two poets, Della Frank and Roberta D. Joe—one of the only examples of a Diné poetry book published on the Navajo Nation; most single volumes of Diné poetry and literature are published either by southwestern university presses or by independent poetry publishers off the reservation. Also in 1993, Anna Lee Walters (Pawnee/Otoe), who was teaching English at Diné College in Tsaile, edited *Neon Pow-Wow: New Native American Voices of the Southwest*, an anthology featuring twenty-two emerging Native American writers, ten of whom are Diné and several of whom are included in this anthology. That same year, Luci Tapahonso published her third book, *Sáanii Dahataał: The Women Are Singing*, which was followed, in 1994, by Nia Francisco's *Carried Away by the Black River* and two books by Elizabeth Woody, *Luminaries of the Humble* and *Seven Hands, Seven Hearts*. In 1995, Rex Lee Jim published *saad*, a second collection of poetry through the Princeton University Library, written entirely in Diné bizaad, and in 1998, Jim published *Dúchas Táá Kóó Diné*, a trilingual collection of poetry in Diné, Gaelic, and English. In 1995, Hershman John and Norla Chee published their first works, followed by Sherwin Bitsui in 1997. In 1997 Luci Tapahonso published her fourth book, *Blue Horses Rush In*, and Irvin Morris published his first, *From the Glittering World: A Navajo Story*. The decade saw the publication of Laura Tohe's second book, *No Parole Today*, and Esther Belin's first, *From the Belly of My Beauty*, winner of an American Book Award. In short, contemporary Diné poets and prose writers in the last four decades of the twentieth century—regardless of how they were introduced to poetics and creative writing—claimed a space in the literary field that is uniquely their own.

A new generation of writers in the twenty-first century has been inspired by these early Diné writers and is producing remarkable work that has garnered the attention of publishers and prize committees alike. The first two decades saw a bounty of Diné single-authored poetry collections, some by first-timers, others from established authors: Norla Chee's *Cedar Smoke on Abalone Mountain* (2001); Rutherford Ashley's *Heart Vision 2000* (2001); Gloria Emerson's *At the Hems of the Lowest Clouds: Meditations on Navajo Landscapes* (2003); Sherwin Bitsui's *Shapeshift* (2003); Laura Tohe's *Tséyi': Deep in the Rock* (2005); Laura Tohe's oratorio, *Enemy Slayer: A Navajo Oratorio* (2007); Hershman John's *I Swallow Turquoise for Courage* (2007); Luci Tapahonso's *A Radiant Curve* (2008); Sherwin Bitsui's *Flood Song* (2009), winner of an American Book Award and the PEN Open Book Award; Orlando White's *Bone Light* (2009) and LETT*ERR*S (2015); Bojan Louis's

Currents (2017), winner of an American Book Award; Esther Belin's *Of Cartography* (2017); Crisoto Apache's *~~GENESIS~~* (2018); Tacey Atsitty's *Rain Scald* (2018); Sherwin Bitsui's *Dissolve* (2018); Rex Lee Jim's *Saad Lá Tah Hózhóón: A Collection of Diné Poetry* (2019); Jake Skeets's *Eyes Bottle Dark with a Mouthful of Flowers* (2019), the winner of the prestigious National Poetry Series prize and the 2020 American Book Award; and Rick Abasta's *All Eyes on Me: A Collection of Diné Poetry* (2020). Fiction and nonfiction works also joined this substantial list of poetry titles. Evangeline Parsons Yazzie published an epic, romance novel trilogy set during the Long Walk: *Her Land, Her Love* (2014); *Her Enemy, Her Love* (2016); and, *Her Captive, Her Love* (2018). Natanya Ann Pulley published her first collection of short fiction, *With Teeth* (2019), the winner of the Many Voices prize. In the memoir *Dog Flowers*, Danielle Geller, a 2016 Rona Jaffe winner, incorporates the essay included in this anthology as well her 2017 essay from the *New Yorker*, "Annotating the First Page of the First Navajo-English Dictionary." Bojan Louis is also working on a collection of fiction acquired by Graywolf Press and slated to be published in 2022.

More and more Diné are completing MFA creative writing degrees as well as PhD programs in English or creative writing, and many of these writers have previously taught or teach at IAIA, at Diné College, at Navajo Technical University, and at universities in the Southwest, including San Juan College, Fort Lewis College, Colorado College, Arizona State University, University of Arizona, Northern Arizona University, and University of New Mexico. Like those who have come before them, they give back to their communities and foster the talent of younger writers. Diné writers have been incorporated into cultural celebrations throughout the reservation. Examples include the Eastern Navajo Nation Fair's Cowboy/Cowgirl Poetry and Storytelling event and the creation of the Navajo Nation Poet Laureate in 2013, sponsored by Navajo Technical University in Crownpoint, New Mexico, and launched by Irvin Morris while he was on faculty there. The inaugural poet laureate was Luci Tapahonso; the current poet laureate is Laura Tohe. Jake Skeets founded a literary salon in Window Rock called Pollentongue, and Manny Loley continues to support and guide the Emerging Diné Writers' Institute; finally, a large number of the writers included here are members of Saad Bee Hózhǫ́ Diné Writers' Collective, a supportive network of writers engaged in discussions about Navajo literature and representations of Diné culture and life in writing by those who are not Navajo.

As The People continue to use English in literary art, the language transitions into a tribal Diné language. This book contains numerous examples of mastery of both languages by Diné writers, including artistic and linguistic devices of code-switching. Sound symbolism, punning, parallelism, quoted speech, and a variety of poetic devices found in traditional Diné oral poetry have been actively incorporated into some contemporary writing as well. Diné writers have also experimented with free verse, sestinas, limericks, haiku, prose poems, creative nonfiction, mixed genres, and other poetic and literary traditions. In public readings of their work, Diné writers can take on the roles of tribal storyteller and hataali (a traditional chanter who, through singing, incorporates healing) when infusing uniquely Diné poetic devices. In many Diné narratives—coyote stories, for example—there may be a sung portion within the narrative, and two writers in particular, Blackhorse Mitchell and Luci Tapahonso, have incorporated song into their poetry readings.

Numerous writers in this book received their first exposure to poetry in school, most likely as a vehicle for grasping the English language and its literary traditions. However, as more Diné are writing poetry and prose and utilizing it as a vehicle to express their existence as Diné, there has been a growing understanding of the intricate and intrinsic power of language within Diné culture from time immemorial. Early observations from Dr. Washington Matthews, a white army surgeon who worked closely among The People in the late 1890s, are noteworthy: he described Diné storytellers and singers (hataali) as "poets" and their songs as "poems." Matthews argued that, if Diné bizaad were written, one would find many poetic devices, if not more than are found in their English counterparts. Hane' (story, narrative) is generally the word in Diné bizaad that translates as something akin to poetry. The descriptive hane' na'ach'ąąh (designed stories) is also used. Hane' encompasses the spoken poetry as well as traditional Diné narratives like coyote stories and emergence stories—and can incorporate song. The function of hane' in Diné society has been expressed by poets Rex Lee Jim and Blackhorse Mitchell as a vehicle "to make one think, to reflect, and that such reflection should then motivate one to proper behavior" and inspire reflection about good and evil (hózhǫ́/hóchxǫ'). Even the full meaning of the phrase "Diné bizaad" offers important insights about the value of language for The People. Common and too-simplified translations of the phrase as "Navajo language" gloss over greater intricacies. Understood more fully, "Diné bizaad" means "Diné their language, languages, voice, voices, word, words, etc." Rex Lee Jim exemplifies this translation in his poem "Saad/Language/Voice" included in this book.

This book project began as a vehicle to demonstrate both the power of Diné literary artistry and the survivance of The People, with beginnings straight from the heart of Diné principles, Sa'ąh Naaghái Bik'eh Hózhóón. This project surrendered itself to this system of values and beliefs. Each editor has their own stories to tell of how gathering this collection of writing together involved nitsáhákees (thinking), nahat'á (planning), iiná (living), and siihasin (reflecting). Each editor individually overcame conflicts, difficulties, hardships, and chaos while working on this project and continued the journey through to achieve greater understanding of the concept of wholeness and completeness. Each editor journeyed with each poem/prose piece to live out the paradigm as bíla' ashdla'ii, committed to the field of literature and language.

Editor Connie Jacobs, now emerita professor, taught from 1993 to 2008 at San Juan College in the border town (towns just outside the Navajo Nation) of Farmington, New Mexico, and too often found that her Indigenous students—predominantly Diné, making up 33 percent of the student population—were not aware of any Diné writers. During her tenure at the college, she introduced her students to the poetry of Luci Tapahonso and Esther Belin, exposing them, often for the first time, to Diné poets who were writing to and for them. This gap led Connie to consider producing a volume of Diné authors to be used especially in reservation schools in the Four Corners region. The idea gained momentum at a Native American Literature Symposium (NALS) conference, when she mentioned it to editor Jeff Berglund, a professor of literature since 1999 at Northern Arizona University, in the border town of Flagstaff. He also shared an interest in teaching Diné writers to his students and had assembled a packet of Diné writings for a reading series at his university. Both Connie and Jeff recognized—long before the #OwnVoices campaign of today—that Diné students would benefit from reading other Diné writers and that all students would gain much from understanding the complexity, beauty, and diversity of Diné literature by Diné writers.

By this time, both Jeff and Connie knew Esther Belin well and had become friends, invited her to their campuses, and frequently taught her 1999 award-winning book, *From the Belly of My Beauty*; each separately conducted and published in-depth interviews with this rising talent who represented in complex, complicated, and beautiful ways the experience of growing up in urban Los Angeles while maintaining deep ties to Diné culture, traditions, and communities. It made perfect sense to invite Esther to help guide and oversee their work with this volume. As a Diné writer and public intellectual, Esther helped forge strong connections among the powerful writers who came before her and the younger writers who were just beginning their careers or still in school. She eventually introduced Anthony K. Webster to the group and invited him to join the editorial team; as a linguistic anthropologist researching Diné poetics since early 2000, he has built meaningful relationships with many of the writers in this anthology, and his extensive publications have brought Diné poetry to the attention of new academic audiences. Jeff, Esther, Connie, and Anthony met up at various conferences, including NALS and Navajo Studies; during a 2010 NALS meeting, Jeff organized a session on pedagogies for teaching Diné literature. In 2011 Jeff hosted a plenary dialogue with Esther, Sherwin Bitsui, Orlando White, and Hershman John at the Western Literature Association conference in Prescott, Arizona. These formal and informal conversations made this book seem not only vital, but inevitable.

Larry Evers's 1980 edited collection *The South Corner of Time* was ahead of its time in arguing "that American Indian literature really consists of many literatures supported by many distinct tribal traditions." Emphasizing the value of the oral tradition and the traditional language of origin common to particular Indigenous cultural groups, Evers writes,

> The oral tradition is a distillation of the shared experience that gives language meaning. Stories, songs, the whole oral tradition of a community, expresses its ideals, wisdom, and humor. In a significant way it is the singers and storytellers who hold tribal communities together, for in their telling and singing they preserve and re-create their community's idea of itself. In this way tribal communities shape, and are shaped by, literature.

More recently, *Tribal Secrets: Recovering American Indian Intellectual Traditions* by Robert Warrior (Osage); *Red on Red: Native American Literary Separatism* by Craig Womack (Mvskoke Creek); *Our Fires Survive the Storm: A Cherokee Literary History* by Daniel Heath Justice (Cherokee); the concept of "tribalography" by LeeAnne Howe (Choctaw); and *Centering Anishinaabeg Studies* by Anishinaabe scholars Jill Doerfler, Niigaanwewidam James Sinclair, and Heidi Kiiwetinepinesiik Star have encouraged the adoption of tribally relevant approaches to interpreting and reading literatures and cultures. Among Diné-produced scholarship, Jennifer Nez Denetdale's *Reclaiming Diné History: The Legacies of Navajo Chief Manuelito and Juanita* (2007); Lloyd Lee's edited collections, *Diné Perspectives: Revitalizing and Reclaiming*

Navajo Thought (2014) and *Navajo Sovereignty: Understandings and Visions of the Diné People* (2017); and Farina King's *The Earth Memory Compass: Diné Landscapes and Education in the Twentieth Century* (2018) have provided vital contributions about theorizing and centering Diné tribal values, cosmologies, and epistemologies.

The Diné Reader, published four decades after Evers's *The South Corner of Time*, profiles and illuminates the expanding written literary tradition of Diné writers and the affinities, continuities, and departures among writers who share common cultural foundations and grounding. It is the first book of its kind to collect writing from a comprehensive range of Navajo authors. Blackhorse Mitchell, Luci Tapahonso, Laura Tohe, Rex Lee Jim, Irvin Morris, Sherwin Bitsui, Orlando White, and Esther Belin have long attracted the notice of readers of contemporary poetry and literature. Alongside their groundbreaking and recent writing, this book presents a whole chorus of Diné voices, some lesser known today, some who are becoming well known, and others who one day will be well known. Without exception, each of the writers included here enthusiastically responded to our request to include them in *The Diné Reader*. Through the years this book has been in production, their enthusiasm for and confidence in the value of our anthology has propelled the editors along.

Designed for readers new to Native American literature as well as readers and teachers who want to expand their knowledge beyond single-author volumes, *The Diné Reader* provides readers with introductions and interviews with writers, relevant historical chronologies, bibliographies, and related reading and writing assignments. There are many ways to organize an anthology such as this; this one is organized primarily in chronological terms, based on authors' first publications. Perhaps even more significantly, after much conversation, the editors have framed its contents to support the integration of Diné perspectives through multiple levels of the education system. Many logistical factors contribute to the works of Diné writers not being taught, even in Navajo school districts; equally, however, underlying prejudicial and colonialist ideologies also sustain the erasure of nonwhite authors in the curriculum at various levels. *The Diné Reader* offers an intervention and addresses this omission. It is the hope that this book will enable teachers to effectively include Diné literature in the classroom. Enlisted to assist in that process—with assignments and resources for teachers—is educator Michael Thompson (Mvskoke Creek), who taught in the border town of Bloomfield, New Mexico, from 1998 to 2012. Dr. Jennifer Nez Denetdale, esteemed Diné historian, currently a professor of American studies at the University of New Mexico, created a chronology that marks important moments in Navajo literary and cultural history.

The Diné Reader draws attention to intriguing themes within contemporary Diné writing. Topics and themes consistent in Diné writing include connections with home and history, especially the Long Walk (1864–68), which is often connected with contemporary concerns about identity, historical trauma, and homeland. Other common topics include the loss of the language, what it means to be a Diné in the twenty-first-century world, and economic and environmental inequalities. Some Diné writers employ poetry and prose as a way to educate non-Diné about important cultural, spiritual, and philosophical issues. The themes of growing up on Diné bikéyah and experiencing government-operated boarding schools continue to be central in Diné poetry and prose. Thus, Diné writing serves as a historical and cultural supplement to the Westernized education that too often excludes The People's presence and contributions to the world. To this end, we have not sought to standardize the spellings of Diné bizaad in the writings presented here. Rather we have seen their variety as an important reflection of historical, social, local, personal, and aesthetic sensibilities and concerns.

May the works of these Diné writers be the foundation for visionaries and the generations to come.

BLACKHORSE MITCHELL

Credit: Blackhorse Mitchell

BLACKHORSE MITCHELL was born and raised on Palmer Mesa, a place known by Diné as Tsé Dildǫ'ii (roughly, popping rock) above Salt Creek Canyon, New Mexico, which is near the Colorado state line in northern New Mexico. He is a Yei'ii Dine'é Táchii'nii born for Naakai Dine'é. His maternal grandfather is Hooghan Łani and his paternal grandfather is 'Áshįįhí. He attended boarding school in Ignacio, Colorado. He received his academic degree from the Institute of American Indian Arts, Santa Fe, New Mexico, in 1964. Mitchell returned to IAIA and received his MFA in literary writing in 1966. In 1978 he earned his BS in elementary education from the University of New Mexico. He later went on to earn his MA from the University of New Mexico College of Education. He has been an educator for more than thirty years. He has also been sheepherding most of his life. Among other avocations, he is also a Navajo blues performer, a comedian, a medicine man/practitioner/sand painter, a moccasin maker, and a potter. He is the author of the landmark publication *Miracle Hill: The Story of a Navaho Boy* (1967; reissued in 2004). He has also released three CDs of his distinctive sheepherding songs: *American Bar* (2002), *Where Were You When I Was Single* (2006), and *Don't Let Go!* (2008).

Reflections on Conversations with Blackhorse Mitchell

All of the writers in *Diné Reader* are indebted to Blackhorse Mitchell as the first published Diné writer. What must be noted is that *Miracle Hill (MH),* which came out in 1967, was published before N. Scott Momaday's *House Made of Dawn*, a novel generally acknowledged as heralding in the Native American literary renaissance. Momaday was an early reviewer of Mitchell's work in the *New York Times Book Review*, recognized his talent, and praised *MH* for its fresh and engaging voice. *MH* laid a path for Native writers in general and Diné writers, specifically, to follow, a path that Mitchell did not have when he began but that he forged himself against many odds. Mitchell's book, started for Mrs. Allen's creative writing classroom assignment at IAIA, became hijacked as a project for the teacher to showcase her talented Native student. Thankfully, through Mitchell's persistence and help from friends such as Laura Tohe, Barney Bush, and Paul Zolbrod, he regained the rights to his work, and the University of Arizona Press, under the guidance of editor Patti Hartmann, after thirty-six years published *MH* with Mitchell's voice reestablished.

What distinguishes Mitchell's work is that *MH* retains the essence of being Diné with its language and structure. The book begins with a Navajo way of thinking of a sheepherder through his Diné English—the very language that Mrs. Allen tried to erase and revise in *her* version of *his* book—Mitchell's language, that gives *MH* its distinctive voice. It is through this voice that Mitchell powerfully communicates to non-Native readers, brought up with a Western set of ideas, that we are all humans, we have a connection, and this book can serve as a bridge for others to view his world just as Mitchell has viewed others' worlds.

Seeing his book into print with its continuing influence has become the work of a lifetime. As an educator with BA and MA of arts degrees in elementary and secondary education, Mitchell continues to inspire students in classrooms by letting them know that he was once a non-English-speaking sheepherder who dared to dream of learning English and going to school. His story can become their story.

Miracle Hill continues its influence with the upcoming stage production in Prague, Czech Republic.* Mitchell's Austrian friend, Alexander Stipsits, is

---

* This would not be the first stage presentation of Mitchell's book. In 1970, Dr. Rose Marie Smith from Arizona State University did a stage reading of *MH* performed by the ASU Theatre Group.

producing this exciting project. He became interested in Mitchell's work when he was in the United States, and he met Mitchell at Red Mesa High School in 1998 when he was teaching a class on media/video, and Mitchell was teaching Navajo language classes. They became friends and, more than that, family. Stipsits has promoted Mitchell's work and music in Europe, especially in Austria and the Czech Republic; to date, Mitchell has had four visits there to perform his music. What has impressed Stipsits so much about Mitchell is how he grew up speaking only Navajo and now moves comfortably in the dominant culture and wants to learn more about life beyond the reservation. In this way, Mitchell serves as a bridge for the younger generation of Diné. Additionally, Stipsits notes Mitchell's lack of anger in his writing and the creative ways in which he mixes poetry, music, and cultural teachings. For these reasons, and others, Stipsits has been working on a script for *MH* to present to Europeans so they can better know Mitchell's Diné culture, without any idealized picture. Stipsits's goal is to one day have the play performed.

I Do Have a Name,

from *Miracle Hill: The Story of a Navajo Boy*

It was in the year of 1943 on a cold morning, the fifth day, in the month of March. A little boy was born as the wind blew against the hogan with bitter colds and the stars were disappearing into the heaven.

The little puff of smoke was gradually floating skyward. The floor of the earth was hard as ever with a few stripes of white snow still frozen to the grey colored ground. With a queer squeaking, the baby awakes. His eyes were as dark as the colors of the ashes. His face is pink.

Following year, it was May and the bright sun shines in the land of enchantment close to the Four Corners, which was about thirty miles away. Four Corners is where the four states meets. They are New Mexico, Arizona, Utah, and Colorado.

The boy stood on his two little fat legs. Part of the time he crawl, but mostly he walks against chairs and his grandmother's loom. Very many lambs jumps and plays near the tent. The boy sometimes play with the lambs and goats. They smell like a wet dry dirt and the smell of corral.

But life was hard. Year after year the boy, his Grandmother, and Grandfather moved to various part of the reservation area. The boy was four now and begins to wonder, as he looks in the yonder valley and in the afar distance. With his sharp, dark brown eyes he would stand against the tree-shade house and look.

Day by day and step by step he learns different things. Very often Grandfather would say, "My beloved child, when you grow big, I got a surprise for you, Little One."

The boy would smile and sits on his Grandfather's lap.

But still, the boy would go to the hill and look into the distance, wondering when will he ever be there to see the place. The days were long, and, as he herd his flock of sheeps, he began to think about things that were around him.

As the summer has gone by suddenly, they moved back to the Mesa where during winter it is warm and partly cold. The winter slowly passes. When the boy herd sheep, he would play with the shepherd dogs and sometimes his pet lamb. Still yet he hasn't learn much, but he knew every tree and mountain passage through the great forest.

Very often when he herd sheep he would play bareback on the branch of a springy cedar branch which would throw him off. When he feel like playing, he would make his own toys out of clay. They were yellow, grey, orange, and blue. These were the color of his toys which are made by his own five fingers.

Many times he hunted rabbit and animals, carrying his four-feet bow and arrow. It belonged to his Grandfather who had given it to him for a birthday present. First, he learned how to shoot the flying arrow. It was taught by his Grandfather. He was very skill at shooting the arrow.

Since the boy is too small, he would sit and put his bow at the front of his feet and stretch the bowstring to shoot the arrow. Surely enough, the arrow flies like a diving eagle bound to catch a rabbit.

With his practice of shooting arrow, it gave him more and more ideas. While herding sheep he would shoot trees, imagining it as a huge lion, bear, and such. With his ability of learning, he quickly learn how to jump from rock to rock. He could run like an antelope when he runs into rocky hills and forest and down the rocky hillside.

When the boy was six years old, of what he has to learn, he never forgets. But he has never seen much of a white man's ways. Then one day he came home, carry a loads of a rabbit in his bag made of buckskin.

Grandmother stood outside the hogan. "How many rabbit did you kill?" she asked, grinning.

"Oh, I kill six."

Then in English she spoke, "Oh, six."

The boy dropped the bag and put down his arrow bag and bow against the hogan. "Grandmother! What's that word mean?"

"What word?" said Grandmother.

"The word 'ce-e-ex,'" said the boy.

Then she laugh as though the whole mountainside crushing. She dance around a little bit and sang an old song, saying, "Oh twinle, twinle, little star."

"Grandmother, are you going nuts or something?" the boy asked, "or is it you feeling happy because Grandfather's coming home today?"

"No, Little One," she said.

Then the boy stand up against the hogan. He didn't know that his grandmother had been a student once. Now, Grandmother never spoke none of a white man's tongue. "Grandmother," he said.

"Quiet, Little One. Go get some water from the spring. Then I'll answer your question," she said.

The boy pick up the bag and runs down the hill into the forest with a white water bag made of goatskin. With his skill, he has no problem of running swiftly and no problem of falling. It was a mile and a half.

At the spring he filled up his water bag and started walking up the hill. He saw his Grandfather riding his horse through the canyon in the yonder hills.

The boy thought of an idea that he would have a race with him. So, with a quick jerk, he put the bag on the shoulder and jumps on the rock. Like he always did, he made the short cut, doing nothing but jumping from rock to rock. When he got home, Grandmother was preparing a meal outside the hogan.

She turns around with her hands on her waist, holding a big silver spoon. "What did you do," she said, "fly or something?"

"No, I ran," he said.

"Impossible," she said.

The boy sits on the log of an old cedar, his pants all dirty and shirt sleeves torn off on both sides, and wearing a white headband with a black eagle feather. He laughs with his grandmother.

"What is it?" she said.

"Oh, nothing," he said, "it just that, I didn't know you can speak a white tongue! So now would you tell me what the word ''six' mean?"

"It means six rabbit," she said. "Six mean six." She picks up a stick and writes figures in the sandy dust—1, 2, 3, 4, 5, 6—counting as she writes.

"One," the boy said, and "six." Then, "What do you call this?"

"Oh that's a bucket," she said. "Now enough of that."

"Ooh, my Grandfather coming," the boy said.

"Where?"

"See, there he is down yonder."

She is stirring up the mutton soup, and on her left hand she holds a dough in a form of a ball. The soup smelled with vegetable and the smell of fried bread made the boy grow hungrier than ever as she stack the brownish bread in a white plate. She was putting another stick and more in the fireplace to burn.

"Little One, get me the broom and I'll teach your Grandfather a lesson that he never forgets," she said. "He never thinks of us. He's always going."

The boy went back to into the hogan and closed the door. As he peep through the opening of the door, Grandfather got knock off the horse, and Grandmother quickly grabs the broom and hits grandfather again. Then she throws the rubbery dough into Grandfather's face.

"Take that," she said.

The boy just laugh in the hogan and suddenly Grandmother said, "Time to eat."

While they were eating, Grandfather said, "We're moving to summer home."

"Where we used to live in a tent?" the boy asked.

"No," Grandfather said. "We are leaving tomorrow noon, and your uncle is coming on the pickup to haul our blankets, dishes, and a few lambs that are small."

Yes, surely enough, it was the next morning. As Grandmother and Grandfather packed the bundle of blankets and suitcases, clothes, putting and setting boxes in place.

It was a good day for traveling.

"Little One, take the sheep out of the corral and get a head start," said Grandfather.

As he opened the gate to let the sheep out, the boy look up the valley and down the steep canyon. He wondered as he stands there, wearing his white shirt, carry a big bow in his hand. The arrow were kind of heavy, but he was used to carrying it all the time. He kept saying the word "six," and "one" and "bucket"as he stroll after the sheeps down the grassland.

It looked like a green pasture with a stream of water. Only the prairie dogs barked in the far distance at the edge of the woods where there is an open sight.

The boy didn't like prairie dogs. The crows flew across the blue sky as the white cloud are moving eastward like a big white sheep in the grazing land.

Down in the canyon he walks and jumps from rocks to rocks as he's going after the flock of sheep. He would ask himself, "What will I do when I'm seven years old next year?"

He wanted to speak English, but how would he learn? He would say, "When I was young, which was two years ago, I used to wondered about that rock down yonder. I have been there a few times but surely there is a way," he said to himself.

Finally he bought his sheep to the edge of the mesa. It was about three o'clock now. All this time he didn't know he has gone many miles with the sheep. The dust of clouds were up in the air like a dust storm. He didn't mind walking in it. Many times he rested.

Then finally it was getting dark as he arrive with his sheep at the next spring which has a bitter taste. It's good only for sheep so the poor boy has to thirst until Grandmother and Grandfather arrive. He waited and waited until late. He heard horse hoofs beating against the hard floor of the earth. The sheep rested quietly and the dogs barked. And the big yellow moon shined as the stars twinkle above.

The rumbling sound grew louder and louder. The owl hoot in the brushes. There were bushes and tall grass. Soon the boy saw them approach. It was Grandmother and Grandfather riding horses along the road. Then they turn off the road and headed towards the spring. As they watered their horses they joined with the boy.

"We'll make it tonight," said Grandfather, "but first, you must eat."

Grandmother built a fire and putted the sandwich aside for the boy to eat. There were roast mutton, baked potatoes and biscuit. Now it was around nine o'clock.

As soon as they had eaten, they started off for another journey which will surely take until the morning. The sheep knew their pack so they were going single file along the road.

The boy fell asleep sitting behind his Grandfather. Part of the time he would almost fall off, his head goes this way and that way. He didn't know that he was asleep until he wake up in a tent where he has never been before, or nor seen the place.

It was morning. Grandfather snores while Grandmother was outside making coffee and tortillas.

The boy went out to see the place, to see what it is like. As for him, he'd never seen a water tower, or a big building, and real green trees. As he runs to the top of the hill, he could now see distance away. For many years he had seen Shiprock stand, but had never looked what was below and beyond. It was for the first time he is seeing buildings and towns. There were smokes going up in the air. In about four miles there runs a river. He could heard many ducks and various kinds of sounds by the river.

He rushes back to Grandmother and asks, "What are the building and great tower like a ball in the air?"

Grandmother said, "They are town, and many people live there, and your mother lives there at the farm."

"My mother?" said the boy. "I don't know her."

Then Grandmother calls to Grandfather, "Get up and tell the Little One about his mother."

"Come, Little One, let's go up the hill and let me tell you about the place," Grandfather said.

The boy and Grandfather first had a cup of coffee, as Grandmother sweeps the hard earth floor outside under the shade house. Grandfather stretch himself and then gets hold of the boy's hand and went up the hill.

At the top, the boy again looks across the hills. Grandfather sat down with his leg crossed. They boy sit besides his Grandfather like a pet dog.

"Your aunt is coming on horseback before noon," said Grandfather, "and she's bringing watermelons and fresh green corns, and a few vegetables."

At that moment, the boy sees his aunt riding in a distance. His Grandfather said, "How do you know it's her?"

"Because I know it's her by the color of the horse." The horse was black and walks like he's about ready to take off on a race track. The boy turns and looks at his Grandfather with his eyes twinkling. "Grandfather?" he said, "tell me about my mother."

"Oh, yes," Grandfather said, smiling at him. "Sit down and let me tell you."

The boy sit against a brush.

"Your mother Emma has left you when you were eleven month old. She only went and took your brother with her."

"I have a brother?" said the boy. "I have a brother," he repeated it several times. "Then Grandmother isn't my mother," he said, "and you aren't, aren't my father."

"Your father was killed," he said, "during World War II in over sea."

"My father was killed." The boy quiet down and looked at his Grandfather.

Then Grandfather looked up and said, "Your father was a very kind man. Before he left, he made many plans, but he was killed." He wipe his tears.

The boy got up and looked below the foot of the hill. There were four kids playing. "Grandfather let's go back to the tent," he said, "and see my aunt."

Grandfather gets up and hold the boy's hand. Grandfather didn't feel too well.

When they reached the house, Aunt Amy greet her father. "Oh father, I was late coming 'cause I was irrigating and plowing the field, and I had planted more corns," she said.

Grandmother was fixing a loom with yarn of colored strings to weave another rug.

The boy stood against a post which was there to hold up the shade house. He wondered why his Grandfather didn't told him more about his mother, or where she is now. Nor he didn't know he had a cousin too until his aunt told him that she had a daughter and she has no father too.

The boy asked, "What has happen to her father?"

Aunt Amy said, "My husband was the brother of your father. He has gone four years ago, and never came back."

"What's her name?"

"Her name is Annie," Aunt Amy said. "And she's coming to see us tomorrow and live here with her Grandmother too."

Later Amy was preparing meal as the sheep were in the green grassland over yonder on the tiny hills. By now it was getting hot, and the ground is getting hotter too. On the north side of the tent there were blooming flowers, colors were red and pink. Very often Grandmother would go out and get the blooming flowers and chop them into tiny bites and cook it and when it's cooled, she would serve it for dessert. It tasted sweet and part sour.

"Aunt Amy," the boy said.

"What is it?" she said.

"Why do they call me Little One?"

"I don't know. I suppose because you're small," she replied.

"Why don't I have a name?" asked the boy as he look at his aunt making a vegetable soup. She didn't stop. She went ahead and continue about her work. And Grandmother was busy rolling up more strings. She was ready to weave. Grandfather sleeps and snores.

"Do I have a name?" the boy said slowly as he looked down at his moccasins.

"Yes," she said.

"I do have a name," he said as he smile shyly.

Amy turned around and grinned. Then she said, "You were named after a colt that was born on the same day you were born. So your Grandfather named you Broneco."

"Broneco," the boy said and giggle with his hand over his mouth.

The Drifting Lonely Seed,

from *Miracle Hill: The Story of a Navajo Boy*

From the casein dark-blue sky,
Through the emptiness of space,
A sailing wisp of cotton.
Never have I been so thrilled!
The drifting lonely seed,
Came past my barred window,
Whirling orbit, it landed before me,
As though it were a woolly lamb—
Untouched, untamed, and alone—
Walked atop my desk, stepping daintily,
Reaching forth my hands, I found you,
Gentle, weightless, tantalizing.
I blew you out through barricaded window;
You pranced, circled round me,
Sharing with me your airy freedom.

Beauty of Navajoland

Beauty of Navajoland
Plastic bags blowing in the wind,
Aluminum beer cans shining in the country,
Flies enjoying waste on huggies disposal,
And
An empty bottle of Zima ornaments the roadsides.

The beauty of Navajoland.
Little big trashes drifting in the gale of dust,
Run over dogs and coyotes,
Vultures feasting on deteriorating smell of meat,
And
The crows flying away with the eyes of the kill.

The beauty of Navajoland,
"you say"
Those polluted dark clouds are not the real clouds,
The rivers and streams contaminated—
By Red Neck piss and dungs
And
Uranium in the flowing, innocent river.

The beauty of Navajoland,
Bra strap hanging on the roadside guide post,
Crucifix with plastic bouquets of flowers
Standing and reminding in humiliation!
And
Coal stripping of mother earth
And flood of acid rain?

Is not the beauty of Navajoland

GREY COHOE

Credit: courtesy of Jessie Cohoe Russell, literary executor of Grey Cohoe estate

GREY COHOE (1946–91) was born in Tocito, New Mexico, and grew up near Shiprock. He is born to Kinłichii'nii and born for 'Áshįįhí. His father was a medicine man. Cohoe attended boarding school and holds this experience accountable for him forgetting valuable aspects of Diné tradition and ceremonial life. In an interview, he noted that he'd eventually find his way back since "It all goes back to medicine . . . to survival on the earth, to the elements of the earth." After high school, he attended the Institute of American Indian Arts (IAIA) in Santa Fe, New Mexico, where he distinguished himself in the fields of creative writing, painting, drawing, and printmaking. He earned a BFA from the University of Arizona in 1971, and an MFA in 1974 before becoming a professor at IAIA. He won top awards for his artwork in the Scottsdale National Indian Arts Exhibition, and his prints have been exhibited both at the Arizona State Museum in Tucson and at the Smithsonian Institution in Washington, D.C. In recent years, after his early death in 1991, his reputation as an artist has continued, with inclusion of his work, especially his printmaking, in several recent exhibitions.

He won numerous awards and prizes for his poetry and prose. The story included here, "The Promised Visit," his first published work, was written while he was a student at IAIA. It appeared in the *South Dakota Review* in 1969. It was later anthologized in the landmark 1971 anthology *American Indian Writers*, edited by Natachee Scott Momaday. Several of his works were included in other landmark anthologies, including *The Remembered Earth: An Anthology of Contemporary American Literature* (1979), edited by Geary Hobson, and *Voice of the Turtle: American Indian Literature: 1900–1970* (1994), edited by Paula Gunn Allen. Notable published works include his poems, "Tocito" and "Awaken Me Redhouse-borne Again," which was accompanied by his artwork in an issue of *Wičazo Ša Review*.

The Promised Visit

It had been a long day at Window Rock, Arizona. I'd shoved myself up at dawn and started from Shiprock early that morning. Today was special day for me to appear for my tribal scholarship interview. I had applied for it in the spring so I could go on to school after my graduation from high school. My brother-in-law, Martin, was considerate enough to lend me his pickup truck. I would still have been there promptly for my appointment, no matter if I'd needed to walk, hitchhike, or crawl the hundred and twenty miles.

After all the waiting, I finally learned that I didn't need their scholarship to attend the school of my choice. I didn't need anything from them. They knew this all the time and didn't write to inform me. I was so sore about the unnecessary trip that I didn't bother to eat my lunch or supper. All I got was waste of time, money, and strength which I would've put to good use on the farm. Well, at least they wouldn't bother me, complaining about their money.

Gradually the warmth at the side of my face cooled off as the sunlight was broken up by long shadows across the plain, then bled over the fuzzy mountainous horizon. The same as yesterday—the usual sunny sky, the same quiet atmosphere, and the daily herding toils handled by the desert people—the daylight disappeared, ending another beautiful day. I didn't bother to glance a moment at the departing sun to give farewell or offer my traditional prayer for the kind sun, thanking him for his warmth and life. I constantly stared over the blue hood of the pickup onto the highway up ahead.

The old zigzagging road lined the shadowed flat region, cooling from a day's heat. It was not until now that the evening wind began to form the woollike clouds, building a dark overcast stretching across my destination. At first, it was obviously summer rain clouds, and even a child could recognize the rolling grayish mass. The white lane markers rhythmically speared under me as I raced toward home.

I rolled down the window about an inch to smell the first rain that I would inhale this summer. The harsh air rushed in, cold and wild. Its crazy current tangled and teased my hair. The aroma of the flying wet dirt tensed my warm nose, a smell of rain. Immediately the chill awakened my reflexes. I balanced my body into a proper driving position according to a statement in the driver's manual. I prepared to confront the slippery pavement.

Because of the long hard day, sitting and wrestling the stiff steering wheel, I was beaten. My muscles were too weak to fight the powerful wind, if a big thunderstorm should come upon me. I lazily moved one of my bare arms to roll up the window. I didn't like the roaring of the air leak. The chill of it made me tremble. I felt no fear of a gentle summer rain, but the dangerous hazards under a vigorous downpour frightened me.

I narrowed my eyes into the mirror to look back along the highway, hoping that someone else would be traveling along, too. Unfortunately, no one showed up. I'd have to go all alone on this road with the next nearest gas station about ninety-eight miles. It was unusual, during such a vacationing summer, to find not a single tourist going on this route. Maybe, I thought, if I wait a few minutes, someone will show up; then I'll follow.

I lazily lifted my foot off the gas pedal and slowly stepped on the brakes. When I came to a stop, I gave a long stretch to relieve my stiffness. Then I yawned. I waited in hopes until the cool evening darkness filled the valley. I stood by the open car door and thought of how mysterious the storm looked. The more I waited, the more time I was wasting. Before long, after giving up waiting, I was on the road again. I sang some Navaho songs, whispered, and fitted my sweater around my shoulder. I did anything to accompany myself.

By now I could sight the lightnings spearing into the horizon, glowing against the dark overcast. I could almost see the whole valley in one flash. The black clouds came closer and angrier as I approached their overcast. Being used to the old reservation road, narrow and rough, and well adjusted to the pickup, I drove ahead to meet the first raindrops.

I thought of a joke and wanted to burst out in laughter, but only a smile came. I used to laugh when I teased my folks about my death. They would scold me and would arouse my superstitions about it. Speaking of your death is taboo. Now, when I wondered whether I'd ever make it to the other side of the storm, it didn't sound funny.

Many people had died along the same highway, never telling us what caused their accidents. Most of these tragedies occurred in bad weather, especially in thunderstorms. Several months ago the highway department stuck small white crosses along the road at each place where an accident victim was killed. This was to keep a driver alert and aware. The crosses became so numerous that it caused more confusion and more accidents. When a person sees a cross, he becomes nervous.

Every time we drove through the cross-lined highway, I would think of a parade. The invisible spectators sitting on their crosses would watch us go along. Many people believe that these ghosts bring bad luck. Of course, we Navahos get cursed by such witchcraft.

The dark clouds formed themselves into a huge ugly mass. It reminded me of the myths the people feared in such angry clouds. The suspicious appearance scared me, making my joints and very soul tremble.

My stomach began to tighten up with a groaning sound. It made me weak. I imagined my sister's cooking at home. We'd butchered a sheep yesterday for meat supply. My sister had probably barbecued some mutton and made some fried bread. I swallowed down my empty throat and moved my empty stomach. The smell and taste of my imagined food seemed to be present in my mouth and nose. Restlessly, I speeded up a little faster.

The dark overcast hid my view of the road, and the area around faded away into darkness, so I had to turn on the headlights. My face was now tired of being fixed in the same direction, down the long, dirty highway. My eyelids were so weak that they closed by themselves. I should have slept longer last night. Again, I rolled down the window. The cold air poured in, caressing me with its moistened chill. It awoke me completely.

I would have brought my brother, Teddy, along to accompany me, but he was fast asleep so I didn't bother. I reckoned he'd rather work in the field than to sit all day long. Somehow, I was glad he hadn't come because I wouldn't want him to fear this killer storm. If anything should happen, I'd be the only one to die. Sadly, I kept on counting the dips, rocky hills, and the zigzagging curves as I drove on.

The sudden forceful blow jolted the car and waved it like a rolling wagon. The screaming wind began to knock at my windows. I clung hard on the steering wheel to fight the rushing wind. I slowed almost to a stop and peered out through the blowing dust at the hood, trying to keep on the road. Flying soil and tumble-weeds crashed against the car. I could not tell what ran beside the highway—a canyon or maybe a wash. The angry wind roared and blew so strong that the car slanted. I didn't know how to escape the Wind Monster. I sat motionless, feeling death inside my soul.

And then the car was rocked by falling raindrops as if it were a tin can being battered by flying stones. The downpour came too quickly for me to see the first drops on the windshield. The whole rocky land shook when a loud cracking lightning shot into the nearby ground.

"Oh, no! The devil is coming." I frightened myself, but I had enough courage to pick up my speed a little, thinking that I might escape his aim. I strained my eyes to see through the glare on the windshield. The pouring raindrops were too heavy for the wipers. It was like trying to look under water. Another swift stripe of lightning exploded into the ground. This time, it was closer. I kept myself from panicking. I drove faster, hoping the devil wouldn't see me.

The storm calmed and turned into a genial shower. Then I could see where I was. In sight, through the crystal rain, a green-and-white lettered sign showed up in the headlights. LITTLEWATER 12 miles; SHIPROCK 32 miles. At last, I felt relieved. I would be home in less than an hour. Never in my life did I ever long for home so much until this day. The windshield cleared and the rain had passed.

Again it was quiet, except this time I heard a splashing sound at the tires. My ears missed the hard rhythms of smashing rain. I felt as if I had been closely missed by a rifle shot.

Even though I didn't see any one of the monsters, still I looked out, but shamefully, for the two rainbows. They weren't there. I scolded myself for looking. It was ridiculous to fear something that didn't exist, like fairies. Yes, I'd heard thunders, seen lightnings, and felt the terrifying wind, but I'd come out alive. Only for a moment was I trapped and my minutes numbered. I'd probably confronted the stormhead.

"Standing ghost," I scoffed, and laughed to myself.

"It's too bad I can't see anything except the light-struck black pavement," I thought. I always rejoiced to see and smell the land where the rain had spread its tasteful water. It's refreshing to watch the plants drink from the puddles around them.

I hoped the rain had traveled across the farmlands near Shiprock. I was supposed to irrigate the corn tomorrow, but luckily the rain would take care of it. I might do something else instead. Maybe I'd go to the store or to the café and eat three or four hamburgers. I liked to see that cute waitress there.

With the scary storm passing, and my being penetrated by the superstition over, I felt as if I'd awakened from a nightmare. My hunger, too, had surrendered, but the crampy stiffness still tightened my body. I didn't bother to stop for a rest. I rushed straight home. I hoped my supper would be waiting. The clouds slid away and it wasn't as late as I'd thought.

By now, some twinkling stars appeared over the northern horizon. The found moon cast its light on the soggy ground as the silky white clouds slid after the rain. The water reflected the light so that the standing water shone like the moon itself. I could see the whole area as if in daylight. I ran the tires through the shallow puddles on the pavement to feel it splash. I imagined myself running and playing along the San Juan river shore. I constantly hastened on, looking for the lights at Littlewater over on the other side of the next hill.

Littlewater is a small store standing alongside the highway. Besides the two trailer houses in the back of the store, there are several hogans and log cabins standing in view of the flat valley, but tonight I can see them only as dark objects at a distance. During warm wintry days, the local people gather together on the sunny side of the trading post walls to chat or watch the travelers stop for gas or supplies. But at this time in the summer, they all move to the cool mountains.

A few electric lights appeared within range of my headlights. Three dull guide lights shone at the store. One larger light showed up the whole front porch. As usual, there wasn't anybody around at this late hour of the night. I slowed to glance at the porch as I passed by. At the same time as I turned back to the road, I saw a standing object about fifty yards ahead. I had always feared dark objects at night. My soul tensed with frightening chill as I trembled. I drove closer, telling myself it would be a horse or a calf.

The lights reached the dark image as I approached. Surprisingly, it was a hitchhiker. I didn't think anything about the person. All that came to my mind was to offer someone my help. Then I saw it was a girl.

I stopped a little way past her.

She slowly and shyly walked to the car window. She was all wet and trembling from the cold air. "Can you give me a lift to Shiprock?" she politely asked in her soft, quivering voice.

"Sure. That's where I'm going too." I quickly offered the warm empty seat.

She smiled and opened the door. Water dripped to the floor from her wet clothes. She sat motionless and kept looking away from me.

I thought she was just scared or shy. I, too, was shy to look, and we didn't talk for a long time. It wasn't until a few miles from Shiprock that I finally started a conversation.

"I guess the people around this area are happy to get such a big rain," I finally dared to utter. "I was supposed to water our farm field tomorrow, but I guess the good Lord did it for me," I joked, hoping she would laugh or say something. "What part of Shiprock are you from?" I questioned her.

"Not in Shiprock. About one mile from there," she carefully murmured, using the best of her English.

She looked uneducated by the style of the clothes she wore. She was dressed in a newly made green velvet blouse and a long, silky white skirt. She wore many silver and turquoise necklaces and rings. A red and orange sash-belt tightly fitted around her narrow waist. She was so dressed up that she looked ready for going to town or a squaw dance.

Her long black hair hung loosely to her small, round shoulder and beside her light-complexioned face. In the glow from the instrument panel I could tell she was very pretty. She didn't look like some other Navaho girls. Her skin was much lighter than their tannish-brown skin color.

Finally I gathered enough guts to offer her my school sweater. "Here. You better put this on before you catch cold. I hear pneumonia is very dangerous," I said, as I struggled about to take off the sweater.

She kindly took it and threw it around herself. "Thank you." She smiled and her words came out warmly.

I looked at her and she looked at the same time, too. I almost went off the road when I saw her beautiful smile of greeting. She was the prettiest girl I have ever seen. I jerked the steering wheel, and the car jolted back onto the highway. We both laughed. From that moment on, we talked and felt as if we'd known each other before. I fell in love and I guess she did, too.

"Where have you been in this kind of bad weather?" I began to ask questions so we could get better acquainted with each other.

"I visited some of my old relatives around Littlewater." She calmly broke her shyness. "The ground was too wet to walk on, so I decided to get a ride."

"I've been to Window Rock to get a scholarship to an art school. I started this morning and it isn't until now I'm coming back. I'm late for my supper because of the storm."

I knew she was interested in me, too, as she asked me, "Where do you live?"

"I live on one of the farms down toward west from Shiprock. I live with my family next to Thomas Yazzie's place." I directed her to the place, too.

"I used to know Thomas and his family when I was very small," she almost cried. "It's always sad to lose friends."

I felt sorry for her losing her friends. Right then I knew she was lonely.

"Where do you live?" I asked, as I looked straight down the lighted road.

She hesitated to answer as if she weren't sure of it. Then she said, "I live about four miles from Shiprock." Then she lowered her head as if she was worried about something I'd said.

I didn't talk any more after that. Again it was quiet. I kept my mind on the road, trying to forget my warm feelings for her beauty.

The night settled itself across the desert land, making stars and the moon more bright. The night sky and the dampness made me sleepy. I felt in a dreamy, romantic mood. The rain still covered the road. It was too quiet for comfort.

"Let's listen to some music," I interrupted the silence as I turned on the radio. I tuned to some rock 'n' roll music. So now, with the cool night, beating music, and our silence we drove until she asked me to stop. It was just about a mile over two hills to Shiprock. I stopped where a dirt road joined the highway.

"Is this the path to your place?" I quickly asked before she departed.

"Yes. I live about three miles on this road." She pointed her lips for direction as she placed her hand on the door handle.

"I wish I could take you home, but the road is too wet. I might never get home tonight. Well, I hope I'll see you in Shiprock sometime. By the way, what's your name?" I tried to keep her there a while longer by talking to her.

She took a long time to say her name. "Susan Billy," she said finally. Then she added, "Maybe I can visit you some of these nights." She smiled as she opened the door and stepped out of the car.

"All right; good-bye." I tried to show how I felt as I said those last words.

I looked back in the mirror as I dropped over the hill. She stood waving her hand. I felt proud to find someone like her who wanted so much to see me again. I already missed her. Or was she just joking about her visit? Why would she want to visit me at night? I smiled, hoping she'd come very soon.

Before I knew I was home, I stopped at our garage. The lights in the house were out, and the rain had wet the red brick building to a deeper red. I couldn't wait to get into the bed where I could freely think about Susan. I didn't bother to eat or wake my folks. I just covered myself with the warm blankets.

Another sunny morning turned into a cloudy and windy afternoon. Rain clouds brought another chilly breeze as they had two evenings ago when I went to Window Rock. I had not forgotten Susan and, deep in my heart, I kept expecting her visit which she had spoken of. Today, though, we must go to the field to plant new seeds. The cold called for a warm jacket. I glanced around the room where I usually placed my sweater, a maroon-and-gold-colored school sweater. I walked through the house, but I didn't find it. I used my old jacket instead, hoping my sweater was in the car at the hospital where my brother-in-law, Martin, was working.

The movements of my arms and legs, my digging and sowing seeds, were in my usual routine for the last few weeks. I could let my mind wander to Susan while my body went on with its work. Suddenly I remembered offering her my sweater on that trip.

"Are you tired already? What are you thinking about? Supper?" my brother asked when he saw me standing with a smile on my face.

"I remembered where I left my sweater. What time is it?" I asked him, wishing the time for Martin to come home with the pickup were near, but I remembered that our noon lunch wasn't even thought of yet.

"Don't know, I know it's not lunch time yet," he joked, and kept on hoeing the small weeds along the corn rows.

It wasn't until late that evening, about six-thirty, that I was on my way to see Susan. My whole life filled with joy. The dirt road leading off the highway where Susan had stood seemed dried enough for the tires to roll on.

Slowly and very nervously I approached the end of the three miles to her place. I rode over the last hill and stopped at a hogan. The people were still outside, eating their supper under a shadehouse. A familiar man sat facing me from the circle around the dishes on the ground. I was sure I'd seen him someplace, but I couldn't recall where. His wife sat beside him, keeping busy frying some round, thin dough. Three small children accompanied them, two older girls and a child—I couldn't tell whether it was a girl or boy. I politely asked the man where the Billys lived. He pointed his finger to the west from his cross-legged sitting position. It was at the next hogan where I could find Susan.

"Their hogans are near, over beyond that rocky hill," he directed me in his unmannered way. His words came from his filled mouth.

"They moved to the mountain several days ago," his wife interrupted, "but I saw a light at the place last night. The husband might have ridden down for their supplies."

Hopefully I started again. Sure enough, there were the mud hogans, standing on a lonely plateau. As I approached, a man paused from his busy packing and stood watching me.

He set down a box of groceries and came to the car door. I reached out the window and shook his hand for greeting.

"Hello. Do you know where Susan Billy lives?" I asked, pretending I didn't know where to go to find her.

"Susan Billy?" He looked down, puzzled, and pronounced the name as if he'd never heard it before. After a while of silence, he remarked, "I don't know if you are mistaking for our Susan, or there might be another girl by that name."

My hope almost left as I explained further. "Two nights ago I gave her a ride from Littlewater to the road over there. She told me she lived at this place."

His smile disappeared and a puzzled, odd look took its place.

"See that old hogan over in the distance beyond the three sage-brushes?" He pointed to an old caved-in hogan. "Susan Billy is there," he sadly informed me.

"Good. I'll wait here until she comes back." I sank into the car seat happily, but why was he looking so shocked or worried?

"You don't understand," he went on, explaining, "she died ten years ago and she is buried in that hogan."

At first, I thought it was a joke. I knew how some parents would try to keep their daughters or sons from seeing any strangers. His black hair and light complexion, not so smooth or whitish as Susan's somehow resembled hers.

Then I knew he was lying. "I loaned her my sweater and I forgot to get it back." I tried to convince him to tell the truth.

He seemed so shocked as he looked more carefully at the old hogan again. "See that red object on one of the logs?" He pointed out that it hadn't been there until recently.

I saw the maroon object. I could instantly recognize my sweater at a distance. My heart almost stopped with the horrible shock. I struggled to catch my breath back. I didn't believe in ghosts until then, but I had to believe in my sweater. I had to believe the beautiful girl who had ridden with me, who had promised to visit me. Still, why hadn't she killed me like the rest of her victims? Was it because of my sweater or because of the love we shared?

From that day, I had proven to myself the truth of the Navaho superstitions. I know I shall never get my sweater back, but on one of these windy nights, I will see Susan again as she promised. What will I do then?

Awaken Me Redhouse-borne Again

I

Image-maker dippers Tocito raindrops

Must make-believer yet as mythic
In this fallow eye
Bename me his only newborn.
Midst reminders rusted in hallowed skull
He kindles magic mind
Of cross-legged fetishes
So might i bridge nomadic moods
Across still crazier eyes.

Wisdom he talks! Walks in robin Beauty
From mica meadow away
So come shade rainbowed brow
And form forth
Thunder's teardrops he spits. i sip.

Squint swift whence eaglet verses call
Whilst unknowing sensation
Blindfolds with dirty instincts.
Remind me odic memoirs
Waken awhile from salty nightmares ago
And begin selfish souls.

Behold! Befool the true-blue owlish
With Whiteman wishbone
And bear his reincarnation
Kissing horny stares in a looking glass
Cosmos-cleared this secret sleep.

You say we betray Navajo grandfathers
Cuz coyote Poetress
Is our only bittersweet seer.

2

Joyous is veil voice from carcass cradle
Re-echoing hailstoned hogan,
Calling me back like lamed lamb romps
Into trickster's passion.

3

Horned Toad at pray i caged

Red Antway anasazi at play i harmony
Since two tiptoes too few
Retracing abalone alleys in eclipse.
He who rhymes wind-eaten wings
Slung a sinew string of emetic effigies.

Basalt bones fingertip angelic lip
Of Dawn Bearer oncoming for flesh warmth.
Wink erotic pass
At nightlong notion he greets anyhow.
Come suckle honeysuckle plumes
In barbwire twist,
Let alight straws of borrowed bones!

4

Over grape-sweet sweats of soot shoulder
i thumb-flick each yellow word
Of Toadlena teach.
Crinkling porcelain chins she wheezes
What hellish way
i'd sharpened my christmas pencil.

Remember tin taste from painted pains
Of january promises
Since thawed by hummingbird hunger.

Whoever mistakens a fawn fete
At slate saliva
But memorized my metaphors may ne'er die.

Twas that boarding school serenader
Who worships missing moons
With dimestore wreath left behind
By coward Creator
Drifting by in stone-blind selfness.

Dearest at apple-red breath
Sabbath rumors arisen
From one-tooth grin of urban indian.

Tis why I weep
Behind cornhusk mask of Fire Dance clown.
Cuss me coyote jokes
But could two-dimensional tongue e'er
Let me laugh in Navajo english?

5

Unearth saltbush Figurine

Unchanging Salamander mellows
With deepest sorrows.
Shaman struts stupor this missing morn
Sowing acorn agates
Into resin rivulet so clearer
Through taboo teardrops in slow flow.

When olden omen insist moonstruck luck
Harken to surprising, uprising
Essence of eternity.

Strew medicine quartz far fossils fields
Where Teec-nospos tillers crowd

Cursing obsidian owlets in oblivion.
Nightmarer in ceramic boots
Returns buffalo-horned warshields.
His 'so what' expression
Enlightened me for uncertain cure.

Magic magpies ricochet
Sewing black ribbon o'er Chuska contours
Of evil eve in disguise
Whereupon lyrist ladybug shall scan
Like crippled crow can.

6

Prettier phrases in rosebud bloom

Given broken brain again
Willow woodpecker
Nostril-nibbling at alabaster nipples
For lilac thrill
Yet drew gloom of handsome hangover
From red-dressed midnights

And sheds faster feathers in april rape
Enliken to snowflake sweats
Downing against coffee can tom-tom

Dainty damselfly bred butterfly fled
From barehanded apache.
Feel unborn feelings from pouch of his
And question if you
Outlived the wiser of enemy's egos.

Warless warrior waning
Caught every hidden thought in icy iris.
Sunglassed sculptor
Preys on your hiding daughter.

7

Some sparrows in a sopor

Breezy breasts tickle sure sanity
Liken to callous caress of her
Sensual shape in moonrising deafness
Reliving a sacrifice;
Some somber impulses prevail us at will.

8

am senile/surreal atlast
On its charcoal belly
Since the first back alley bed-wetted
Where motherly sis smothered
From empty breast
As gracious, glorious story lied
From telltale jukebox for a green penny.

Through embers of Milky Way gone
Triplet crickets track
Leather lighting he outsang. i ran
From self-immolation
In juxtaposition of elegy/effigy
You just praised.
Shroud to sober her in burlap blanket
And toss Tokay bottle.

Answer ancient ants with epic puzzle
Of reaching the Fifth World.
Cross-eyed lizard in mesquite muscles
Shows my divine distances.

Across kissing creeks I callow chase
for sixteenth sin

She forgiven herself for defaced virgin
And spewed that first lollipop.

Beseech upon muted mountains
Chalcedony bowl of perfumed crayons
And dipper drink
For this clay child in my misty mirror.

9

Shaman without a seashell

'Salt Clan' sons encircle my daystars
For geometric embers.
Brave the sacrilege of the grave i loved
And sacrosanct sip
Herbed street senses concerned for him.

10

Sanostee Sandpainters say

Turquoise stone at Yeii ear i dangle
For cousin to comic chanter
From same watering hole
Where 'tis said his squash sprouts
Glisten in morning motion
Splendid as Cracker Jacks things.

Pollen Boy painted in Tsa-nostee sands
Redhouse rainwater erased.

10A

Sandstone stars in gourd-rattle i jingle
For Peyote dream-makers

Buried 'neath baby-bluish flowerets
In thirsty tranquil
As icicle crescents reborn burning

Look back how they sewn fetish seeds
Beading my cradleboard stolen.

11

Through Bosque Redondo ashes
We hear fox-tailed Cheyennes in homage
Exchanging cattail arrows
Mildewed in blood-red acrylic
From left-fisted battles.

'Long Walk' grandchild in copper chains
Choosen to mask in cornsilk rainbow
To winnow december dewdrops
From emerald eyes of saint soldier.

Fetch for Manuelito
Canyoncito Bonito drum in brassy beats
With Ft. Sumner vengeance in mind.

12

In superstitious say-so
Comes Harrison Begay in appaloosa saddle

Gather against pollen puff
Of calmous cumulus
Gabby gang of gusty goats of his
And antelope riders from sheepshear ago.

Baby bluejays in silly show
Turning pastel tassels of yucca yon.

Autumn aunt far Pinon noon
Entwining melodic loom with winter wool.
Stubborn newborn, casein cat
With fly-freckled faces giggling on
At polkadot dog
Stalking juniper spiders.

i smudge Squaw Dancers in ochre footdust
For his secretive stare
And those sage-singed silhouettes
Of Lukachukai lullabyers
Return me to Tocito
In riding songs still so emotional.

13

Cedar cheeks a Caddo-Kiowa loosen
Sweet-talking my Purity girls.
His hoof-belled spurs stir
From tipsy vision in tricksy victory.

Feathered Flutist in fragrant footpaths
Awaits from Ft. Still daydreaming.
His stinkbug sedan splinters
Down sunset shadow of watercolor wogan
And wanders on into my yesterday.

Daisy-dazzled thicket near
Silkshirted raven in toy-trinket top hat
Titter tips Nehi bottle
Offering candy these deadly souls.

Gesturing jests i glint
Rhinestone roses on violet velveteen.
Rather be handshaken
Enemyway Artist in rebellious silence

Than be a driftwood doll
Dangling for a newspaper dollar.

14

Toadlena twilight over thorn horizon

am yet uncaught Cicada long gone
From domino deepest of cryptic canyons
Creeping in coppery cadences.

Two-stepping a twin twister
Antlered ancestor
Wily whispers from here, from o'er there,
"Intaglio winds must be so truer
As sagebrush brushstrokes
And paper dandelions before real rain."

Search skunky sky after Gallup suns die
And dip-up tumbleweed skeleton.
Let go forevermore
Saturday sinner a neonlit firefly led
Yet wisdom he walks matures us.

15

Till i pain poetic a Redhouse heal
Could transparent Coyote listen fore'er?

GLORIA J. EMERSON

GLORIA J. EMERSON (b. 1938) is a Diné matriarch of Tse Daa K'aan. Her clans include Tsé nahabiłnii, doo Tó'aheedlíinii, Hooghan łání, and Kin yaa'áanii. She grew up in Shiprock, New Mexico, and continues to live on her family's homestead. She attended Fort Lewis College, transferred to the University of Denver, where she received her BA. Later she earned an MA in education from Harvard School of Education. In the late 1980s, she also attended the Institute of American Indian Arts, where she earned a certificate in studio arts. She has held numerous jobs on the Navajo Nation, Albuquerque, and Santa Fe during the 1960s through the 2000s in the fields of educational administration and community action programs. She owned a coffeehouse and art gallery in Shiprock on the Navajo Nation from 2004 to 2009, which provided a place for poetry readings and for local artists to display their work, as well as a place to express themselves both aesthetically and politically. Sonja Horoshko says, of Emerson's career, she was "one of the original culture workers of the late 1960s. . . . All [her] paintings and writing begin with a conscious issue at the core." Emerson says of herself, "I may be the oldest Diné woman painting today in what I call cultural expressionism."

Emerson's first published poems appeared in the *Indian Historian* in 1971, and her landmark book of poetry, which features her own paintings, *At the Hems of the Lowest Clouds: Meditations on Navajo Landscapes*, was published in 2003. Emerson's mastery is in her ability to reveal hidden landscapes in the synergistic forms of poetry and painting; each form uncovers different dimensions of her artistry.

Interview

How does the Navajo language influence your work?

I am a passive speaker who understands the Navajo language well. I worked at IAIA as a director of a cultural exchange program, and when I'd drive back and forth from Santa Fe to my home in Hogback, I'd practice my Navajo and make up stories and songs. At this time, I became active in promoting Native languages on a national level. Part of my mission is to help preserve the language. I've written concept papers to help teachers in border towns boldly use the language that should be fun for the kids to learn, and they need practice using it.

Who or what inspires you?

Wallace Stevens, and Simon Ortiz's *Sand Creek*. I have made several paintings to go with Simon's poems, and it was anguish for me to paint them. I have started working again on one of the paintings, entitled *Guernica in America*, which is influenced by Simon's book.

You've had a wonderfully varied and important career as an educator, consultant, member of several important boards, yet what stands out to me in stark contrast to all this work is the five years you ran a coffee shop in Shiprock. Tell us about that experience.

The coffeehouse was a gathering place for artists of all kinds. I hung their paintings on the walls, organized poetry readings, and helped gather people together to discuss aesthetics and politics. It was a good time.

In your book, At the Hems of the Lowest Clouds: Meditations on Navajo Landscapes, *you effectively mix genres: a brief introduction to a particular reservation landscape, which you describe through poems and paintings. You even include notes for your readers. This is very powerful. Tell us about creating this book.*

I was awarded a three-month artist-in-residence at SAR [the School for Advanced Research] in 2002, where I had the freedom to write and paint. This book came out of my time there.

You have been described as "the invisible thread" in political and community activism and "one of the original culture workers of the late '60s" (Horoshko). Tell us about your long commitment to activism and the issues that you felt compelled to protest against and work on.

I have already spoken about the need for preserving the Navajo language. We are living under the siege of corporate America and their greed for minerals. Navajos care about the earth, but corporate America does not, and they are destroying our ecosystems. We used to walk in beauty, but now we walk in filth and trash with our land and waters polluted.

Your first poems were published in the Indian Historian in the early '70s. What other Diné writers were publishing at this time?

I knew about Blackhorse Mitchell's book, and there was a lot of excitement around its publication. The *Indian Historian* brought Navajo writers to California in the '70s and published my early work as well as the work of Irene Nakai, Nia Francisco, and Grey Cohoe.

What advice do you have for beginning writers?

Just write, don't have restrictions. Use music, walking, the sounds of nature, and even arguments to get started.

÷

Iron Track City

Iron track city
Gray by day, we're on display
Doing your cigar Indian stance
While others dance
Disjointedly
At Eddies and Milan's.

O the red hot pleasure
Of findin' friends,
talkin' it all out
in expletive spurts
before we get hauled away
down that lonesome road to somewhere.

Shapeshifting

A deer turned into prairie dog
turned into horned toad
turned into man
who flashed into a sparkle
and vanished into rainy clouds
that circled circled
                    northward, northward.

Early next morning
they knelt where deer had stood,
they carried corn pollen bags
searching for something, for something.
At last they found
a tiny hoof print and a cosmic wrinkle.

Although the women prayed, prayed
Darkness turned northward, northward

And way over there
Hair bundles loosened into long strands of rain.
Although the women prayed, prayed
Darkness turned northward, northward
And way over there,
Hair bundles loosened into long strands of rain.
The hoof print crumbled into dust
And Earth Mother thirsted, thirsted,
And parched and parched.

Grace's Hairnet

Grace put her black hairnet on her dresser before she left.
No one wears black hairnets anymore.
The old women who used to wear them
Seem to have all left Shiprock.
But the black hairnets return every winter,
Stretched out, twirling in the sky,
Forming cylinders, diving, bouncing onto brown farmlands,
And just as suddenly
Bouncing back into cold blue skies,
Diving and playing
Perhaps remembering the old women who wore them
When the women were young and joyful
Laughing and dancing even in the coldest winters in Shiprock.

NIA FRANCISCO

Credit: Nia Francisco

NIA FRANCISCO (b. 1952) is Tł'ááshchí'í, born for 'Áshįįhí. Her maternal grandfather is Kinyaa'áanii and her paternal grandfather is Ta'neeszahnii. In 1971, two of her untitled works were published in *Arrow III*, edited by T. D. Allen and funded by the Kehoe-Mamer Foundation. Although this publication acknowledged the winners of a creative writing contest, for Francisco it was an incentive to express, write, and give a voice to Native American women. She has published two books of poetry. *Blue Horses for Navajo Women* (1988) chronicles Diné life, especially the strength of women and the closeness of the Diné family. These poems, especially those on the Holy Beings, reflect the poet's deep spirituality. *Carried Away by the Black River* (1994) is a powerful and disturbing book that engages the reader with accounts of childhood abuse and its effect on the victim. She has also co-edited with Anna Lee Walters "Navajo Traditional Knowledge" in *The Sacred: Ways of Knowledge, Sources of Life* (1977); Peggy Beck is also a co-editor on the book, which is now in its sixth edition. Nia Francisco has been a recipient of a National Endowment for the Arts grant as well as being recognized by the Arizona Commission on the Arts. Navajo is her first spoken language, but

English is her first written language. Early in her writing career, she also began writing in Navajo. The poem "táchééh," written in the spring of 1977, was published in the journal *College English* and was one of the first poems published in Navajo. She has taught at the Navajo Community College in Shiprock, served as an educator around the Navajo Nation, and worked in Tribal Family Services, Division of Social Services, for about twelve years.

Interview

You, Luci Tapahonso, Tina Deschenie, Della Frank, Roberta Joe, and Gloria Emerson were the first Diné women writers who paved the way for the young female Diné writers today. Who or what inspired you to write?

In my early writing, I was obsessed with telling the world that we are not a vanishing race, which I convey in "iridescent child." In those early years, I was mostly writing for self-expression, an opportunity to be heard, since nobody seemed to be asking Native people for their opinions. Also, because Navajos tend to be quiet, writing allowed me to express myself.

In the 1970s, we were trying to find an outlet for our work. My good friend Tina Deschenie took some of my poems and sent them to the *Indian Historian* in San Francisco, which was publishing work of Native poets. Also, the [Northwest] New Mexico Arts Council sought poetry, which they xeroxed and sent out. There weren't many Diné writers then, and we were trying hard to get our work published.

There is a need for women to have a community of writers. Leslie Marmon Silko successfully brought awareness to women's writing.

Blue Horses for Navajo Women (1988) is a collection of my poems which I put together after attending a gathering of writers sponsored by Navajo Community College where Simon Ortiz and Gary Snyder were speakers. They were inspiring and really grabbed the audience, and I wanted then to get my work out to the public. My book contains poems which encompass key aspects of a woman's life: birth and death, motherhood, love in all its many forms, and family ties. Now that I am a grandmother and retired, I have been going through boxes of my old work and picking out some to rework. I want to add humor and now write with a grandmother's voice speaking in Navajo.

There are still many issues to reflect on, and we want young Diné to see themselves as writers.

When you are writing, how does the Navajo language affect your work?

I was raised by my paternal grandmother, and my first spoken language is Navajo, but my first written language is English, although now I also write in Navajo. "táchééh/sweat house," published in the 1970s, is one of the first poems written in Navajo for a general audience. I appreciate the communication which happens between Navajo and English and feel this is good for all people.

You attended IAIA in the early 1970s. How was this time influential to your writing and to your life?

In a creative writing class at IAIA, a teacher told me to throw out all the rules and keep a journal. It took me a long time playing with words and structure until I finally found my voice and I could go from "we" to "I." Once I had my voice, I could share it with the world, which was gratifying.

While at IAIA, I was able to travel with other students to conferences, and I found my work well received. I did lots of reading and was consumed by the book *Dune* and its sequel series. Most likely, the young Diné writers attending IAIA today are not from the boarding school era like elderly Native Americans experienced. It's been a long journey from then to Native students writing today.

Who was the first Diné author you read?

Blackhorse Mitchell.

Carried Away by the Black River *(1994) is very disturbing, and, at times, hard to read. Tell us more about how your years as a social service worker prepared you to write this book.*

I worked with Tribal Division of Social Services in the Family Services Unit for about twelve years. I always worried about the families and the social problems they were facing. During this time, I wrote these poems and was able to share pieces, which became this book, at a woman's conference, where I brought up scenarios of sexual abuse of children on the reservation. Writing this was difficult for me to do. The title is a metaphor for what it is like when children are sexually abused; a strong current carries them away in a black, not clear, river. I do not read poems from this volume in public.

"ode to a drunk woman" is a very powerful poem. What do you want readers to take away from reading it?

I was protesting in this poem. The drunken woman is still our mother. I remember a bar, the Navajo Inn, on the border of Navajo land boundaries, where I saw this woman. This incident stayed with me, and I wanted to remind readers not to be so judgmental about other people's lives. It is a strong poem and my statement. We have our issues here, and I wanted to write about alcoholism from a different perspective, a woman's view.

≑

táchééh

ałk'idą́ą́ "tóníłts'ílídi"
"tsék'ishalíní" holyéígi
nízhónígo ha'a'ágo
shinálí yęę táchééh
yá deidiłjah
tsézhin yik'í deidiłjah

chizh éí tsinaabas yeeniiyéé
áádó táchééh yá deidiłjah

áádó
dłohníléeł lii
tsinaabąs yeeniiyéé

éí yá
táchééh biyi' góné niiłjah
ákó shįį́ nizhónígo
bik'i nidahjíizt'ą́ąłeh
diné ałtsé táchééh yijah

áádó
sáanii bikeedó
táchééh yijah

sweat house

it was long ago

"where clear crystal stream comes up"
a place called "flowing from between rocks"
when sunrise is beautiful

my paternal grandfather he was for the sweat house
for it he would build a fire
on the black lava rocks
he would build a fire

the wood he would bring in the wagon
and he would build a big fire for it

and
"the grass that smoothly slides"
he hauls in the wagon

that one that one
in the sweat house he lays it inside on the floor

and that way it is comfortable on it

the men they go in first
and
after they have left
the women follow
they sweat bathe

iridescent child

Call me Diné asdzaaní

I am child of winter nights
growing in rhythm of summer thaw
I am the one you will see walking before dawn
and dancing after rain dew has dried

Call me
Southwest child

recently Earth greeted us
a hand shake   an earth tremor
near Farmington NM and Tsaile AZ
south of Aneth Utah and Towaoc Colorado

the Earth said, "It's been years since
I stretched and yawned . . ."

there is a rainbow
encircling my stomping ground
(like an embrace)
entrance from the east, from dawn's step
the rainbow stands
a rainbow with a face and limbs
a Rainbow   a proctor and my shield

Call me
decadent child
decades ago   and everyday   now
BIA, FBI (and other like wise)
devour my heart   a heart they ripped out
of my ancestors a hundred years ago
leaving our blood spots as legal documents
of victory   reflecting distorted faces
In the subtle blue shadows   the Sun never sees

BIA and Olta' decapitate a thousand children
in the thickness of sage brush shrubs
leaving confused faces on the ground

Call me
        Artifacted child

        amongst Native people
missionaries are trying to change
        coyote stories into parables of recent times

But now   Indians are expected to act indian
            for the glamour and benigned donator

            (it is foreign to be Indian from India!)
besides it is too dam   expensive to buy back
                    our pawned jeweleries
        even our hand-made jeweleries,
            moccasins and native clothes

Or to rob those museums full of them costumes
(and to xerox one sheet is fifty cents each!!!)

Call me
        Child-bearing child

I am a child of winter stories
        feet bundled with warmest, driest rags
        borne into a blizzard
Named for surviving in a cradle board

Now a grown woman
        a grown woman touching
            a man of experience
                his experience of killing plants, animals
                and VC people

His experience of raving, raging
raging about his male pride and manliness

and I am making copies of him for him
(carbon copies)
producing innocuous eyed males
(our sons)

Call me Incorrigible female

My body is curved and carefully carved
by the touch of the wind
chipped and sculptured like sexy mesas
and sand stone cliffs

My hair black like storms clouds
and you will often see black birds
flying through my thoughts
and gestures
I am the land and the land
is me
My breath is the rain essence
my finger nails are chips of abalone shell
and I have a purple shadow
like a hedge hog cactus
and I've been cured
by the smoke of cedar bough

ode to a drunk woman

1

dear lady earth
with
swollen lips
your beauty
comes and goes
those shoes you wear
muddy "tennies"
you don't know a tennis game
not even in an experience of that game

but those tennies stagger
to a bootlegger's joint

2

dear lady dusty
bundled warm this warm day
you stand by a highway
possibly hitching
from eddie's, to tropic's, to navajo inn

i saw you wearing your scarf
red yellow flowers covering your head
a scarf shadowing your dark skin

a face that is only a face
and in the shadow of the scarf
blood shot eyes sparkle
sad and thirsty

3

dear lady
with "roma" delusions
my ancestors beaded inside you
you are my mother

mother see us
we are sober   but drunk
with pain
caused by the same damn shame you learned

4

as your children we'll stay
and our delusions

are colorful
red yarn tied around braids
our minds twisting
in rage to overcome
that same damn shame you learned

5

and
only now i see
we remain like you mother
again hitching again
from albuquerque to gallup to window rock, chinle

and the shadows
of distant clouds
hiding our red tired faces

6

dear lady drunk

we are together again
unalike
and we love you still
as our mother clan

naabeeho women with blue horses

Friends of sky birds peppery hot spirits flying high
Friends of rain clouds huge shadows standing over the
land
Shadows descending tall over the early morning clouds
Devotees of Holy Ones tending to night fires all night long
who says that we Naabeeho women with blue horses must
be ready
for the great storms to pass thru our lives during our middle ages
For the great secret of old women medicinal ways of
knowing
to be the protectors of the younger generations

Friends of sky people grant salvation to drunken women
to medicine men
they have walked away to drink that liquid that eats the
brain
that liquid that takes away the heart and inner land, its people
that liquid that eats away the wombs and fetuses

Are we preparing? getting decorated dressing up young
Naabeeho women
for the passing of age no one warned us of a threatening passing
a flower frails and falls off blowing into the western winds
Friends of Sky birds I love seeing the wonderful colors
in my soul
in the child of Water people rainbow dew in Water
Sprinkler's hands
and the blue spruce needles around his neck and wrist
dew the soft dew
unwrinkled faces of Naabeehos the great powerful people
revived to its
original strength
I must see these I must smell I must touch and hear their songs

Must we talk about our tasks   or our fastings ways of four
        sunrises
let's talk about the tiny pinon nuts which once were the breasts
        of a maiden
who was given salvation thru self-sacrify and thrown to the Four
        winds
tell our stories until White Dawn yellow corn meal for female
        white corn meal for male in prayers for all to ascend
abstaining from human joys   fleshy desires   or christian woes

Naabeeho women with blue horse drink the sleep the sleep that
        Rested
the woman who moaned and cried to give life a brand new
        human being
or every woman who selfishly took from her lover's hand that
        brand new
turquoise necklace with its ear ring beads hanging . . . and drink
        sleep sleep

i hate elvis presley

here it goes again
tell me what happened?

i don't care what happened by now
feel real   ugly   that's
all
that lady who came by yesterday
she looks so nice   i
wonder
if she   feels like that inside
        she asked me about this stupid sore on my knee

i remember that pain
i got a safety pin and stuck it into my skin

my friend thinks i'm crazy
heck she's the one who is going nuts she's
in love with elvis presley
i hate elvis   i hate men   i
hate boys too and my mother hates me
when i ask her to get some money from my father
          for me to buy shoes she starts throwing
dishes, and ends up yelling at me am i the
only teenager
who has to work for a place to stay

i wish i could live some other time
and another place   away from
here   not here i
shouldn't never   never told
                                   never told Aunt
Jackie   what that drunk
man did to me
maybe   he was too drunk to remember he was my father

TIANA BIGHORSE

Credit: John Running, Courtesy of Northern Arizona University, Cline Library John Running Collection

TIANA BIGHORSE (1917–2003) is Bį́įh bitoodnii and born for Tsé deeshgizhnii. She was the daughter of Gus Bighorse, Asdzą́ą́ Łį́į́ Yiishchįįh Biyáázh or Son-of-the-Woman-Who-Is-Expert-with-Horses, who was born in 1846 and lived until age ninety-three. Tiana grew up north of Tuba City, Arizona, and attended Tuba City Boarding School. In 1968, Tiana met her writing collaborator, Noël Bennett, a non-Diné woman who became her apprentice of sorts. Together, they published several collaborations, including *Working with the Wool: How to Weave a Navajo Rug* (1971) and *The Weaver's Pathway: A Clarification of the "Spirit Trail" in Navajo Weaving* (1974). Tiana was also a contributor to Bennett's book, *Halo of the Sun: Stories Told and Retold* (1987).

At the age of seventy-three, Tiana collaborated with Bennett again to publish *Bighorse the Warrior* (1990). The book records eyewitness accounts of the Long Walk from Tiana's father, Gus Bighorse. As Diné historian Jennifer Nez Denetdale notes, "His narratives impressed upon a young Tiana the meaning of warrior. To be a warrior means to be compassionate and loving and to defend Dinétah. Grandmother Tiana's goal, to remind present and future Diné generations of their ancestors' courage." In her editorial curatorship, Bennett was instrumental in maintaining the unique voices of Tiana and her father "to preserve the storyteller's essence in this culturally rich manuscript" by refuting editorial regularization of English grammar. Susan Brill de Ramírez, in *Native American Life-History Narratives: Colonial and Postcolonial Navajo Ethnography*, notes, "Her diction, voice, grammar, and rhetoric reflect the Navajo world of her stories and are part of the very warp and woof of the stories' fabric. Thereby, listener-readers are brought that much more closely into the Navajo world of her father, his father, and the times of the Long Walk. . . . [These choices produce] a storytelling voice that has the conversive closeness of an intimate storytelling; it is as if Tiana Bighorse is sitting right next to her listener-readers, relating her father's stories directly, comfortably, and perhaps most importantly, in her own Navajo voice."

Selections from *Bighorse the Warrior*

INTRODUCTION

I am a Navajo of the Bįįh Bitoondii (Deer Spring) Clan. My name is Tiana Bighorse. I am seventy-one years old. My home-town is Tuba City, Arizona.

I started to weave when I was seven, and when I was eight I went to school. I went up to ninth grade in the Tuba City Boarding School. Then my mother got sick. I'm her only daughter, and I got three brothers. There was nobody else to take care of her. Good thing I did. She lived just a few more years. I was twenty-one when my father died and twenty-two when my mother died.

After my parents died, a year and a half later I met a man and we got married. I was twenty-three years old. His name was Fred Butler, Jr. But there were no jobs where we were so we had to go to Utah to support ourselves. We worked on the sugar beets. While we worked on hoeing the sugar beet fields, I still wove rugs in between the work. I always weave wherever I go.

Now I got seven children. When I was raising them, I didn't have a regular job, I just wove. I bought food and clothes for them. My weaving always supports us. Weaving comes from our ancestors. To the Navajo it's very important to hold onto weaving and the Navajo culture. That way it won't be forgotten.

I promised my mom I would never set aside what a great culture she taught me, and so in 1971 I made a book about weaving. The name of the book is *Working with the Wool*. It's a great book for the young generation. They are using the book to teach children in boarding school and even college students.

My father's name was Bighorse. He was of the Tsé Deeshgizhnii (Rock Gap) Clan, and his father was Tábąąhá (Edgewater) Clan. They called him Asdzą́ą́ Łį́į́ Yiishchįįh Biyáázh—Son-of-the-Woman-Who-Is-Expert-with-Horses.

When I was small I just listened to my father's stories. I am really interested in them, and what he is telling. Sometimes he is just telling stories and nobody else is listening—I'm the only one sitting there and listening to him. Sometimes he is telling lots of men what it is to be a warrior. Sometimes he is telling us when we are by ourselves, just talking to my brothers while I'm lying in bed. They don't want me to listen because it's just the men that are supposed to be listening. They think about it that way. They don't like it when I'm listening, so my brothers say, "She's not supposed to be listening. Make her stop." So my father says not to listen. He tells me the stories are not for me to hear. So I just pretend I'm asleep. But after a while, my father finds out. He finds out I'm the only one who is really listening. The only one who is remembering the stories. So after a while, when my brothers say, "Make her stop listening!" my father says, "It's okay let her listen. She knows two languages, Navajo and English, so maybe it's good that she's listening, and maybe someday you will have forgotten and have to ask her, and she can tell you. She's a girl, and if she has kids, then she'll tell them stories she heard from me. They will be told to my great-grandkids." That's what he said.

The stories my father tells us, they are scary stories—how the cavalry was there and how everyone gets killed, and how the kids and the ladies get killed.

The way my father tells the stories, it's like it's happening right there. That's how I don't forget it. I remember. It makes me think what a brave man he was, and all the other warriors, how brave they all were. And what good leaders we had—Manuelito and all the chiefs. They give the warriors and their people courage to stand on their feet and not give up.

My father fought for the Navajo land with hundreds and hundreds of Navajo warriors, with bows and arrows. And lots of Navajos did their job. And now what he said is right. I ask my two older brothers about our father's stories, but they don't remember any.

I love my father. Maybe that's why he gave me all that memory of the stories he told. Maybe that's why it's in my mind all this time. It's in my heart and in my living. It's important to the Navajos when you know these kinds of stories. They can keep you going. These are brave stories, and knowing them can make you brave.

I don't want to just throw away what he told us. Right now the young generation knows nothing. They don't know stories about anything. They just think that this is our land and it was given to us by the Great Spirit. But their great-grand-ancestors didn't tell them. The reservation was fought for.

I decided to write another book. I want people to know the warriors are brave to fight with the enemies. I want the world to know that the Navajo warriors were heros. They fight against the cavalries. Lots of Navajos shed blood. I make this book for the young generation to read and know the courage of the Navajo warriors, what our ancestors did for us. They fight for what they believe in. They suffer hardship at Fort Sumner. They pay for our land with their lives.

I want everyone to remember how the Navajo got this big reservation. They will tell their grandchildren, and our warriors will not be forgotten.

WHY I TELL MY STORIES

I want to tell my life story. My name is Gus Bighorse, and I am Tsé Deeshgizhnii (Rock Gap) Clan. And my father's clan is Tábąąhá (Edgewater) Clan.

I was born near Mount Taylor around 1846. I'm the only child in my family.

I am old now. Some days when I am herding sheep I can't see too well 'cause it looks like it's foggy. I just say I'm not ready yet. My time is coming, but it's okay. Someday it will be the end of my journey, but I've had a long life, and I will live through my children and my grandchildren and my great-grandchildren and even three times great-grandchildren. And I am happy and I love every one of them.

I have survived wars and many hardships. I never thought of going this far. And I am thankful for all my clan children. I'm not going to let my grandchildren suffer what I suffered. I shuddered *for* them.

I survived the great war of Navajo and cavalry. And after the peace came, that's when I got married and got these kids. On top of it, my first wife died and I got only the kids. And the next wife was her sister, and I got more kids, and I think how I can support my children. They were small when their mother dies, and I have to take care of them. And I plant corn and watermelon and raise horses and sheep, and that's how I have to take care of them. And the farming was really good for me to support my children. And that time there was rain, and it was really plentiful for my livestock and my crops. That's how I raised my kids, and that's how I really did my job on this earth. I'm thankful for the guidance I have, and for this long life that I have.

There will be war again someday. There won't be peace all the way. The white people were going to take the land away from us, but we fought for it and kept part of our own land.

Or maybe not war. Maybe someday the white people will give you something you like that will be getting rid of you. This is an old Navajo word that they always say, bááhádzid, danger. It means you think it's harmless, but you have to be careful. Something will sting you, like a scorpion or an ant. But don't try to bother with it. Don't try to touch it. It's just the same as an enemy. It kills people.

I always say, life will not be easy. But, as bad as it is, we Navajos know we were the least unfortunate of all the western Indians. We started our living again, we struggled to survive. And the only thing in the world we have is our own life and the land we want to keep to live on.

Nowadays the men and the boys should be thinking about how they could survive like I survived. It just be in your thinking and in your life to be brave and be safe.

CHOSEN TO BE A LEADER

I am very happy my father already took me everywhere when I was young to look at all those places on the Navajo land. Now I have to fight for our land, and I already know where to hide, where to get food, where there is water.

One of the chiefs I know really well. His name is Dághaa'ii Mustache. He has a Mexican name too—Delgadito. Manuelito and Delgaditio are the chiefs of all the warriors. They have leaders under them to tell the warriors where to go. Delgadito chooses me to be a leader of the band of warriors. I think of my father's words, "Someday you'll be a brave leader." Now my father and mother are dead. I am an orphan. I remember my father's words when he was living. I remember that he took me all over the Navajo land. If it were someplace else, I would worry, but I know this land well. And I'm supposed to be brave if I'm a leader, so I just do what the chief says and take the men. I'm the head leader, and there are about seven or eight leaders that are under me to take care of all the people—the men, women, and children.

In every group there should be a runner. There always has to be somebody on hand to take a message to where the warriors are. They do it in relay on horse or on foot. Manuelito is the main leader, and he always knows where the warriors are. He sends the messenger, and within a week or so the warriors have to be ready for the attack. We are always ready. That is what we do.

There are many enemies of the Navajo: Utes, Apache, Mexican, Paiute, and Comanche. Sometimes these guys even fight on the side of the white soldiers. The Navajo call the Comanche Naałání Dziłghą'í. They are the meanest, most ruthless of the enemies. They shoot anyone on sight—little kids, women that are pregnant, and old people. One time these enemies chased many Navajos from the Shonto area up to Navajo Mountain. Some people went to a place called Raw-Face and another place called Underarm. Both were canyons near Navajo Mountain. These people stayed there for two years.

And it isn't only the other tribes we have to look out for. Even our own people work against us. That's the way it is with Ahidigishii. He is Navajo, the enemy of his own tribe, raiding upon us. With him travel several men and women. They are a tough gang. He is the leader. If they happen to come upon someone herding sheep, they catch a sheep and butcher it and have a feast.

There is a Navajo family on Grey Mountain that is forced to move to Fort Defiance. They start moving east from south of the Grand Canyon. They go through some woods, and they come upon the camp where Ahidigishii's gang are. Ahidigishii shoots a horse while the lady and her son are riding. The horse falls. The lady and the son take off on foot and tell the family what happened, and the family just stops there, and they try to hunt for the main leader. There are two men in this family. One man has a gun and the other has a bow and arrow. They finally find Ahidigishii sitting on the rock. He has just finished a feast, and he is picking his teeth with a toothpick. The men ride up to him without fear.

Hastiin Łistoii Ts'ósí says to him, "Ahidigishii. Why did you kill our horse?" Ahidigishii won't speak a word. So Hastiin Łistoii Ts'ósí gets off his horse and walks up to him and strikes him on the head with his rifle butt. Ahidigishii slumps to the side. Hastiin Łistoii Ts'ósí shoots him and leaves his body there. His band disappears quickly. That is how Ahidigishii got killed. Nobody found out what clan he was. His gang went raiding other tribes and made enemies against the Navajos. He made innocent people suffer and pay with their lives.

Sometimes the Navajo warriors who are captured give us trouble. Sometimes they tell the enemy where the hiding place is for the Navajo, how many are there, and all that. And what chief's name is there holding the warriors there. And Manuelito gets really mad to the people. He says, "Just because they capture you and even take your life, it's just you and not all your people who will suffer. When you get captured, you just tell them, 'Go ahead and kill me, and I will shed my blood on my own land, not some strange land. And my people will have the land even if *I* die.'" Manuelito talks to the people all the time. He tells them, "Love your people and love your land. There's four sacred mountains. We are supposed to be here. The Great Spirit gave the land to us. So don't tell the enemy where the warriors are. And don't give up."

There are many warriors and other chiefs besides Delgadito and Manuelito who hold onto the brave thoughts of never allowing the enemy to take the land from the people as long as any one of us is still living.

Now a messenger runner tells us the Nóóda'í (Utes) are coming to attack us. We get the message, and so we take all the kids and women and some warriors and some food and go hide in Canyon de Chelly. We are told the Utes are mean people. They got guns and arrows, and they have long hair, not tied.

In Canyon de Chelly there are families that do farming where there is enough water. They plant corn and peaches and look after the crops until they ripen. When we get to Canyon de Chelly we tell the families the enemy is coming, but some don't believe us. They keep saying, "We never do any harm to anybody." They say, "Nobody in this world will try to take away our land." We tell them to hide and take all their kids someplace to hide, but they stay. Some other families say they will go to the mountains before the winter and stay there because they don't want to see their favorite peach orchards burn.

There is another chief, Dághá Yázhí, which means Little Beard. He has a Mexican name too—Barboncito. He and his warriors are up on top of the rim, guarding these people who are down in the canyon. Barboncito and his warriors see a wagon coming toward the canyon. They think that the wagon is going to attack the families down below, so Barboncito and his warriors attack this wagon and run the mules off to the canyon, where we use them for winter meat supply. They kill these soldiers who are coming on the wagon. They are carrying supplies for the army. Barboncito gets the horses and the supplies that they are carrying—guns too.

Canyon de Chelly is a sacred place for the Navajos. This is where the Mother Earth keeps her children hiding from the enemy. In Canyon de Chelly no enemies will kill all her children, for there are lots of hiding places. Some places the rocks are like underarms, and we call it our Mother Earth's

Underarm. That is where our hiding place is. I have to find safe places for the people to hide.

Sometimes I think the Great Spirit is guiding me, telling me, "Don't go there, go this way." I think it is my father's spirit guiding me. I mean my real father—and my Father Sky.

HIDING BEHIND THE MOUNTAIN

But there are Navajos that don't get captured. They are hiding in Grand Canyon, and on top of Black Mesa near Kayenta, and down to the Colorado River in their own homeland. And all this time, war is going on. All the warriors are in hiding with Manuelito, and some of them are guarding him not to get killed.

One day Manuelito comes to talk to me. He tells me to take my warriors and lots of families and move over there to Colorado River behind Navajo Mountain. He says, "You will be the leader to these families and warriors. The families have to hide down there and plant food." We stay there four years, all the time Hwéeldi is going on. All that time we have to guard the families from the rim of the river. The families plant corn down there, and watermelon, even peaches. That's how they support the warriors.

Here are some warriors that stay up in the mountains with me; there are many more:

Hastiin Deenásts'aa'	Ram-Sheep
Hastiin Bilátsoohii	Big-Thumb
Hastiin Bizhí Dizhah	Big-Voice
Hastiin Ayóo Ndiilii	Big-Man
Hastiin Hadah Adeetiin	Road-Goes-Down
Hastiin Bilį́į' Lání	Many-Horses
Hastiin Tádídínii	Corn-Pollen
Hastiin Hadilch'áłí Sání	Old-Talker
Hastiin Bilį́į' Łizhiní	Black-Horse
Hastiin Bilį́į' Łigaii	White-Horse
Hastiin Bidzaanézii	Mule
Hastiin Lók'aa'ch'égaii	Lukachukai
Hastiin Tł'aaschí'í	Red-Bottom-People-Clan

Hastiin Ntł'aaí	Left-Handed
Hastiin Tł'ízí Łání	Many-Goats
Hastiin Atsą́ą́' Béheestł'ónii	Ribs-Tied-To
Hastiin Tódích'íí'nii Sání	Old-Bitter-Water
Hastiin Tł'ahnii Bidághaa' Łichíí'ii	Left-Handed-Red-Whiskers
Hastiin Yistł'nii	Spotted-Man
Hastiin Bitł'ízí Łigaii	White-Goats
Hastiin Tł'aaí Nééz	Tall-Lefthanded
Hastiin Béégashii Łání	Much-Cattle
Hastiin Ndaaz	Heavy
Hastiin Biłóodii	Sore
Hastiin Nééz	Tall-Man
Hastiin Béésh Łigaii	Silversmith
Hastiin Béésh Łigaii Yitsidi	White Silversmith
Hastiin Bigodí	Wounded-Knee
Hastiin Chishí Nééz	(Navajo Clan)
Hastiin Bidághaa' Łitso	Light-Beard

From time to time new people come in our camp. They bring their family and their herds and tell us the story of how they get over here and how they get away from the enemy. Here is Hastiin Bigodí's story:

He is living on the west side of Black Mountain. He is a medicine man, and people call him Hataałii. He is living peacefully on the other side of the mountain. He is head of about seven families, and they have livestock and horses and mules and donkeys. They live in once place for about five years, and they herd their livestock on the mountain in the summer, and they bring them down in the fall. He doesn't know some Navajos are having trouble with all these different tribes of Indians, or there is killing going on.

One day somebody brings him bad news. That there are soldiers who are going to kill all the Navajos. He tells his family to more toward Navajo Mountain, all together. While they are moving in a bunch, the dust rises from the herds of sheep and horses, and they are seen by the soldiers. Some families don't move fast enough. They get trapped by the soldiers, who catch them and force them to Fort Defiance. Men get killed while protecting their herds and their families. Hataałii is way ahead with three families, and they get away. They go to a canyon just before Navajo Mountain. It is a long way from Black Mountain to Navajo Mountain. They stay there for nearly a year, and they hear that lots of Navajo are going to hide behind Navajo Mountain. But some have already gone to Fort Defiance.

One day, Hataałii goes out of the canyon to see what's going on. He runs about four or five miles. He doesn't realize that he has run that far. He runs from hill to hill. Then he sees a herd of Navajo horses running. Soldiers are riding behind the horses. He hides behind a bush.

He spends a night there, and next day he sees something moving across the wash from where he is walking. He runs to hide and throws himself in another bush. That's where he gets shot. The soldiers think he is killed—don't come to see, just leave.

He stays there for two days. He is shot up above the knee, but the bullet doesn't hit the bone. He crawls around there to find a medicine plant to put on it. He is okay then, and he can find water and some berries to eat. And he finally finds strong sticks to walk with. So he starts back toward camp down in the canyon.

He has been gone for four days, and there are four men of his family searching for him. When he gets back near the canyon, he knows somebody is looking for him. The men have been searching for a day, but they can't find him. This day they try again. They don't dare yell or make a fire. They think the enemies are near. These men have bows and arrows, and they walk close together. They think he isn't close by. While they walk they listen to every sound. One man hears somebody calling out. They stop and look around. Hataałii is sitting on a rock on top of a little hill. He has just gone up there to see around. They go up to him. His body is okay, but just his knee is wounded. Then one man says to him, "Your name will be Hastiin Bigodí (Wounded-Knee)." He gets his name like that.

One man from the camp has brought an extra horse for Wounded-Knee, and he gets on and they all take off. When they get back, all the families are really happy to see him. They all talk about how lucky he is—the bullet missed his bone, just went through his flesh.

The next day a messenger comes to the camp. Manuelito wants them to move behind Navajo Mountain. They leave right away. They move their herd all night till they get to the foot of the mountain. They rest for a day, and the next day get down into the canyon with us. Lots of people are already here.

We tell them the Navajos left for Hwéeldi three days ago, and the soldiers are looking all over for the Navajos that are hiding. Wounded-Knee says, "We are here in a safe place now." He holds a prayer for all the people—those that are here, and those that are still hiding in the canyon, and those that are marching to Hwéeldi. He prays they will be safely returned to their land.

He is a young man about thirty-four years old. He knows lots of stories. He knows how to make saddles and bridles and how to braid ropes from hides. He likes to tease around, and everybody calls him Our Son-in-Law.

His families bring lots of livestock into the canyon. They tell us, "We found lots of sheep and goats down in that canyon. Nobody was around. Maybe the people who went to Hwéeldi lost their herds. Maybe the herds got frightened and ran into the canyon. So we just put the sheep and goats with our herd. I think they were put there for us to bring them here to help us survive. We should all think about how we will survive. I don't know how long we will be here, and we men down here have to get to work and feed our warriors good so they will be strong and healthy. They are not afraid to fight. They can face their enemies face-to-face to fight them. And we have our work to do too." And he lets the boys clear the bushes where they will plant. Just a few days later the ground is all ready to plant on.

The people at the camp always listen to him. He is a great man, and he can say a kind word to the people that lose their relatives and those that their men get killed by the soldiers. He says, "We lost lots of our relatives. Some of them are killed and some are forced to go to Fort Defiance. But we are all here, and we all are in one family. We love each other and will help each other."

We warriors know him really well. He comes and talks to us too. He is always saying, "Thank you very much for your guarding us." Sometimes he brings lots of food for us to eat. He is young but wise.

All these people behind Navajo Mountain are wondering when these people will return to their homeland from Hwéeldi. The medicine man named Many-Whiskers and another called Old-Arrow go to the top of Navajo Mountain to pray to the Holy People. They pray that these captured Navajos will come back to their homeland safely, soon be free. At this time there are lots of medicine men. They pray every time before they eat—the whole family, all the time praying for the safe return. When they cook mush or any kind of corn food to eat, they use the stick, ádístsiin, that they stir it with. When they are finished, they take that stick out, with the mush on it, and they pray with it, too, for the safe return. And they can pray to the fire too. The charcoal that they use to cook with, they pray with it for their people to come home safely. They use corn pollen. And some of them use the corn that's ground. They do this every day and every night, before the sunset and after the sunset—white corn before the sunset, and yellow corn after the sunset. And they pray for the warriors that are protecting them and for the white people who are holding all those people captive, pray to soften the white soldiers' hearts to let these people go free.

TINA DESCHENIE

Credit: Tina Deschenie

TINA DESCHENIE (b. 1955) is Ta'neeszahnii, born for Tó'aheedlíini. Her cheii are the Tewa from First Mesa in Arizona, and her nálí are Bit'ahnii. She grew up in Crystal, New Mexico (her maternal family home), and in the Becenti community near Crownpoint, New Mexico (her paternal family home), and is married to Michael Thompson (Mvskoke Creek), a retired educator. They have four grown children and several grandchildren. She has written poetry since her high school years, publishing her first work in 1973 in Northfield Mount Hermon School's *Mandala* arts magazine.

She has read her work locally in the Four Corners area for many years, often in K–12 schools. Deschenie received a BA in business from Fort Lewis College, an MA in education from the University of New Mexico, and an EdD in education administration from New Mexico State University. She is proud that her dissertation includes some of her poetry. In 2008 she received the Governor's Award for Outstanding New Mexico Women.

Deschenie was the first Diné woman provost at Navajo Technical University, serving from 2013 to 2016. She worked in Indian education for nearly thirty years in numerous schools and at the Department of Diné Education until she retired in 2019 as administrator of the Dream Diné Charter School in Shiprock, New Mexico. She feels her work with the Navajo language teachers was the most important in her educational career.

Another first for Deschenie was serving as editor of *Tribal College Journal* for three years, noting, "I was the first Native editor, and I enjoyed assembling stories from writers all over the U.S. and Canada, including Esther Belin, Sherwin Bitsui, and Elizabeth Cook-Lynn. I was also proud to feature students' work from the tribal colleges. Our stories are always so powerful." She has been a lifelong advocate of Native poets by hosting readings in schools and by promoting their published works wherever possible.

Interview

In your poem "We Are Corn," you talk about the importance of the Diné language. How, as an educator, have you been able to promote and strengthen the use of the Diné language?

"We Are Corn" was written as a reflection for Diné-language educators that I worked with at Central Consolidated schools in Shiprock, New Mexico. An elder came to speak to us, and as I reflected on that day, I truly felt how he had nourished me with Diné words. We as educators were the corn, nourished by the elder's words. I was strengthened from my involvement in organizations and positions that directly supported Diné language learning. From teaching Diné at the Native American Prep School, holding a position as bilingual director, and serving on the boards for the Diné Language Teachers Association and the Navajo Studies Conference, I find educators want to use materials in Navajo and need more resources using the Diné language.

What do you feel are some of the specific poetic devices you use when writing Navajo poetry?

There's a reference to ceremonial language, ceremonies, sounds, protocols, having fun with language and its uses, writing as chant and as a directional. My early work reflected a repetitive mode, from chanting, but not so much anymore. I use imagery. I build on stories I know. I included four of my poems in my dissertation even when my committee questioned why. My poems mark specific sections of my study. Luckily there was precedent from other universities that made this possible. Poetry can help keep the language alive, and I always look for ways to share my poetry in whatever setting possible. My poetry is an extension of my thoughts and experiences. My point of view attempts to express my individual experience as a Diné woman.

When you write, do you have an audience in mind?

At first I wrote for my kids, teaching them stories about family. Then my audience got broader, and I started modeling writing that I felt bilingual teachers could use. Through my poetry readings, I've come to realize that my writing is for anyone, really.

What advice do you have for young writers?

It is so important for instructors to praise especially the shy, quiet youngsters. That was me. I would rather write than talk, and growing up, praise from my teachers for my writing was positive reinforcement that encouraged me to write more. Reading is also a key to becoming a writer. I had an educated uncle who took me from rural Crownpoint to the library in Gallup, and the access to a pile of books every month was a big influence.

Who was the first Diné writer you read?

I read Nia Francisco's poetry early on since we traded our writings back and forth as friends. Later, when I was in Luci Tapahonso's poetry class at UNM, hers was the first Diné published work that I read.

What was your favorite book in high school? What are you reading now?

I liked books by Jane Austen, Louisa May Alcott, and Anne Frank, among others; perhaps Jane Austen was/is a favorite, especially *Pride and Prejudice*. *Bury My Heart at Wounded Knee* was assigned to me by a high school teacher; it was not my favorite, but I was strongly impacted by it. Coming from mostly BIA schooling, I had little knowledge of Native American history until I read that book. I'm reading *There There* by Tommy Orange right now. I read most any new work by Native writers.

÷

In the Best of Dreams

Inspired by "In Praise of Dreams" by W. Szymborska

In my dreams
I write better than Sherman Alexie.

I can sing in Lakota, Dakota and Nakota
and not just about love.

I recognize lines
from every classic anybody has ever read.

At another tribe's casino
I hit the biggest jackpot on record.

I can mesmerize:
I drum heartbeats on a hollowed-out log covered with animal hide.

I can run marathons,
always in the fastest time, never losing the lead.

I ride fast, lathered black stallions
bareback in Monument Valley.

I can jump off canyon cliffs
and always sink gracefully into the deepest sand.

I can see everything
in the blackest of nights, and days, too.

I have absolutely no questions.
I trust your answers.

In my sleep,
I always smile and wake up laughing.

I am proud to be a brown woman of blood,
and I never have to explain that.

Some years ago
I saw a flying saucer hovering over a windmill.

And just yesterday a brown spider.
In stark contrast against the white of my sink.

You Bring Out the Diné in Me

After Sandra Cisneros's "You Bring Out the Mexican in Me"

You bring out the Diné in me—
that repressed giggle
urge to hide behind the folds in someone's skirts
or to run away never looking back,
but then, maybe,
that's just because you are the one I'd run away to,
leave my cluttered house for, give access to my secrets.
A few of them at least.

You bring out the Chief Manuelito's wife in me, Juanita,
the one who stares back from the 1868 photograph, unflinching.
The Diné woman warrior in me,
the one who could stand her ground
against the U.S. army marching over Narbona Pass.
The grinding stone in me, heavy and rough,
crushing kernels down to fine white powder.
The shit kicking, ass whipping,
fling-you-around-the-dance-floor vixen in me.
The pounding, mounting, insistent non-stop,
arm-deadening drumbeat in me.
You do. Yes. You do. You do. You do. You do.

You bring out the Long Walk tragedy in me,
the pain of it, the confusion and horror of it, all of it.
The uranium mining, coal-fired plant threat in me,
the dread of politicians, the emptiness of campaign promises,
the lure of quick casino cash.
You bring out the onslaught of poverty in me,
the reliance on low rent HUD housing and General Assistance checks,
the numbness of food stamps and WIC vouchers.
The fear of talking to my own kids,
the fear of their possible arrogance,
their possible disregard of all that I believe in.
You bring out the cultural struggle in me,
the frustration with each new season
of TV amorality and movie blockbusters:
shoot 'em up, drink it down, and smoke it up.
The hatred for every singer screaming,
"Treat my woman like a bitch."
Ohhhhh, you do.

Thankfully, you also bring out in me
the woman who can still roll corn-husked smokes,
burning her lips to keep little fires sparking at the tip.
The fantastic smell of roasted mutton wrapped in soft tortillas in me.
The hope of snow-crested sacred mountains,
their names in me, their songs, which hum in me all on their own.
You bring out the white shell in me, the turquoise in me,
the pollen in me, the First Woman in me.
The my-little-sweetie-sweetie grandma in me,
The one who longs for tiny hands to hold on to.
The Diné woman in me.

Yeah, you do.
You bring out the slam-that-damn-door-shut in me.
You conflict me.
You bring out the arrogance in me.

You bring out the I-will-fight-back-no-matter-what in me.
Even though my enemy is sly and cunning, both loud and silent,
articulate in other languages, present in body, in music, in words,
in print, on screen, in cyberspace,
and as oppressive as fog falling from sky to earth, cloaking all,
like nothing and everything.
Even so, I will fight back.

And I will wait for you as faithfully
as the sun and moon trade light and fire and power.
And oh, all the time,
my smile will be sweet and my looks demure.
Shy.
Yeah, right.
You bring it all out in me. Here!

We Are Corn

Just last week, a man came and shared sacred old stories
of the Diné people
with a group of us interested educators.
So thirsty we were, we drank in his stories,
fortified our souls with the information.
At our lunch break, he instructed us to eat some corn-based food,
he said, "So the stories will stick better, and stay with you."

After we were nourished in that way, it seemed
almost as if our group itself became a field of corn,
each one of us an individual stalk,
with our different colored ears, our tassels long and silky, waving.
His words, all in Diné, were the seed, the sun, the rain we needed,
and through the stories, we'd grown, become corn itself,
because our language is our corn, our food, our sustenance.
And what are we without our language?

Near Crystal

My heart always quickens at this place.
From the south,
it's when I see Sǫ' Sila, "Star Lying On the Ground."
From the north,
it's when I see Ḅeesh Nał Daas, "Metal Fallen to the Ground."
But especially,
it's when I see Tse' Hii Ts'oozi Yazhi, "Little White Cone."
Among these landmarks,
my roots nestle deep in the dark reaches
and a smile always curves my lips.

LUCI TAPAHONSO

Credit: Connie A. Jacobs

LUCI TAPAHONSO (b. 1953) is Tódik'ǫzhi and Todich'inii. She grew up in a family of eleven children and was raised traditionally on the family farm in Shiprock, New Mexico. After her schooling at Navajo Methodist School in Farmington, New Mexico, and after high school in Shiprock, New Mexico, she attended the University of New Mexico, where she met the novelist and poet Leslie Marmon Silko, who recognized Tapahonso's talent and encouraged her to publish her first work, "The Snake Man" (1978). After receiving her MA in creative writing, Tapahonso taught English literature and language at the Universities of Kansas, Arizona, and New Mexico. She is the author of three children's books and six books of poetry, including *Sáanii Dahataal: The Women Are Singing* (1993), which brought her an international audience; *Blue Horses Rush In* (1997); and *A Radiant Curve* (2008), which was awarded the Arizona Book Award for Poetry. She was featured on two Rhino Records CDs, *In Their Own Voices: A Century of Recorded Poetry* and *Poetry on Record: 98 Poets Read Their Work.*

The Native Writers' Circle of the Americas named Tapahonso the 1999 Storyteller of the Year. She has also received a Kansas Governor's Arts Award and Woman of Distinction awards from the National Association for Women in Education and the Girl Scout Council of America. She was honored as the Grand Marshal for the Northern Navajo Fair Parade (1991, 1999) in her hometown of Shiprock. In 2006, she received the Lifetime Achievement Award from the Native Writers' Circle of the Americas and a Spirit of the Eagle Award for her key role in establishing the Indigenous Studies Graduate Studies Program at the University of Kansas. In recognition of her work as both educator and poet, Tapahonso was named the inaugural Navajo Nation Poet Laureate in 2013 and received a Native Arts and Culture Fellowship in 2018.

Interview

What books or writers influenced you as a young reader or writer?

Even before I learned to read, I was surrounded by stories and the language of traditional rituals and memories that formed a blueprint. When I was eight or nine years old, I learned to read and would copy stories. I loved replacing characters and settings with familiar people and places.

What advice do you have for beginning writers?

We all have stories, and so we're all storytellers. I think we are like vaults ready to be opened. As Navajo people, we tend to think about ourselves and our identities in terms of hané or stories.

Why do you write?

I write because I can't not write. Writing is essential, thus I am always writing. It was a blessing to teach at universities and to be surrounded by people who love reading and writing as much as I do. I retired in 2016. My work offers a glimpse of a single Navajo perspective and shows the interconnectedness we Diné share and how we relate to each other. The Diné language is the basis for this connection.

My job as a writer is to take everyday details and memorialize it. The poem should present an image which reminds you of someone in your life. Like in my poem "Hills Brothers Coffee," seeing that coffee can reminds me of my uncle. One image or situation in a poem can bring a flood of memories for the reader.

In 2013, you received the very special honor of being named the inaugural poet laureate of the Navajo Nation. What was the most memorable part of that honor?

It came as a complete surprise when they contacted me. I very much regard this as an honor for my family: my parents, grandparents, and community. My work is a collective reflection of Navajo life, and I honor that idea. The poet laureate honor provided many opportunities to travel. My book *Blue Horses Rush In* was translated into Italian due to various international trips.

When you gather with your family, what is your favorite food to eat or to cook?

Mutton remains a favorite food. However, family gatherings are about being together and telling stories. We take delight in seeing the new babies and telling family stories.

Do you have a favorite poem that you wrote?

No. My favorite is always the poem in progress. I do have a fondness for my first poems, "Hills Brothers Coffee" and "Raisin Eyes," which I wrote as a student at the University of New Mexico in Leslie Marmon Silko's class.

What is the best part about being a poet? Are there any downsides?

I will always be a poet. When I was teaching, I would discover and rediscover various forms, images, allusion, and other aspects of poetics with every class. The downside is that there never seems to be enough time.

She Sits on the Bridge

When Nelson was still running around and drinking
years ago, he was coming home from Gallup
hitch-hiking late at night
and right by Sheepsprings Trading Post—
you know where the turn to Crystal is?
Well, he was walking near there
when he heard a woman laughing somewhere nearby

It was dark there
(there were no lights at the trading post then)
        he couldn't see anyone but he stopped and yelled out
        Where are you? What happened to you?
but she kept laughing louder and louder
and then she started to cry in a kind of scream.

Well, Nelson got scared and started running
then right behind him—he could hear her running too.
She was still crying and then he stopped,
she stopped also.

She kept crying and laughing really loud
coming behind him and she caught up with him.
He knew even though he couldn't see her.
She was gasping and crying
right close to him as if she was trying to catch her breath.

He started running faster and off to the side
he saw some lights in the houses against the hill
and he ran off the road towards them
then she stopped and stayed on the highway
still laughing and crying loudly.

When Nelson got to the houses
he heard people laughing and talking
they were playing winter shoe games inside there.

But a little ways away was a hooghan with a light inside
he went there and knocked
Come in a voice said
An old man (somebody's grandpa) was there alone
and upon seeing him said
Come in! What happened to you?
He started to heat up some coffee.
Nelson told the old grandpa about
the woman crying on the road.

You don't know about her? he asked.
She sits on the bridge sometimes late at night.
The wind blows through her long hair.
We see her sitting in the moonlight or
walking real slow pretending to be going to Shiprock.
We people who live here know her and
she doesn't bother us.
Sometimes young men driving by pick her up—
thinking she wants a ride and after riding a ways
with them—she disappears right in front of them.
She can't go too far away, I guess.

That's what he told Nelson
as he stirred his coffee.

Nelson stayed there in the hooghan that night
and the old grandpa kept the fire going until morning.

Hills Brothers Coffee

My uncle is a small man.
In Navajo, we call him, "shidá'í yaazh,"
my mother's brother.

He doesn't know English,
but his name in the white way is Tom Jim.

He lives about a mile or so
down the road from our house.

One morning he sat in the kitchen,
drinking coffee.
I just came over, he said.
the store is where I'm going to.

He tells me about how my mother seems to be gone
every time he comes over.
Maybe she sees me coming
then runs and jumps in her car
and speeds away!
he says smiling.

We both laugh—just to think of my mother
jumping in her car and speeding.

I pour him more coffee
and he spoons in sugar and cream
until it looks almost like a chocolate shake.
Then he sees the coffee can.
Oh, that's the coffee with the man in a dress,
like a church man.
Ah-h, that's the one that does it for me.
Very good coffee.

I sit down again and he tells me,
Some coffee has no kick.
But this one is the one.
It does it good for me.

I pour us both a cup
and while we wait for my mother,
his eyes crinkle with the smile and he says,
Yes, ah yes. This is the very one
(putting in more sugar and cream).

So, I usually buy Hills Brothers Coffee.
Once or sometimes twice a day,
I drink a hot coffee and

it sure does it for me.

In 1864

In 1864, 8,354 Navajos were forced to walk from Dinétah to Bosque Redondo in southern New Mexico, a distance of three hundred miles. They were held for four years until the U.S. government declared the assimilation attempt a failure. More than 2,500 died of smallpox and other illnesses, depression, severe weather conditions, and starvation. The survivors returned to Dinétah in June of 1868.*

While the younger daughter slept, she dreamt of mountains,
the wide blue sky above, and friends laughing.

We talked as the day wore on. The stories and highway beneath
became a steady hum. The center lines were a blurred guide.
As we neared the turn to Fort Sumner,** I remembered this story:

A few winters ago, he worked as an electrician on a crew
installing power lines on the western plains of New Mexico.
He stayed in his pickup camper, which was connected to a generator.
The crew parked their trucks together and built a fire in the center.
The nights were cold and there weren't any trees to break the wind.
It snowed off and on, a quiet, still blanket. The land was like
he had imagined it from the old stories—flat and dotted with shrubs.
The arroyos and washes cut through the soft dirt.
They were unsuspectingly deep.
During the day, the work was hard and the men were exhausted.

* "Dinétah" means "Navajo country" or "homeland of The People."
** Fort Sumner was also called "Bosque Redondo," owing to its location.

In the evenings, some went into the nearby town to eat and drink
a few beers. He fixed a small meal for himself and tried to relax.
Then at night, he heard cries and moans carried by the wind
and blowing snow. He heard the voices wavering and rising
in the darkness. He would turn over and pray, humming songs
he remembered from his childhood. The songs returned to him
as easily as if he had heard them that very afternoon.
He sang for himself, his family, and the people whose spirits
lingered on the plains, in the arroyos, and in the old windswept plants.
No one else heard the thin wailing.
After the third night, he unhooked his camper, signed his timecard,
and started the drive north to home. He told the guys,
"Sure, the money's good. But I miss my kids and it sure gets lonely
out here for a family man." He couldn't stay there any longer.
The place contained the pain and cries of his relatives,
the confused and battered spirits of his own existence.

After we stopped for a Coke and chips, the storytelling resumed:

My aunt always started the story saying, "You are here
because of what happened to your great-grandmother long ago."

They began rounding up the people in the fall.
Some were lured into surrendering by offers of food, clothes,
and livestock. So many of us were starving and suffering
that year because the bilagáana* kept attacking us.
Kit Carson and his army had burned all the fields,
and they killed our sheep right in front of us.
We couldn't believe it. I covered my face and cried.
All my life, we had sheep. They were like our family.
It was then I knew our lives were in great danger.

We were all so afraid of that man, Redshirt,** and his army.
Some people hid in the foothills of the Chuska Mountains

---

* "Bilagáana" is the Navajo word for Anglos.

** Kit Carson's name was "Redshirt" in Navajo.

and in Canyon de Chelly. Our family talked it over,
and we decided to go to this place. What would our lives
be like without sheep, crops, and land? At least, we thought
we would be safe from gunfire and our family would not starve.

The journey began, and the soldiers were all around us.
All of us walked, some carried babies. Little children and the elderly
stayed in the middle of the group. We walked steadily each day,
stopping only when the soldiers wanted to eat or rest.
We talked among ourselves and cried quietly.
We didn't know how far it was or even where we were going.
All that was certain was that we were leaving Dinétah, our home.
As the days went by, we grew more tired, and soon,
the journey was difficult for all of us, even the military.
And it was they who thought all this up.

We had such a long distance to cover.
Some old people fell behind, and they wouldn't let us go back to help them.
It was the saddest thing to see—my heart hurts so to remember that.
Two women were near the time of the births of their babies,
and they had a hard time keeping up with the rest.
Some army men pulled them behind a huge rock, and we screamed out loud
when we heard the gunshots. The women didn't make a sound.
but we cried out loud for them and their babies.
I felt then that I would not live through everything.

When we crossed the Rio Grande, many people drowned.
We didn't know how to swim—there was hardly any water deep enough
to swim in at home. Some babies, children, and some of the older men
and women were swept away by the river current.
We must not ever forget their screams and the last we saw of them—
hands, a leg, or strands of hair floating.

There were many who died on the way to Hwéeldi. All the way
we told each other, "We will be strong, as long as we are together."
I think that was what kept us alive. We believed in ourselves
and the old stories that the Holy people had given us.

"This is why," she would say to us. "This is why we are here.
Because our grandparents prayed and grieved for us."

The car hums steadily, and my daughter is crying softly.
Tears stream down her face. She cannot speak. Then I tell her that
it was at Bosque Redondo the people learned to use flour and now
fry bread is considered to be the "traditional" Navajo bread.
It was there that we acquired a deep appreciation for strong coffee.
The women began to make long, tiered calico skirts
and fine velvet shirts for the men. They decorated their dark velvet
blouses with silver dimes, nickels, and quarters.
They had no use for money then.
It is always something to see—silver flashing in the sun
against dark velvet and black, black hair.

Raisin Eyes

I saw my friend Ella
with a tall cowboy at the store
the other day in Shiprock.

Later, I asked her
Who's that guy anyway?

Oh Luci, she said (I knew that was coming),
it's terrible. He lives with me
and my money and my car.
But just for a while.
He's in AIRCA and rodeos a lot.
                And I still work.

This rodeo business is getting to me, you know,
and I'm going to leave him.
Because I think all this I'm doing now
will pay off better somewhere else,

but I just stay with him and it's hard
because
    he just smiles that way, you know
    and then I end up paying entry fees
    and putting shiny Tony Lamas on lay-away again.
    It's not hard.

But he doesn't know when
I'll leave him and I'll drive across the flat desert
from Red Valley in blue morning light
straight to Shiprock so easily.

And anyway, my car is already used
to humming a mourning song with Gary Stewart,
complaining again of aching and breaking,
down-and-out love affairs.

Damn.
These Navajo cowboys with raisin eyes
and pointed boots are just bad news,
but it's so hard to remember that all the time,
she said with a little laugh.

This Is How They Were Placed for Us

I

Hayoołkáałgo Sisnaajiní nihi neł'iih łeh.
Blanca Peak is adorned with white shell.
Blanca Peak is adorned with morning light.
She watches us rise at dawn.
Nidoohjeeh shá'áłchíní, nii leh.
Get up, my children, she says.

She is the brightness of spring.
She is Changing Woman returned.
By Sisnaajiní, we set our standards for living.
Bik'ehgo da'iiná.

Because of her, we think and create.
Because of her, we make songs.
Because of her, the designs appear as we weave.
Because of her, we tell stories and laugh.
We believe in old values and new ideas.
Hayoołkáałgo Sisnaajiní bik'ehgo hózhónígo naashá.

II

This is how they were placed for us.
Ałní' ní' áago Tsoo dził ánii łeh, "Da'oosá, shá'ałchíní."
In the midday sunlight, Mount Taylor tells us,
"It's time to eat, my little ones."

She is adorned with turquoise.
She is adorned with lakes that sparkle in the sunlight.
Jó éi biniinaa nihitah yá'áhoot ééh.
Tsoo dził represents our adolescence.
Mount Taylor gave us turquoise to honor all men,
thus we wear turquoise to honor our brothers,
we wear turquoise to honor our sons,
we wear turquoise to honor our fathers.
Because of Tsoo dził, we do this.

We envision our goals as we gaze southward.
Each summer, we are reminded of our own strength.
T'áá hó' ájít' iigo t'éiya dajiníi łeh.
Tsoo dził teaches us to believe in all ways of learning.
Ałní' ní' áago Tsoodził bik'ehgo hózhónígo naashá.

III

This is how they were placed for us.
E'e'aahjigo, Dook'o'oosłííd sida.
To the west, the San Francisco Peaks are adorned with abalone.
Each evening she is majestic.
She is adorned with snow.
She is adorned with the white light of the moon.

The San Francisco Peaks represent the autumn of our lives.
Asdzání dahiniłnii doo.
Dinééh dahiniłnii doo.
In the autumn of our lives,
they will call us woman.
In the autumn of our lives,
they will call us man.

The San Francisco Peaks taught us to believe in strong families.
Dook'o'oosłííd binahji'danihidziił.
The San Francisco Peaks taught us to value our many relatives.
E'e'aahjígo Dook'o'oosłííd bik'ehgo hózhónígo naashá.

IV

This is how they were placed for us.
Chahałheełgo Dibé Nitsaa, "Da'olwosh, shá'áłchíní," níí łeh.
From the north, darkness arrives—Hesperus Peak—
urges us to rest. "Go to sleep, my children," she says.
She is adorned with jet.
She is our renewal, our rejuvenation.
Dibé Nitsaa binahji' laanaa daniidzin łeh.
Hesperus Peak taught us to have hope for good things.

Haigo sáanii, dahiniłnii doo.
Haigo hastóíí dahiniłnii doo.
In the winter of our life, they will call us elderly woman.
In the winter of our life, they will call us elderly man.

In the winter of our life, we will be appreciated.
In the winter of our life, we will rest.
Chahałheełgo Dibé Nitsaa bik'ehgo hózhónígo naashá.

This is how the world was placed for us.
In the midst of this land, Huerfano Mountain
is draped in precious fabrics.
Her clothes glitter and sway in the bright sunlight.
Gobernador Knob is clothed in sacred jewels.
She wears mornings of white shell.
She wears midday light of turquoise.
She wears evenings of abalone, the light of the moon.
She wears nights of jet black.

This is how they were placed for us.
We dress as they have taught us,
adorned with precious jewels
and draped in soft fabrics.

All these were given to us to live by.
These mountains and the land keep us strong.
From them, and because of them, we prosper.

With this we speak,
with this we think,
with this we sing,
with this we pray.

This is where our prayers began.

Náneeskaadí

When the weather is nice, we sit under the trees with covered bowls
of warm dough and make bread on grills set over glowing ashes.
More often, we sit in my mother's kitchen

and take turns placing flattened circles of dough on the hot griddle.
The stack of bread alternately grows, then shrinks,
depending on how many people are around.

These days I drive home in the darkened evening to a quiet house.
The cats greet me with a glance and yawn. They look repeatedly
at their food bowls; they want canned food. "It seems like everyone
wants something from me," I complain while filling their bowls.
Dexter Dudley Begay purrs in response. I wish for beans or warm stew,
but then I just wash my hands and line up ingredients,
as I learned to do in home economics years ago.
"Never start cooking without everything being in order,"
Mrs. Bowman preached.
I mix the dough and cover it, then let it set while
I change clothes, turn on lights, and fix a glass of ice water.
Then I search the refrigerator for something to accompany the
náneeskaadí.
"It goes with everything and anything," my inner Martha Stewart reassures me.

The process is simple. Take a few handfuls of flour,
preferably Blue Bird or Navajo Pride.
Toss with a bit of salt and a palmful of baking powder. Mix well.
Ponder the next ingredient awhile, but then go ahead
and add two fingertips of lard—
not too much, just enough to help the texture.
Mix very well. Then pour 1½ cups of very hot water
(as hot as you can stand) and mix quickly.
Mix until the dough forms a soft ball and the remaining flour
lifts away from the sides of the bowl. Rub olive oil on a griddle
and heat it until very warm; then take a ball of dough
and pat it into a disk. Stretch it gently,
while slapping it back and forth from hand to hand.

After a few minutes, a rhythm emerges from the soft, muffled slapping
combined with the pauses to lay the dough on the griddle, flip it over,
its removal from the hot grill, and its quick replacement.

Soon the kitchen warms, and the fresh scent of náneeskaadí drifts through
the house. The cats are now sleeping circles of fur; the door opens;
my husband comes in smiling. He is savoring náneeskaadí and melting butter.

"Ná. Here." As in "Ná, k'ad yiłwoł. Here, now go run along."
"Ná. For you."
"Díí ná ishłaa. I made this for you."
"Ná, díí ná iishłaa. Here, I made this for you."
"Ná 'ahéésh kad. I slapped this dough into shape for you."
"Díí náníínsííł kaad. This warm circle of dough is spread out for you."
"K'ad la'. There. Łikanish? Is it good?"

The Motion of Songs Rising

The October night is warm and clear.
We are standing on a small hill and in all directions,
around us, the flat land listens to the songs rising.
The holy ones are here dancing.
The Yeis are here.

In the west, Shiprock looms above the desert.
'Tsé bit'a'í, old bird-shaped rock. She watches us.
'Tsé bit'a'í, our mother who brought the people here on her back.
Our refuge from the floods long ago. It was worlds and centuries ago,
yet she remains here. Nihimá, our mother.

This is the center of the night
and right in front of us, the holy ones dance.
They dance, surrounded by hundreds of Navajos.

Diné t'óó àhayói.
Diné t'óó àhayói.

We listen and watch the holy ones dance.

Yeibicheii.
Yeibicheii.
Grandfather of the holy ones.

They dance, moving back and forth.
Their bodies are covered with white clay
and they wave evergreen branches.
They wear hides of varying colors,
their coyote tails swinging as they sway back and forth.
All of them dancing ancient steps.
They dance precise steps, our own emergence onto this land.
They dance again, the formation of this world.
They dance for us now—one precise swaying motion.
They dance back and forth, back and forth.
As they are singing, we watch ourselves recreated.

Éí áłts'íísígíí shił nizhóní. The little clown must be about six years old. He skips lightly about waving his branches around. He teases people in the audience, tickling their faces if they look too serious or too sleepy. At the beginning of each dance, when the woman walks by to bless the Yeis, he runs from her. Finally, after the third time, she sprinkles him with corn pollen and he skips off happily. 'eí shił nizhóní.

The Yeis are dancing again, each step, our own strong bodies.
They are dancing the same dance, thousands of years old. They are here
for us now, grateful for another harvest and our own good health.
The roasted corn I had this morning was fresh,
cooked all night and taken out of the ground this
morning. It was steamed and browned just right.

They are dancing and in the motion of songs rising,
our breathing becomes the morning moonlit air.
The fires are burning below as always.
We are restored.
We are restored.

The Canyon Was Serene

Tonight as the bright moon fills the bed, I am certain I can't rise
and face the dawn. These dreams of Chinle and the mountains urge me to drive
back to the rez. My family knows why I left, but my husband's gentle horses
must wonder where he went. Since it happened, there has been no way to weave
this loneliness and the quiet nights into that calm state called beauty.
Hózhǫ́. Maybe it doesn't exist. These days it makes me sad and jealous

that some Navajos really live by hózhǫ́ǫ́jí. Yes, I am jealous
of how the old ways actually work for them. They wake, rise,
and pray each morning, knowing they are blessed. For me, the Beauty
Way is abstract most of the time. At dawn, I rush out and drive
to work instead of praying outside. They say we should weave
these ancient ways into our daily lives. Do you remember the horses

his mother gave at our wedding? Those horses
were such exquisite animals. We heard that people were jealous,
but we dismissed it. Back then, I rode horses for hours and used to weave
until sunset each day. Once we went camping in Canyon de Chelly. The moonrise
was so bright, we could see tiny birds in the brush. The four-wheel drive
got stuck in the sand, and two guys helped push it out. That night the beauty

of the old canyon, the moon, and the surprise rescue proved that the beauty
the elders speak of does exist. Late that night, a small herd of wild horses
came to our camp. They circled and sniffed the worn-out four-wheel drive.
It smelled of gas and sweat. The canyon was serene. It's easy to be jealous
of the people who live there. How much more substantial the sunrise
blessings seem there. During those summers, it was easy to weave

that story and many others like it into my rugs. Back then, I used to weave
and pray, weave and sing. The rhythm of the weaving comb meant that beauty
was taking form. Nights like that and his low laughter made my rugs rise
evenly in warm, delicate designs. Once, I wove the colors of his horses
into a saddle blanket. He teased me and said that my brother was jealous
because I had not made him one. Often memories of his riding songs drive

me to tears. Whatever happened to that saddle blanket? Once, on a drive
to Albuquerque, the long, red mesas and smooth cliffs showed me how to weave
them into a rug. I was so happy. Here, I was sometimes frustrated and jealous
of weavers who seemed to live and breathe designs. I learned that beauty
can't be forced. It comes on its own. It's like the silky sheen of horses
on cool summer mornings. It's like the small breezes, the sway and rise

of an Appaloosa's back. Back then, we drove the sheep home in the pure beauty
of Chinle Valley twilight. Will I ever weave like that again? Our fine horses
and tender love caused jealousy. He's gone. From his grave, my tears rise.

ELIZABETH WOODY

Credit: Joshua Seaman Photography

ELIZABETH A. WOODY (b. 1959) was born in Ganado, Arizona, and is an enrolled member of the Confederated Tribes of Warm Springs, Oregon, of Yakama Nation descent, and is born for the Tódích'íinii of the Navajo Nation. Her paternal grandfather's clan is Mą'ii deeshgiizhinii. She holds a BA in humanities from Evergreen State College and studied creative writing and two-dimensional arts at the Institute of American Indian Arts. In June of 2012 she received an Executive Master of Public Administration through the Mark O. Hatfield Executive Leadership Institute of Portland State University. She has worked in many programs nationwide, leading workshops and jurying, mentoring, lecturing, and consulting. Her poetry was first published in 1978 in *Spilyay Tymoo*, a biweekly newspaper published by the Confederated Tribes of Warm Springs, Oregon. She received the American Book Award in 1990 for her first book of poetry, *Hand Into Stone*, as well as the William Stafford Memorial Poetry Award; her *Luminaries of the Humble* won the Pacific Northwest Booksellers Association Award for poetry and was a finalist for the Oregon Book Awards in 1995. She served as Oregon Poet Laureate from 2016 to 2018, the first Native woman to hold that position. Woody has published poetry, short fiction, and essays and is also a visual artist; she illustrated Sherman Alexie's poetry book, *Old Shirts and New Skins*, and as an artist has exhibited regionally and nationally. Her book *Seven Hands, Seven Hearts* (1994) is an updated and expanded edition of *Hand Into Stone*. In an autobiographical essay in *Reinventing the Enemy's Language*, Woody discusses the importance of the various medias for her work: "It is this blessing of being able to make things that reconstructs my life, that gives me the knowledge to restore myself. . . . These messages—that beaded birds, horses, trees, stars, and geometric abstractions—are like prayer, a prayer for our present world to know again the root connection to our existence."

Interview

What do you hope readers learn from your writing?

I have a strong attachment to the ancestral lands of the Northwest and the Southwest. The beauty found in light on land, the water of the rainscapes and the dry creeks, lively rivers, and springs bring emotions that are hard to describe, so I spend a great amount of time writing on perception, over and over. Colors, and the wind's power to change focus, the sun's intensity on the eyes, and the scent of the earth, the heat and chill of separate seasons. One needs to be on the land. Not as an observer, as a participant, a species, and power in one's thoughts impact the environment.

When you are writing, does the Navajo language influence your work?

The Navajo language, Diné bizaad, is the first language I heard. As I formed, it was spoken all around my mother. My father spoke this to me while I was in my mother's womb. I hear it in my body memory. I have other languages in this memory. The Kiksht, Ichishkiin, of my maternal grandparents. The first years of my life this is the homeland's song that nourished my brain.

You have been publishing poetry for over three decades. Who or what inspires you to write?

I write from the core belief the word of our ancestors still reverberates in our present. It is a whisper in the grasses moving in all directions. My grandmothers, both Native language speakers, have told me volumes in my dreams in their language of what I need to know. I have English as my tool. This language is inflexible in its depth. I make it work into patterns of sound that is felt inside as I speak it, a medium for the maternal wealth of intrinsic genius with art. The making of their hands, the ova from where I triggered into being, repeated in a new manner by my existence. I live to honor the power of their resilience through language.

What advice do you have for beginning writers?

There is no weakness in the work you make. Sometimes, it is only practice, but the act, the vigor, the courage you have is the best impetus to write from. You can plot out writing like a map or in segments; however, the best surprises are the unconscious literacy you build from experience and from reading great works over your lifetime. Keep your ears open and listen to others in their conversations, listen to the birds, the sound of water in its movement. I think there is the influences of land that is always around one, even in the city

What was your favorite book in high school? What are you reading now?

When I was in high school, I read a great deal. There were paperback pulp fiction in the supermarket. The high school librarian ordered incredible books he would show me at the start of the school year. I do recall walking around with *Going for the Rain* by Simon Ortiz that my uncle's friend brought back from college. I annoyed my friends by reading from it on the bus to them.

Who was the first Diné author you read?

The first Diné author I read was Luci Tapahonso. Of course, this was in the early nineties. She was in various anthologies. Her books of poems are classics.

How does your poetry inform your art and vice versa?

My poetry is visual in its content. I started out as a photographer. It was my passion to look and explore and wear my camera as a mask. It was my excuse to be in places. No one questioned me with a camera. As an eavesdropper, it was a different matter. I loved listening to my family and the ceremonial gatherings' rhythm. In the longhouse on my maternal side, there is a calling through the drums. It is visceral and powerful synchronization finding the heartbeat in our bodies. To be ready for the spirit to move and the power of the creative will to unite with others in the room. It is a poem in sound. The feeling of feet and body weight jumping on the floors. A rising of harmony that takes everyone together to unified devotion and endurance. We go for days in this state.

Chinle Summer

Loneliness for me is being a daughter of two landscapes,
distant from the horizon circling me.
The red earth completely round.
The sky a deep bowl of turquoise overhead.
Mother and father. Loneliness
rising up like thunderheads. The rain pours over
the smooth rocks into the canyon that is familiar.

This is the road that leads to my father's home.
After twenty years I stand on the threshold of his mother's hogan.
Grandmother sits in the cool dark, out of the light
from the door and smoke hole. She talks softly
in the Diné language.

Talking to me as I grew in her warmth, my mother
lowered herself into this canyon, barefoot and unafraid.
She walked miles in high heels to church by this road
that runs alongside Canyon de Chelly.
She was a river woman walking in dust.

The Recumbent Woman whispers inside different languages.
I am one story. Beauty walked South then North again.
Beauty sparked physical creation.

A strong and wild will draws up the land into the body.
My journey circles back, unraveling, remaking itself
like the magnificent loom work of my grandmother's center.
My grandfather once told me, "Lizzy, I was busy singing
over there . . . you were here. So I came home to see you."

Rosette

Beading a story
is like weaving,
a spiral, space making itself in the light
and colors pick up
what one loves on the needle
like a song.
Over and over,
the repetition is solace.
A vibrant note in the thread
moves through this fabric.

Wind's Movement

Father tells me the wind is still free
I am bound, measured, corralled
by comparison. Enslaved
by the lack of direction.
The limit is my
vision,
which cannot twirl or encounter the meaning
of patterns in the scrolls of its
temperament.
I cannot leave my matters
attached to others by experience,
made less by the exclusion of imprisonment.

IRENE NAKAI HAMILTON

Credit: Irene Nakai Hamilton

IRENE NAKAI HAMILTON (b. 1954) is Ta'neeszahnii and born for Bit'ahnii. Her maternal grandfather is Tábąąhí and her paternal grandfather is Naakai Dine'é. As a Utah Diné, Hamilton is a continuous San Juan River valley resident and grew up near Bluff, Utah. Today she splits her time between there and New Mexico. Hamilton attended boarding school from the age of six. She graduated high school from Colorado Rocky Mountain School and in 1986 earned her BA in education from Abilene Christian University in Texas. She taught for nearly thirty years, most recently at Kirtland Central High School in Kirtland, New Mexico, where she taught Navajo Language I, II, and III. She was a member of the Diné Language Teachers Association and is an advocate for Diné bizaad's survival in perpetuity.

In 1980, four of her works were included in the landmark book, *The South Corner of Time: Hopi, Navajo, Papago, Yaqui Tribal Literature* (1980), edited by Larry Evers and published by the University of Arizona Press; two of these works are included here. Evers's book was conceptually and theoretically ahead of the time, as it emphasized the value of understanding writing in relationship to artistic and literary traditions within particular tribal cultural contexts. In one poem, "Bridge Perspective," Hamilton comments on the role of herself as a contemporary Diné poet:

i must be like a bridge
for my people
i may connect time; yesterday
today and tomorrow—for my people

In 1995, Nakai Hamilton published a book for young readers, *Sacajawea: Translator and Guide*, part of a unique series of books that was produced under the leadership of a Native editorial board and that emphasized heroic Native peoples' accomplishments. Retired from thirty years of teaching, Nakai Hamilton now devotes time to outdoor education, ethnobotany, community literacy, and travel writing. She is working on a memoir, a novel, and collecting her poetry. Recently, a number of her poems have appeared in *Canyon Echo: A Journal of Southeastern Utah.*

Interview

What do you hope readers learn from your writing?

Stories have rooted our culture and have inspired us to prevail, even in the worst of situations. As a writer and storyteller, I try to continue and push forward healing language. As a young reader, I searched for affirmation of identity, turned stones of shared history and travail as well as seek shaded paths determined to survive. As a Diné citizen, who best to tell our stories without apology?

How does the Navajo language influence your work?

Diné bizaad is my first language and its music blessed the first six years of my life before I left for BIA boarding school where I seriously began mastery of English, my second language. The elders in my family were a loquacious bunch and their speech and wordplay very poetic! Often, I recall an utterance and it lends me key to storied verse. Growing up adjacent to a border town community, I was also nudged into juggling the two languages as a young translator/interpreter. These days, I hunger to speak my first language but opportunities are spare and fleeting!

Who or what inspires you?

The natural world is my refuge. My father, mother, and grandmother were herbalists but I was absent too much to learn from them. Still, I'm a gardener and like to make things grow. Words are metaphorically similar; we grow stories to entertain, inspire, and give comfort and hope.

What advice do you have for beginning writers?

Keeping a journal is an easy start. I would advise beginning writers to write, write, and write. Read abundantly from the menu of classical and modern writers. Read profusely of international works and in other languages. When in a writing lull, reading other people's work always inspires me. Live. Writers often write what they live; be open to new adventures, add to life's ventures.

Who was the first Diné writer you read?

Luci Tapahonso was the first published Diné writer I read. Before her, I read English translations of Diné songs and prayers.

What was your favorite book in high school? What are you reading now?

In high school, I fell in love with short stories, some by Albert Camus. Short stories were palatable and concise. I liked that. Loved the satire and escape of Richard Brautigan's books. Currently, I'm reading *The Hidden Life of Trees* by Peter Wohlleben. It is nonfiction and full of lovely information about trees.

You live part of the year in Bluff, Utah, down the San Juan River near Shash Jaa' / the Bears Ears, in Diné ancestral homelands. How does this place inform your understanding of who you are?

During 1970s college life, I researched homeland issues cloaked by a visible termination effort; termination of Indian reservations. I was intrigued by the politics of the extractive industries. Some of my writing has been descriptive of the natural word and in defense of the Creation—flora and fauna.

Currently, I am also a citizen-scientist volunteer to observe, catalogue, and describe who and what is living on the Colorado Plateau. We defend our cultural heritage embedded in the expansive landscape of Shash Jaa'/ the Bears Ears region, which has been inhabited by Indigenous people for millennia, and it holds intangible resources. Our spoken, written-on-paper-and-screen words add to the collection of ancestral stories etched on sandstone canyon walls.

Story of a Cricket, Spring 1978

Little sister Eilene and I were looking, with amazed eyes, at the blooming desert flowers in the gray rock garden expanses near Kenneth Bi Dził. We heard a cricket, and we started to look for him. He was sitting under a flat, gray tsé' áwozí. Strange, it seemed, that he would be making a noise in the heat of a late spring afternoon.

Eilene took the rock off the cricket; the cricket was black and shiny. Exposed to the light, our interruption ("pardon us"), he stopped singing, and ran around looking for shade. Eilene put back his roof. The cricket took a breath and resumed his singing.

Sometimes, I see the black, shiny cricket so suited to have sung the first note of the song of creation; in dark directionless space, everyone waiting, then one chirp to make an announcement, "K' iz . . . something is happening. We are becoming!" Nahak' ízii.

Sunrise Flight into Acid Rain/Cancelled

I woke up my mother, father and little cousin around one-thirty in the early morning. My luggage was packed and already in the trunk of the car. Around two o'clock, we bumped down the short dirt road drive to the highway. From there it was a smooth two hours' cruise to Cortez, from where I was to catch my plane to Denver. My mother drove, I sat beside her, and my cousin Victoria and my father were in the backseat. Once in a while, someone spoke, sang a song or told a story. It was a novel experience, traveling in the predawn darkness. Only one car passed us on the road and it was going the opposite way.

We arrived in Cortez in a seemingly short time and got some gas at a truck stop. We also had some coffee and sweet rolls in the adjoining cafe. The cafe had only two other customers when we entered and it was very quiet. Sitting across from me, my mother looked sad so I told her a funny story and she smiled.

At five-thirty, we left the cafe and drove to the airport. I checked in and had my luggage tagged. I barely had time to wash my face again when suddenly it was time to go. I went through security check, came back through and hugged my mother, father, and cousin: "goodbye and I will be back, soon." I remembered my horse and told my cousin to take care of him while I was away. As I walked through the glass door, and past the armed security guard, I was also going through a "time warp."

On the plane I sat at the far end, in the smoking section, although I do not smoke. I had heard from my sister that that part of the plane offered a better outside view, she was right. The stewardess mumbled her well-memorized jargon about airbags and emergency exits as the plane ambled down the runway. Minutes later, we were over Mesa Verde. Down below, there were the still-bald spots from the forest fires of 1970, a drought year. The sun was peeking over the horizon, lighting the eastern slopes of the high mesas of junipers and pinon pines, and already behind, in the northwest lay the Sleeping Ute Mountain, Dzil Naajinii. Looking south over Dinétah, my people's homeland, I saw it enveloped in an ugly, green cloud—the dreaded smoke from the Four Corners Power Plant in New Mexico. In mourning, I also saw the furrowed alkaline hills north of the power plant. There were also the septic-green pools of dammed water, not sparkling like living water. South of Farmington, on the mesas, I saw for the first time the green hay fields, the product of an optimistic and colossal irrigation project. I questioned, "Would those fields be irrigated with an acid rain? Would the well-known sandstone pillars and mesas of Dinétah be drenched with the same deteriorating rain and would we wake up one day, in a flat dead land? No! No, it must not be." There was only mourning in me as the plane lifted off again, from Farmington, into the north, the mountain country of Colorado. The mountain country scenery was more pleasant but it was remote, now, National Forest/Private/No Trespassing land. Somewhere over central Colorado, we flew over aspen forests and high mountain meadows over-run with cloud shadows. The forests were bright green clumps, the texture of a shedding pony's back. Another time, while over some still snowy mountains, I looked down and noticed the gray-dusted-no-longer-white snow.

Shortly after the gray snow, the little plane left the mountains, and Denver and the plains came into view. The cityscape was the same rather monotonous domino trails of squat buildings arranged in rows and patches of small green lawns—paradoxical tributes to a once free Earth.

My black horse runs fast; one ear back,
one ear forward and his mane tangled by
the wind. I would whistle to the meadow
larks, mountain bluebirds, and all the
tsídii in the sagebrush and the junipers, and
we had talked.

Back in Denver, the plane descended, bumped along the runway and taxied to a stop. Slowly, I collected my carry-on bag, tennis racket, and purse, and walked down the steps of the plane and up again into an eight o'clock already-busy terminal. There was a breeze blowing, warm air bouncing off the paved-over Earth. No, it must not be. It shall not be.

Summer Coup, 1973

We arrived at the south rim of the Grand Canyon in a dark green pickup truck, the parents and five children of assorted ages. At the park entrance, all must pay a fee. Our aged father said, "No, I will not pay. I am a Native American. Áłtsé Kééhat'íinii nishłį.

I will not pay to see what is my birthright."

We, the children of Eddie Nakai cowered and sunk low into the seats, our spirits quivering, having been intimidated by the thrashing of BIA boarding school trauma whatever they may be. We held our collective breath.

Our gray haired father persisted. He was not flustered. He was a warrior looking the enemy in the eye. "We will not pay to see what is ours. This land belonged to our ancestors."

Then suddenly, the ranger waved us in. We sighed, and rose up in our seats.

The Grand Canyon is a geological marvel. What our dear father did there that day was also marvelous. From outside and within ourselves, courage rises to slay the ghosts of wrongs that have been wrought. That small fatherly gesture had redeemed us.

Dishwasher

The electric dishwasher has been inoperable for about a year, now.
The Maytag wonder had finally croaked,
choked by mineral deposits or circuits fried!
Never minding,
I mix a plastic tub of warm chlorinated water,
sprinkled with a capful bleach.
Roll up my sleeves and looking out the window at the unfolding vernal
    vegetation,
I rinse the dog licked, slimy bowls,
"Only bleach takes off the slime," I tell my husband,
whose culture has no qualms
about letting dogs lick bowls of whipped egg residue.
Fondling the plates and cups,
I bathe them in soapy water and rinse them,
and rest them in dish drainer to dry,
in their own time.

Growing up in the desert,
there were no excuses
for girls not doing the dishes!

Our dear Navajo mother, frustrated,
would finally burst out sarcastically,
"Doo hanii łeets'aa' t'óó ni'góó ninóhníił da! Bini'dii lééchaa'í deełnaad!"
"Why don't you just put the dirty dishes on the floor
and let the dogs lick them clean for you?"
As it was, in our culture, dogs were not even allowed in the house.
So I imagine,
dogs licking dishes were an insult of high degree!

Shibeedí tánásgis, tł'óógóó díníshįį'go.
I cleanse my precious kitchenware,
bowls that cradled nourishing sustenance and,
I remember Grandmother's prayers that gave special mention of "beedí,"
precious cooking utensils.

Outside, an easterly breeze tickles pine branches,
the snow has melted, the grass is greening up.

Cleansing one's dishes must have been a holy ritual.
"Tsx'íį̨łgo łeets'aa' ha'naa naanaojeeh."
"Herd the dishes across the flowing water, quickly!"
The dishes are done!

LAURA TOHE

Credit: Laura Tohe

LAURA TOHE (b. 1952) is Tsé Nahabiłnii and born for the Tódích'ii'nii. Born in Fort Defiance, Arizona, Tohe grew up at Crystal, New Mexico, near the Chuska Mountains on the Diné homeland. Her father was a Navajo Code Talker. In an interview, she notes, "I grew up speaking Diné as my primary language. . . . While growing up I heard stories all around me. As we drove down the dusty reservation road, my mother told many Diné stories." Tohe graduated with a BA in psychology from the University of New Mexico in 1975 and earned an MA from the University of Nebraska in 1985 and a PhD from the University of Nebraska in 1993. She was the first Navajo person to earn a doctorate in English. At Arizona State University she was professor with distinction and is now professor emerita.

Tohe has written or edited five books and published poetry in the United States, Canada, and Europe. Tohe's first publication, in 1981, was *Ceremony of Brotherhood*, edited by Rudolfo Anaya and Simon J. Ortiz. Her published books include *Making Friends with Water* (chapbook); *No Parole Today*, a book on boarding schools; *Sister Nations: Native American Women Writers on Community*, co-edited with Heid E. Erdrich; *Tséyi' / Deep in the Rock*, in collaboration with photographer Stephen Strom; and *Code Talker Stories*, an oral history book created with some of the remaining Navajo Code Talkers. She wrote a commissioned libretto, *Enemy Slayer, A Navajo Oratorio*, for the Phoenix Symphony, which was called "a triumph" by *Opera Today*. In April 2019, another libretto, *Nahasdzáán in the Glittering World / Mother Earth in the Glittering World*, premiered at Normandy's Opera de Rouen in France.

Arizona Humanities awarded her the 2006 Dan Schilling Public Scholar Award. In 2015 Laura was honored as the Navajo Nation Poet Laureate, a title given to her in celebration and recognition of her work as a poet and writer. In 2020, Tohe was the recipient of an Academy of American Poets Laureate Fellowship. Anthony K. Webster, co-editor of this volume, has published in-depth scholarship on her writing; her work has also been the central focus of graduate theses and dissertations.

Interview

What do you hope readers learn from your writing?

My work can't necessarily be categorized as Native American literature, though generically it can be called that. I prefer Navajo or Diné literature. The Diné people have a long heritage of storytelling and poetic traditions that have sustained and maintained our lives and culture for centuries. My work originated from that tradition, as it does from place, language, education, and life experience. I also have a PhD in literature, so my writing reflects that education as well. I hope my readers see that my work makes the invisible visible. My work isn't all about celebration of culture or about tragedy, those stories and poems about a people who have survived or are trying to survive brutal attacks on their land, community, and language. On the other hand, there are also the stories and poems that act as shields against that onslaught. There are also the stories, poems, and language that claim and validate our voices and our lives. I hope that readers see that my work contributes to a world literature.

How does the Navajo language influence your work?

I'm deeply grateful to my parents who taught and dressed me in the Navajo language. Diné bizaad enables me to see through that lens that is at once artistic, poetic, and is a beautiful language that has many uses. Diné bizaad is medicine for healing, was used as a secret code by the Navajo Code Talkers, and has blessed me in writing poetry, stories, essays, and now writing librettos for operas. It has grounded me to Navajo culture, spirituality, and community. Without it, I would be a different person.

Who or what inspires you?

As a writer everything around can inspire me—images, lines, films, other writers and poets, my sons, my students, animals, mountains, music, and the list goes on. Having curiosity about the world inspires me. The other night I saw an old western film in which Elvis Presley was part Kiowa and I wanted to write a poem about it.

What advice do you have for beginning writers?

Read, read, read contemporary and writers from past eras and from other countries. Growing up during a time on the rez I didn't have access to the world like today. Reading was a way for me to escape and visit the world through fairy tales, comic books, Nancy Drew, and later through more mature literature. Reading can take you all over the world.

Keep a journal and *make time* to write in it. I found a writer whose work I admired and I tried to imitate her writing when I was putting my first words on paper. This was a useful way for me to find my own voice and something to do on a trial basis, because you will want to find your own unique voice and not be a copycat of someone else. Eventually, I abandoned this practice. To be a writer, you have to become a loner but in a good way. To be a writer you have to practice being a writer and that means making the time for it and not expect that it will come easy. Many of us had to work really hard and put in the time to get where we are. And if you find that writing is not your cup of tea, that's okay. You can find something else that you're good at and that will motivate you.

Take creative writing classes and/or form a writing group, which can be one or more of your peers, people who share your interest in writing. You can go to this group for support. They can read your work and give feedback, and you can discuss each other's work, all things that will help you grow as a writer. My group is only made up of one writer, and she meets my writer needs.

Publish in small presses to begin and don't give up if you get a rejection. We don't like rejection, but it is part of being a writer. Rejoice when you do get an acceptance.

Who was the first Navajo writer you read?

That was myself. I read my first poem. Other than myself, I think it was Luci Tapahonso.

What was your favorite book in high school? What are you reading now?

I had a teacher in fourth grade who told us Edgar Allan Poe stories after lunch every day. I loved story time and because of Mr. Rivera, I grew to love Poe's stories and still do. When I got to high school, I found his books in the school library, checked them out, and indulged myself. Right now I'm reading *The Handmaid's Tale* by Margaret Atwood; essays in *The World of Yesterday, an Autobiography* by Stefan Zweig; and poetry in *Sing*, edited by Allison Hedge Coke.

So many of your boarding school–related poems touch readers and move them to share their stories with you. What have these responses taught you about the role of literature/art?

I think literature, which includes oral literature, brings us together. Ancient peoples all over the world always had oral traditions. Humans have been telling stories for so long that we are wired for it. What I came to realize is that stories from my community are invisible. At least two or three generations of Native peoples attended boarding schools and yet there were no stories written about it until recently. People who've read my book *No Parole Today* or heard me read my boarding school poems will say they laughed because they could identity with it and, sadly, some say the trauma of their boarding school experiences are still with them. The people (mostly Navajo people) who find humor or tragedy may find a kind of validation in the poems because it speaks of their experience; it makes their stories visible. For the Diné people, oral and written literatures are means of healing.

⩧

Our Tongues Slapped into Silence

In first grade I was five years old, the youngest and smallest in my class, always the one in front at group picture time. The principal put me in first grade because I spoke both Diné and English. Because of that, I skipped Beginner class.

All my classmates were Diné and most of them spoke only the language of our ancestors. During this time, the government's policy meant to assimilate us into the white way of life. We had no choice in the matter; we had to comply. The taking of our language was a priority.

Dick and Jane Subdue the Diné

See Father.
See Mother.
See Dick run.
See Jane and Sally laugh.
oh, oh, oh
See Spot jump.
oh, oh, oh
See Eugene speak Diné.
See Juanita answer him.
oh, oh, oh
See teacher frown.
uh oh, uh oh

In first grade our first introduction to Indian school was Miss Rolands, a black woman from Texas, who treated us the way her people had been treated by white people. Later I learned how difficult it was for black teachers to find jobs in their communities, so they took jobs with the Bureau of Indian Affairs in New Mexico and Arizona in the 1950s and 60s.

Miss Rolands found it difficult to adjust to living in a mostly Diné community, connected to the outside world by only a dirt road that was sometimes impassable in the winter.

See Eugene with red hands, shape of ruler.
oh, oh, oh
See Eugene cry.
oh, oh, oh

See Juanita stand in corner, see tears fall down face.
oh, oh, oh

In first grade we received the first of our Dick and Jane books that introduced us to the white man's world through Father, Mother, Dick, Jane, Puff and Spot. These and other characters said and did what we thought all white people did: drive cars to the farm, drain maple juice from trees, and say oh, oh, oh a lot.

Oh see us draw pictures
of brown horses under blue clouds.
We color eyes black, hair black.
We draw ears and leave out mouth.

Oh see, see, see, see.

Miss Rolands, an alien in our world, stood us in the corner of the classroom or outside in the hallway to feel shame for the crime of speaking Diné. Other times our hands were imprinted with red slaps from the ruler. In later classes we headed straight for the rear of the classrooms, never asked questions, and never raised our hand. Utter one word of Diné and the government made sure our tongues were drowned in the murky waters of assimilation.

Joe Babes

Joe Babes, the ones named
Jolene, Rena, Mae, Juanita or Loretta.

Some teased their hair
into bouffant hairdos and
wore too much makeup.
Others wore outdated dresses and shoes,
and washed their hair with detergent soap.
They spoke in broken Indin-glish and
we used to laugh at them.

Joe Babes sat quietly
in the back of classrooms
even when they knew the answers
were described as shy, dumb, angry, or on drugs
by the teachers.

These were the ones who stood in corners
for speaking Indian
until the government said it was okay.
Then they sang in Indian Clubs
and danced at pow-wows.
Joe Babes were given pernicious looks
by the cashier in the public school cafeteria

as they went through the line
because she thought they got free meals from the
government.

Joe Babes
laughed too loud
and were easily angered
when they got drunk.

Joe Babes
were the one that left the reservations
for the cities, for the schools, for the jobs.

We were the Joe Babes.
All of us.

Easter Sunday

Driving to the mountains at noon
  through sagebrush and pinon trees
children gather wood uncle builds fire
  mother and daughters prepare food

flames burning good and hot
  coals ready grill on push coals around

stew on stir it now and then
  skillet ready for fry bread watch smoke rise
  slap dough into large thin circles edges lumpy
  pull dough make holes it's okay
  put in skillet anyway watch it floating
  makes bubbles turns brown turn it over
  feel heat on face and hands

Grandma scolding Aunt doesn't know how
  to cut mutton ribs Grandma fixes puts back
  on grill watch ribs sizzle brown turn over
  drop in ashes dust it off put back on grill
  hope Grandma didn't see

Fry bread stack getting higher
  push more coals under skillet
  my son moves closer to the fire raises hand
  "hot hot" he says uncle comes
  takes him away from cooking

stew boiling over hisses and drips into the coals
  take lid off coffee steaming
  grounds bubbling
  breeze blowing carries away coffee smell

Ribs cooked coffee boiled fry bread stacked
stew boiled stomach grumbling mouth watery
anticipation

plates full sit down under tree
family together
give thanks
we eat now.

Within Dinétah the People's Spirit Remains Strong

On this historic occasion 130 years after the signing of the peace treaty of 1868. Within Dinétah the People's spirit remains strong in 1998. These words are for my people, the Diné, who endured colossal hardship and near-death and continue to endure.

In the people's memory are the stories
This we remember:

I

Ałkidą́ą́' adajiní nít'ę́ę́',
They say long time ago in time immemorial:
the stories say we emerged from
the umbilical center of this sacred earth into
the Glittering World
smoothed by Twin Heroes,
sons of White Shell Woman,
who journeyed to find their father
and aided by Spider Woman who taught them
how not to fear the perilous journey.
They say the sun, father to the Twin Heroes,
gave them the knowledge to slay the monsters
so that the world would be safe.

We lived according to the teachings of the Holy People
to dwell within the sacred mountains:
Sis Naajiní rising to the east,
Tsoodził rising to the south,
Dook'o'oosłíid rising to the west,
Dibé Nítsaa rising to the north

We raised our families,
planted our corn,
greeted the dawn with our prayers,
and followed the path of corn pollen
Every day was a new beginning
. . . in Beauty
. . . in Beauty.

II

The ancestors predicted it would happen,
that the wind would shift and bring
light-colored men from across the big water
who would shatter our world.
They would arrive wearing metal coats
riding strange beautiful animals,
would arrive in clothes that brushed the earth
carrying crossed sticks to plunge into Dinétah.
In their zealous urge they sought cities of gold.
Later we learned they came to take
our land, our lives, our spirits.

Did they not know we are
all created from the same elements?
Rainclouds for hair,
fingernails formed from beautiful seashells,
the rivers flow through our veins, our lifeline,
from wind we came to life,
with thunder voices we speak.
We fought back to protect ourselves
as we had fought with other enemies.

The world changed when
the light-colored men brought their women.
It was then we knew they meant to stay.
They invented ways to justify what they wanted,
Manifest Destiny, assimilation, colonization.
And, most of all, they wanted the land.

One day a man wearing red clothes appeared.
Bi'éé' Łichíí'í, Kit Carson, sent by Wáashindoon.
He brought many soldiers.
They spoke with thunder sticks
that tore into everything that we loved
to burn our beautiful peach orchards,
to slaughter our sheep in front of us,
to starve us out from Dinétah,
to do unspeakable things to us,
to wrench us from our land.
What strange fruit is this that dangles
from the trees?
We feared for our lives
and hid among the rocks and shadows
gathering food and water when we could.

III

What was our crime?
We wanted only to live as we had
within our sacred mountains
seeking harmony, seeking long life
. . . in Beauty
. . . in Beauty.

Others had their death march:
The Trail of Tears, Auschwitz,
The Door of No Return in the House of Slaves.
We are Diné.
We too had our death march forced on us.
When The Long Walk began, we witnessed our women
murdered and raped
our children and relatives swept away in the rushing currents
of the Rio Grande

We heard explosions that silenced mothers giving birth
behind the rocks.
We saw the newborn and the elderly left behind.

We saw our warriors unable to defend us.
And even now the land we crossed still holds
        the memory of our people's tears, cries, and blood.
Kit Carson marched us three hundred miles away.
In the distance we saw our sacred mountains
        becoming smaller and smaller.
We were torn from the land that held our birth stems.
We were taken to the land that was not us.
We were taken to the desolate place without trees or vegetation.
Where the men picked out undigested corn from animal dung
    to eat.
Where young women were raped.
We called this place Hwéeldi,
this place of starvation,
this place of near-death
this place of extreme hardship.

IV

We returned to our land after four years.
Our spirits ragged and weary.
And vowed that we would never be separated from Dinétah;
        the earth is our strength
We have grown strong.
We are the children of White Shell Woman.
We are the people of the original clans she created.
We are female warriors and male warriors—
    Manuelito, Barboncito
We are the Code Talkers who used our language to help
    save America.
We are Annie Wauneka who taught us to have faith
    in the white man's medicine.
We are the sons and daughters of activists and other
    unsung heroes
        "when Indian men were the finest men there were."
We are the hands that create fine turquoise and silver jewelry.
We are the women who resisted relocation
    when the government came with papers and fences.

We are teachers, cowboys, lawyers, musicians.
We are medicine people, doctors, nurses, college professors.
We are artists, soldiers, politicians, architects, farmers.
We are sheep herders, engineers, singers, comediennes.
We are weavers of baskets and exquisite blankets.
We are bus drivers, welders, ranchers, dishwashers.
We are the people who offer prayers during the cycles of the day.
We are Diné.
In Beauty it was begun.
In Beauty it continues.
In Beauty,

In Beauty,

In Beauty,

In Beauty.

Tsoodził, Mountain to the South

You arrive in the bright of morning
carrying music in your eyes
and the breath of mountains in your hair

We travel the path of thunder beings
passing above stories where Twin Heroes slayed monsters
proof lies in the dark mounds of lava trails
streaming south from Tsoodził
near the meadow where spring begins and calls forth
yellow horses to graze among the cattails

I would tell you, beloved, these stories
on nights when the scent of orange blossoms lingers in the air
would tell you how brave locust smoothed the earth for humans
stories congealed into landscape
and how places mark existence

I want to travel all the colors of the worlds with you
to arrive in this Glittering World
held in your swollen male clouds
and your hand on my thigh
that causes the world to grow
again and again
without fine,
without end
your sweet music
pouring forth like
    rain
        rain
            rain
                rain . . . .

Deep in the Rock

I.

Deep in the rock, the tamarisk and monkey-egg trees have dug in to prevent erosion. Like the Diné, they refuse to leave. These newcomers prefer a symphony of crows playing against a solid backdrop. They spread themselves, thick as thieves, drinking away the water for the sheep. Someone lights a match to them. Too late, their roots have memorized the canyon's endoderm. When the flood came, their arms groped for the sky as they sank into the muddy chocolate waters. A mass of tangled hair rose when the canyon emptied. Then a shivering silhouette of branches, like cracks in the sky.

II.

Deep in the rock, the interplay of texture and color. Iron and manganese dribble down the rock face. Will it matter to this land, carved by steady wind and rain, after our bones have crumbled into dust?

III.

Deep in the rock, crows make echoes, gáagii, gáagii. Their name is pure onomatopoeia. Gáagii are everywhere, picking up the remains of what humans leave, even the stuff that isn't intended for them, like the boxer shorts stolen from the clothesline. My cousins laughed so hard when they fluttered away beneath the gáagii's grasp. Gáagii are everywhere and are taken for granted. If they were to leave, they would be missed.

Niłtsą́ Bi'áád

Niłtsą́ bi'áád
    Shá' di'ááhdę́ę́'go dah naaldogo 'alzhish
        k'ós hazlį́į́'
            honeezk'ází
                níłtsą́ bi'áád bitázhool bijooltsą́
                    áádóó níłtsą́ bi'áád biyázhí bídii'na'

Naaniiniiłkaahgo
    níłtsą́ bi'áád biyázhí hazlį́į́'
        ch'íl látah hózhóón dahtoo' bee 'ałch'į' háazhah
            áádóó nihik'inizdidlą́ąd

Female Rain

Female Rain
    Dancing from the south
        cloudy cool and gray
            pregnant with rainchild

At dawn she gives birth to a gentle mist
flowers bow with wet sustenance
            luminescence all around

REX LEE JIM

Credit: Del Ray Photography

REX LEE JIM (b. 1962) was born and raised in Rock Point, Arizona. He is of the Kin Lichíí'nii, born for the Táchii'nii; his maternal grandparents are the Kin Yaa'áanii and his paternal grandparents are the Naakaii Dine'é. Jim studied at Princeton University, Middlebury Bread Loaf School of English, and Oxford University (England). He is a poet, playwright, and medicine man. He was also a council delegate for the Navajo Nation Tribal Council and, after that, vice president of the Navajo Nation. He is fluent and literate in Navajo, Spanish, and English. In the early 1980s he was among the students at Rock Point Community School who produced *Between Sacred Mountains: Navajo Stories and Lessons from the Land* (1982). His poetry has appeared, among other places, in *Diné Be'iina': A Journal of Navajo Life*, the *Journal of Navajo Education*, and *Broadsided Press*; his essays and creative work have also appeared in *Here First: Autobiographical Essays by Native American Writers* (2000) and *Voices from Four Directions: Contemporary Translations of Native Literatures of North America* (2004). In 1989, under the pen name Mazii Dinéłtsóí, he published his first book, *Ahí Ni' Nikisheegiizh*, followed by *saad* in 1995; both were published by Princeton Collections of Western Americana and written entirely in Diné bizaad. His third book, *Dúchas T'áá Kǫ́ǫ́ Diné: A*

Trilingual Poetry Collection in Navajo, Irish and English (1998), published in Ireland, contains poems in Diné bizaad, English, and Gaelic. His most recent book of poetry, *Saad Lá Tah Hózhóón: A Collection of Diné Poetry* (2019), published by Salina Bookshelf, is a bilingual collection of poems in Diné bizaad and English. Some of the poems in that collection had appeared in earlier collections, but many of the translations are new and some of the Diné bizaad poems have been reworked as well.

Interview

What do you hope readers learn from your writing?

I write primarily in Navajo. I initially wrote to explore my own thoughts and feelings. As more and more Navajos and others began to read my work, I became conscious of writing to help build a nation, the Navajo Nation. I want my readers to question traditions, norms, and customs in order to reflect and learn from them. I also want them to explore and learn from their own experiences and retell their own stories in ways that contribute to hope, strength, and resiliency, to endure as a people and a nation.

How does the Navajo language influence your work?

The Navajo language is who I am. Whether I write in other languages like English or Spanish, the Navajo language is the core, the root, the foundation. It speaks to fundamental values of spirituality, family, earth and sky, prayers, songs, and rituals that are essential Navajo.

Who or what inspires you?

My source of information is all possibilities and opportunities that the imagination can create out of who we are, individually and collectively. Writing allows me to explore and experience what the power of the creative imagination can do with who and what we are. The imagination knows no limits of any kind; it allows us to grow and expand. In Navajo, we sometimes refer to the muse and the imagination as nílch'i biyázhí, the little wind, which essentially is the instinct, the gutsy feeling of what we truly want, of who we really are.

What advice do you have for beginning writers?

Read, read, read. Then write, write, write! And study the masters, truly study the masters, not just read them. Study them. Learn from them.

Who was the first Diné writer you read?

Miracle Hill by Blackhorse Mitchell.

What was your favorite book in high school?

The Heart of Darkness by Joseph Conrad.

What are you reading now?

The Secret Life of Pronouns: What Our Words Say About Us by James W. Pennebaker, *Words Can Change Your Brain* by Andrew Newberg and Mark Robert Waldman, and *Sapiens: A Brief History of Humankind* by Yuval Noah Harari. I'm actually reading several other books as well.

⩧

Saad

Hodeeyáádą́ą́' honishłǫ́
Adą́ą́dą́ą́' honishłǫ́
Dííjį́ honishłǫ́
Ahóyéel'áágóó honishłǫ́
Saad shí nishłį́
Saad diyinii shí nishłį́
Saad diyinii díí shí nishłį́

Shee nitsáhákees
Shee nahat'á
Shee tsohodizin
Shee ni'dit'a'
Shee yáti'

Saad shí nishłį
Saad diyinii shí nishłį
Saad diyinii díí shí nishłį

Ts'ídá t'áá ał'ąą ánísht'éego honishłǫ́
Shinahjį' nitsáhákees ał'ąą át'é
Shinahjį' nahat'á ał'ąą át'é
Shinahjį' tsodizin ał'ąą át'é
Shinahjį' sin ał'ąą át'é
Shinahjį' saad ał'ąą át'é
Saad shí nishłį
Saad diyinii shí nishłį
Saad diyinii díí shí nishłį

Shinahjį' iiná ałtaas'áí hólǫ́
Ó'ool'įįł ałtaas'áí yisht'į
Yódí ałtaas'áí yisht'į
Nitł'iz ałtaas'áí yisht'į
Díí biniiyé nohokáá' dine'é baa ádinisht'ą́
Nohokáá dine'é diyinii
Nohokáá dine'é ílíinii
Nohokáá dine'é jooba'ii
Díí biyi'dę́ę́' hahosiists'įįhgo
Iiná doo nídínéeshgóó k'ee'ąą yilzhish
Díí biniiyé nohokáá' dine'é baa ádinisht'ą́
Saad shí nishłį
Saad diyinii shí nishłį
Saad diyinii díí shí nishłį

Ahóyéel'áágóó honishłǫ́
Yiskáągo honishłǫ́
Díįjį honishłǫ́
Adą́ą́dą́ą́' honishłǫ́
Saad shí nishłį
Saad diyinii shí nishłį
Saad diyinii díí shí nishłį.

Language

In the beginning I was
Yesterday I was
Today I am
Tomorrow I will be
Forever I will be
        Language I am
        Sacred language I am
        Sacred language this I am

People think with me
People act with me
People pray with me
People sing with me
People speak with me
        Language I am
        Sacred language I am
        Sacred language this I am

I come in many different forms
Because of me people think differently
Because of me people act differently
Because of me people pray differently
Because of me people sing differently
Because of me people speak differently
        Language I am
        Sacred language I am
        Sacred language this I am

Because of me there are many different cultures
I value different ways of doing
I value different goods
I value varied hard goods
These are why I gave myself to the earth surface people
A holy people
A respected people

A compassionate people
From within them I sound
In this way life continues to expand
These are reasons why I gave myself to the earth surface people
Language I am
Sacred language I am
Sacred language this I am

Forever I will be
Tomorrow I will be
Today I am
Yesterday I was
In the beginning I was
Language I am
Sacred language I am
Sacred language this I am.

Voice*

In the beginning I am
Yesterday I am
Today I am
Tomorrow I am
Forever I am
Voice I am
Sacred voice I am
Sacred voice this I am

People think with me
People pray with me
People sing with me
People speak with me
People plan with me

* 2019 translation of saad

People live with me
Voice I am
Sacred voice I am
Sacred voice this I am

I come in many forms
Because of me people think differently
Because of me people pray differently
Because of me people sing differently
Because of me people speak differently
Because of me people plan differently
Because of me people live differently
Voice I am
Sacred voice I am
Sacred voice this I am

I value different ways of living
I value different ways of doing
I value different soft goods
I value different hard goods
These are reasons why I gave myself over to the
earth surface people
A holy people
A respected people
A compassionate people
When I sound from within them,
Without falling apart, life ceaselessly expands
These are reasons why I gave myself over to the
earth surface people
Voice I am
Sacred voice I am
Sacred voice this I am

Forever I am
Tomorrow I am
Today I am
Yesterday I am
In the beginning I am

Voice I am
Sacred voice I am
Sacred voice this I am

Tó Háálį

Hodiyingo lá haz'ąą nít'éé'ni
T'ah bénáshniih
T'ah ánísts'ísígo shicheii ákǫǫ bikéé nisíyáa ni'
Ndi doo ayóo bénáshniih da
Ákondi hastįį éí náadiidzáa nii'
K'ad doo bąąhtééhgóó naaghá
Hastįį sání silįį'
T'ah bénáshniih
Éí hastįį ákǫǫ bił nisiikai ni'
Nitł'iz ła bits'ájaa'go
Éí yoojihgo ákǫǫ naazh'áazh ni'
Shí éí t'áá nízaadęę chidí niilbąązgo
Ii' síndá shi'diníigo t'áá áadi ii' sédáá nít'éé'
E'e'aahijigo désh'įį'go
K'os nidaalzhood ni', níłtsązhool nida'ajooł ni'
Áajigo nida'di'ni' ni', nida'dilch'il ni'
Kéyah t'áá si'ąą nít'éé' tó bee disǫs ni'
T'óó hózhóní yee' ni'
'Aoo', hózhóní yee' nít'éé'

Ts'ídán shįį kwe'é át'é
T'ah bénáshniih
K'ad éí kwe'é béésh íí'á
Níyol béésh náyoołbał
Tł'oh deiyítso yęęgóó łeezh t'éí deiyíchii'
Ayáásh ałtaas'áí nídadildah yęęgóó
Gáagii t'éí dahnidahaltsaad
Nitł'iz nidahajáhąągóó
Sáanii naazk'ai'go béésh bik'i nidaask'ee'
Tsodizin bee yádaati' yęęgóó
Adláanii t'éí dadilwosh
"Fuck you" t'éí dadiits'a'
Nahasdzáán shimá ha'níigo
Tóyisdzáán shima ha'níigo
K'é bee yádaati' yęęgóó

“You want a good fuck?
Go see Sue or Mama,”
T'éí bee ak'eda'ashchį́
Tó bee dahodisǫs yę́ęgóó
Bizhéé' hólóní bizis t'éí nida'diłdlaad

Hodiyingo lá haz'ą́ą́ nít'éé ni
T'ah bénáshniih
T'óó nízaadę́ę́ ni'niłbą́ązgo
Nídiisdzohgo ii' sédá

Hodiyingo lá haz'ą́ą́ nít'éé' ni
Ndi doo ayóo bénáshniih da

Spring

The place used to be sacred
I still remember
I was only a kid when I followed my grandfather there
But I don’t remember everything
Still the man got well
Now he is healthy, walking about
He has become an old man
I still remember
We went there with this man
Hard jewels were selected for offering
They went there, carrying the jewels
My grandfather and that man went there
To that spring out in the middle of nowhere
I sat in the truck parked some distance away
I was told to stay in the truck so I stayed behind
And I looked to the west
Clouds floated about; showers drifted about
To the west thunders rolled and lightning flashed
The whole land sparkled in water

The whole land was beautiful
Yes, it was beautiful

I think this may be the place
I still remember
Now a windmill is standing here
The wind spins the metal
Where the grass grew, sand dunes roll
Where the young birds used to travel
Only crows hop about
Where sacred jewels were offered
Naked women spreading their legs are depicted on metal
Where sacred songs were heard
Only drunks yell
Where prayers were offered
People scream 'fuck you'
Where people prayed
'Earth my mother'
'Water woman, my mother'
Where people related to the place,
'You want a good fuck?
Go see Sue or mama,'
Are scribbled onto metal barrels.
Where the earth sparkled in water
Wine bottles reflect in the sun
Beer cans shine up the place

The place used to be sacred
I remember
I am parked some distance away
Sitting in my truck, taking a slug now and then

The place used to be sacred,
But I don't remember everything.

Na'azheeh

Tłig
Niyol nee ní'į́į́'
Tłig
Nibeedí nee ní'į́į́'
Tłig
Tséghájooghałii nee ní'į́į́'
Tłig
Nikéyah nee ní'į́į́'
Tłig
Nidiyin nee ní'į́į́'
Tłig
K'ad łą́ą,
        dah náá'diit'áhígíí bii' doo
        áadi sǫ' łichíí' bidáádidoogááł

Hunting

Click
I stole your breathing
Click
I stole your survival tools
Click
I stole your living goods
Click
I stole your land
Click
I stole your gods
Click
Now all is ready
        For the next shuttle flight
        The red star will keep it from returning.

Three Short Poems

1.

dibé naakai léi'
tsin ałnáosdzid
hanii eegai nisin

sheep wandering
rows of white crosses
i thought
they were

2.

náhookǫs
nidi
náhookǫs

big dipper
even
turns

3.

ni éiyá
yáah ni

you you are
awe
is yours

IRVIN MORRIS

IRVIN MORRIS (b. 1958) is Tábaahí, born for Tótsohnii; his maternal grandfather is Tó'áhaní and his paternal grandfather is Kinyaa'áanii. Originally from Naschitti, New Mexico, Morris holds an AFA in creative writing from the Institute of American Indian Arts, a BA from the University of California, Santa Cruz, and an MFA from Cornell University. He has taught at Cornell University, SUNY-Buffalo, the University of Arizona, and Navajo Technical University, and he is currently on faculty at Diné College on the Navajo Nation. In 2014, Morris worked to create the BFA in creative writing at Navajo Technical University and was a founding member of the Navajo Nation Poet Laureate Program.

In a guest-edited issue of the *Tribal College Journal*, Morris characterized the inspiring role writing by Native authors has had in his own life: "As I grew older, I discovered Native writers. I was inexorably drawn to the works of Momaday, Ortiz, Silko, Erdrich, Vizenor, and others. I latched on to each new discovered work like the lifelines that they were. For a time in my youth, I drifted in the uncertainty and malaise that many Native young men succumb to, but there was always some part of me that persevered. I can honestly say that a large part of that was due to the words of the authors I sought out so eagerly. Their words saved me."

Morris published his first work, "The Homecoming," in *MAAZO Magazine* in 1988. In 1997, Morris published his influential book *From the Glittering World: A Navajo Story* (University of Oklahoma Press), which is excerpted here. As one of the few full-length works of prose (fiction and nonfiction) written by a Diné author, Morris's work has inspired and continues to inspire many writers. *From the Glittering World* begins with creation stories, transitions to stories focused on the Long Walk/Hwééldi, then to a focus on Morris's childhood and adolescence in his beloved homeland (Shikéyah), his young adulthood in Los Angeles and Gallup, and then on to experiences in college in

Santa Cruz, California; Albuquerque and Santa Fe, New Mexico; and Ithaca, New York. The book's concluding section features short fiction.

In a substantive review of Morris's book, literary scholar Susan Brill de Ramírez explains that *From the Glittering World* "is not a pretty story, but it is real. Morris tells us much about the reality and consequences of the glittering world today. This is Morris's true story, a story that he remembers, lives, and imagines, a story that is his people's and his own, too. . . . Does Morris tell us 'the' Navajo story? No, as he makes very clear in his title, this is 'a' Navajo story. This is his story of his people, his land, and his life, and as such, it is a quite remarkable story, . . . [one that] profoundly demonstrates the survival and continuance of the Navajo people today and into the future."

Selections from *From the Glittering World*

SHIKÉYAH (MY HOMELAND)

From my house, on a clear morning—because we are situated high up on the alluvial apron fronting the Chuska Mountains—I can see a wide sweep of my beloved homeland. From there, I am reminded of who I am: I am not alone, nor am I the first. The land has birthed and sustained all my grandmothers and grandfathers.

Áhéhéé'.

But I have also lived outside the holy rainbow circle and learned of those who do not regard her as a living, sacred entity. Their roots do not penetrate the soil. Perched inside a shiny jet skimming high above the clouds, I have seen my mother, the earth—*Nahasdzáán shimá*—lying below, "conquered."

Outside the circle of the sacred mountains, I have known spiritual hunger and longing for the sound of desert thunder, for turquoise sky, dry air, and radiant sun. And for many years, until I realized what I was doing, I was using hurtful words to describe my mother: *landscape, wilderness, nature*.

The land is ripe with the stories of my people. I can hear their voices on still nights, on summer nights when lightning flashes soundlessly in the distance; on winter nights when the land rests quietly under pristine snow; and in the spring and fall when the mountains speak with a low, murmuring wind voice. I can see their campfires away in the distance, tiny points of light quivering on the plain.

T'ÁÁ SHÁBIK'EHGO (SUNWISE)

Ha'a'aah. To the east, beyond the broad, nameless valley and the badlands rising on the other side, past the pale sandstone turrets of White Rock thirty miles distant, and the yellow rim of Chaco Canyon twenty miles further, are etched the faint outlines of the Sierra Nacimiento and the Jémez Range, nearly half the state away. Those mountains are sacred to some of my ancestors from Jémez and Santa Clara pueblos who were sent to live with the *Diné* in the years before the Pueblo Rebellion of 1680, and the Spanish "reconquest" of New Mexico twelve years later, young women who formed new clans within *Diné* society.

From the badlands, the land rises in a gentle incline toward the south in broad, grassy terraces. There, the dark low platform of the Lobo Mesa, a piñon-and-juniper-clad formation that occupies most of the southeastern horizon, lifts abruptly from the flat grassland. The cliffs edging the mesa rise from a point directly behind Crownpoint, a BIA agency town located forty miles southeast of my house. Beyond the mesa—over one hundred miles away—rises the bare peak of *Tsoodzil,* our sacred mountain of the south. At its base are the remains of *Yéi'iitsoh bidil*, the petrified tide of blood left where the monster son of *Jóhonaa'éí* was killed by the Twins. The Twins, also sons of the Sun, vaulted into the sky from there on rainbows and sunbeams.

Next on the horizon is *Ak'idahnást'ání,* a square piñon-covered butte that thrusts up out of the plateau summit. This prominence is known as Mirage Stone Mountain in the *Diné* creation story. Mapmakers have labeled it Hosta Butte. From isolated perches atop this towering landmark, sentinels have kept watch on the land since time immemorial. From there, the whole circle of the earth can be seen: Naalyé silá, the Chuska Mountains to the west; the San Juan Basin to the north; the rugged snowy ranges of southern Colorado to the northeast; and the Rio Puerco Valley and the Zuni Mountains to the south.

Shádi'ááh. To the south, the rounded blue swells of the Zuni Mountains float in perpetual haze. At their northern tip, wedged between the red sandstone hogbacks and the mesa foothills to the north, is the narrow Rio Puerco Valley. In its trough lies the notorious border town of Gallup, New Mexico, a seven-mile-long stretch of bars and nightclubs, tourist traps, gas stations, fast-food joints, Indian jewelry stores, bars, cafés, laundromats, strip malls, and motels.

East of Gallup, is *Shash bitoo'*, Bear Springs, now known as Fort Wingate, the point of departure for thousands of *Diné* forced on the infamous Long Walk in 1863. The fort, now closed, was for many years a major ordinance depot, and the large military reservation surrounding it is dotted with thousands of concrete bunkers once used to store ammunition. The land is rocky and covered with piñon and ponderosa pine forests. The numerous canyons eroded into the mountainsides are banded with maroon, white, buff, and gray clays. Ancient *Anaa'sázi* settlements, oil refineries, abandoned uranium mines, natural gas wells, recreation areas, and *bilagáana* homesteads share the land with hundreds of *Diné* families. At night, orange gas flares lapping the air over refineries light up the valley and the mountainsides.

E'e'aah. To the west, and stretching for fifty miles to the north, are the rugged foothills and the great forested wall of *Naalyé silá*—a name that might be translated as something like "Lying-Down-Wealth." The meaning does not parallel anything in the materialistic Western view, since it refers to the spiritual significance of the range as well as its role as larder and pharmacopoeia. The Chuska Mountains, as they are identified on maps, are the major geological formation on the reservation. They rise to an elevation of nearly ten thousand feet above sea level.

The mountains form an archipelago of well-watered islands in the desert, a stopping-over place for migrating birds. The flat summit supports forests of pine, spruce, fir, gambel oak, and groves of quaking aspen. Numerous ponds and lakes dot the hollows. There are black bear, mountain lion, bobcat and mule deer. The summit provides the best grazing land on the reservation and we are lucky to have a place there. I spent my childhood summers exploring the woods, learning the names of mountain plants and animals, riding my horse, coming to know the land like a relative. I remember splashing in the ponds; scaling the sandstone cliffs that lift the summit a thousand feet above the lower slopes; picking wild strawberries; climbing the towering pines; and seeing the brilliant stars crowding the skies at night. I remember listening to the stories told over the snap of campfires—frightening accounts of the feats of *Diné* warriors who battled *naakaai*, the Spanish, and later, *bilagáana*s. There were also stories about *Nóóda'í* and *Naałání*, the Utes and Comanches.

Parts of the mountain have various names and stories associated with them. *Béésh łichíi'ii bigiizh*, which is the *Diné* name referring to the reddish chert found there—now known as Narbona Pass—is the major east-west passage through the mountains. The new name is the fruit of many years of work by *Diné* students who petitioned to have the offensive name changed. As far as I know it is the only instance in U.S. history, thus far, where Indian people have been able to influence the change of a placename from something that was seen as offensive to something positive. Formerly, the gap had been known as Washington Pass, named after Colonel John T. Washington, an officer in the U.S. Army who played a major role in an infamous incident that took place in the pass.

In the summer of 1849, Colonel Washington and his troops had been dispatched to *Béésh łichíi'ii bigziih to* negotiate peace with the *Diné* headman Narbona. Proceedings were going well until one of Washington's officers claimed that he recognized a stolen horse in the *Diné* remuda. The accusation was quickly and vehemently denied. Tensions flared and the negotiation was abruptly halted. Narbona urged caution, but when several *Diné* began riding away, Colonel Washington ordered his troops to open fire. In the ensuing melee, Narbona, sixty-eight years old at the time and a well-known pacifist, was shot in the back.

Naalyé silá is the male partner to *Dzil yíjiin*, Black Mesa, a lower range to the west, which is identified as female. It is said that they lie facing each other, head to feet. Their bodies form a powerful and sacred circle. This relationship reflects the *Diné* worldview in which duality and reciprocity is elemental.

Black Mesa is now being strip-mined. Millions of tons of high-grade bituminous coal are extracted annually to fuel power plants that light up parts of Las Vegas, Phoenix, and Los Angeles. Megawatt power lines carry the electricity right past the impoverished *Diné* homes. The companies have renewable leases from the federal government and the mining has continued nonstop since the mid-sixties. The coal is crushed into a powder, mixed with groundwater, and sluiced through huge pipes to the Mohave Generation Station on the Nevada-California border. This slurry-pipeline technology is cost effective for the companies that run the mines, but the operation siphons off millions of gallons of precious water daily from the ancient aquifers under Black Mesa. Natural recharge is modest in this arid terrain, and the toll on the land is immeasurable: the water table at Black Mesa has dropped tremendously. Sacred springs have dried up.

Náhookos. To the north is a sea of grass sloping down from the mountain foothills to the San Juan River, the northern boundary of our homeland. The river itself is hidden below the level of the plains, in a narrow valley choked with cottonwood, tamarisk, Russian olive, and Siberian elm. It is the best agricultural land on the reservation, known for abundant harvests of sweet melons and white and yellow corn. Midway between the river and the mountains rises *Tsébit'a'ii*, the Winged Rock. To the outside world, this basaltic monolith soaring seventeen hundred feet above the surrounding plain is known as Shiprock. It has been featured on innumerable postcards, calendars, and magazines, its twin craggy peaks silhouetted against a red-and-purple sunset. Before it was finally closed to climbers, many *bilagáanas* lost their lives on its treacherous heights because of unpredictable winds, crumbling rock, rattlesnakes, and fatigue.

It is said that long ago, in some primordial time, the people were in danger and fled to the rock for safety. Like an enormous bird, it rose up and flew away with them. It settled here, its gigantic wings spread to the north and south. Some say it will come to life again, should the need arise.

In the distance to the north are snow-capped peaks. The La Sal Mountains in Utah are an encampment of white tipis. Sleeping Ute Mountain near Cortez, Colorado, resembles a large breast, as its *Diné* name, *Dzil abe'*, describes. Mount Hesperus, in the La Plata Mountains of southeastern Colorado, is a mass of frosted stone pinnacles. It is called *Dibé ntsaa*, Big Sheep Mountain, and it is our sacred mountain of the north. Extending southward from behind *Dibé ntsaa* is a distant ribbon of snowbound peaks that culminate in the Mount Blanca massif, *Sisnaajiní*, in south-central Colorado. That mountain is our sacred mountain of the east.

Much closer, below the great ranges arrayed on the horizon, is *Dinétah*, our Holy Land. That is where we emerged into this place, the Fifth World, the Glittering World, as it is known. The actual spot where some *Diné* say that the Twins left this world is presently submerged under the Navajo Reservoir, a huge lake formed behind Navajo Dam, an Army Corps of Engineers project that supplies water to the San Juan River Valley, the 110,000-acre Navajo Indian Irrigation Project, and the city of Albuquerque. Southeast of the river is the low, square nub of *Dzilná'oodilii*, Huerfano Mesa, where the Twins—the sons of Changing Woman—were conceived and grew to manhood. *Ch'ooli'ii*, Spruce Knob, the birthplace of Changing Woman, is a few miles away behind the mesa. Across the valley directly east of my home, the Chaco River emerges from between the clay bluffs of the badlands and turns north to join the San Juan River. Forty miles upstream are the silent stone towns of Chaco Canyon: Pueblo Bonito. Pueblo Alto. Pueblo del Arroyo. Casa Rinconada. Peñasco Blanco. Chetro Ketl. Hungo Pavi. Wijiji.

I have seen these landmarks every morning of my life, whether or not I am actually home. These mountains and formations are as real and as alive for me as are the stories that animate them. Better than anything else, they tell me who I am.

KÉÉHAST'ÍNÍGII (WHERE I LIVE)

In the summer, the sun rises directly to the east of my home, straight up from between the tan bluffs guarding the mouth of the Chaco River. The bluffs are topped with red clinker, the remains of an ancient fire that swept through coal seams exposed here and there in the eroded hills of the badlands. Depending on the position of the sun, the bluffs are blue-gray, tan, yellow-white, or reddish orange over the course of a day. Groves of salt cedar embroider the riverbanks, and dark green deltas mark the mouths of arroyos feeding runoff from the mountains into the river. In spring and fall, strange birds—storks, cranes, herons, and pelicans—visit the ephemeral wetlands and scattered stock ponds. Their plumage is carefully gathered and used in ceremonies. The badlands are sculpted layers of shales and clays containing fossils, which some say are the bones, teeth and claws of *Naayéé'*. Feral horses and donkeys share that eccentric land with branded Herefords, Brangus, Charolais, Brahma mixes, and Beefmasters. Bobcats, foxes, coyotes, and other predators inhabit those bluffs too, as do raptors such as hawks and owls. In summer, the valley fills with heat waves and the land appears submerged. A brief rainy season, normally in July and August, brings moisture north from the Gulf of Mexico. Now and then a great storm will half-drown the basin and leave it shining with water.

Higher up, on the west side of the valley closer to the foothills where I live, short grasses and shrubs predominate. There is chamisa, four-wing saltbush, pygmy juniper, sacaton grass, Russian thistle, and snakeweed, to name a few. Siberian elm, Lombardy poplar, globe willow, Russian olive, and maples shade newer homesteads. There are hundreds of acres of neglected fields—the legacy of the CCC programs of the 1930s—surrounded by rusted barbwire fences, clogged with sand dunes, reclaimed by greasewood and saltbush, littered with the weather-beaten remnants of windbreaks and orchards.

The village called Naschitti—*Nahashch'idí* in our language—sits beside U.S. Highway 666, a half-mile east of my home and a mile east of the Chuska foothills. Local church groups are agitating to have the number assigned to the highway changed. They blame the cipher 666 for the numerous accidents on the highway—never mind that the reservation is dry and that the highway links two border towns where alcohol is sold. In the village there is a public elementary school and teacherage, a Christian Reformed Church mission, a Catholic church and bingo hall, a trading post, a telephone switching station, water tower, tribal meeting hall, senior citizen's center, tribal police substation, laundromat, greenhouse, low-rent apartments, and a cluster of ranch-style HUD houses. A few private homes circumscribe the village proper.

It is said that a long time ago, there was a drought and the people were suffering. Then one day, a family of badgers digging their burrows in Black Rock Wash struck water and the people were saved. That's how this place came to be known as Nahasch'idí, *after the fierce little animal.*

The school is dying, the HUD houses are deteriorating, and the scattered trees, shrubs, hedges, and rose bushes have assumed curious postures in their fight to survive. The elevation is six thousand feet above sea level where I live, and the word *steppes* is often used to describe the climate. Summers are hot and winters are cold; temperature swings of twenty degrees or more in an afternoon are not unknown. The average yearly precipitation is about twelve inches.

A dirt road, graded now and then by the BIA Roads Department, veers west from the village. It is infamously rocky. The graders have long since scraped away the thin topsoil and exposed the underlying alluvial rocks and gravel. The white house on your right is my brother's. You can tell he is a miner because the house is new, large, and attractively stuccoed. There is a satellite dish, horse trailers, campers, and a fancy metal corral holding a quarter horse gelding and a buckskin mare. A few yards further sits my cousin's green house with yellow trim. That place has started to go to pieces since he died of a heart attack several years ago. After spending most of his adult life working on sugar beet farms in Idaho, he retired and returned to the homeland—only to last three summers.

My uncle's gray double-wide mobile home is next on the road, along with his neglected cornfield and immaculately kept NAC meeting ground. A *cha-ha'ooh* sits in the front yard, offering cool shade in the summer and a convenient rack for storing things in winter. After that is my mute aunt's one-room hut. The bus route turns north, and a short road splits off toward the west and the huddle of structures harboring my extended kin.

My mother's house stands out because it looks like a gingerbread house, mocha brown with white trim. A do-good organization painted it those colors over the summer; *bilagáana* kids from the east who spent two weeks on the reservation fixing up Indian homes. They wandered about our hovels wide-eyed, bewildered, agog at the condition of our homes. But if anything, they learned that true poverty is unknown to us. There is the land; and we have *K'é*, the intricate and enduring clanship ties that provide us with relatives wherever we go on the reservation; and we have our language, our stories, and our songs.

The older, back part of my mother's house is made of logs covered with chickenwire and stucco, while the front section is made of conventional lumber. This summer we tore out the wallboards in the back rooms for remodeling and found an inscription on the cement chinking between the logs: PETER A. BEGAY, ALL AROUND COWBOY, 1963. The letters, etched into wet cement with a nail, encircled a line drawing of a bull's head. The imprint was so clear it could have been scratched in just moments ago.

The logs of the house have an interesting history. Some of them belonged to my maternal grandmother, whom I never saw. She died in childbirth when my mother was twelve. My grandmother's *hooghan nímazí* was dismantled while my mother was away at Saint Catherine's Indian School in Santa Fe. When she returned years later after my grandmother's death, she was able to locate only a few of the logs. The rest had simply disappeared. The other logs in our house were hauled from the mountains by my mother and her first and only husband after their wedding. They chopped down ponderosa pines and smoothed and shaped the timbers by hand. She took the logs with her after their divorce and had the house reassembled at my grandfather's place, where we lived for a while. But tensions between her and my grandfather's new wife forced her to once again dismantle the cabin and move us to the foot of the mountains where we now live. It's been our home for over thirty years. Four generations have lived in it: my mother, my siblings, my nieces and nephews, and now their children.

Tóbaahí nishlí, doo Tótsohnii éí báshíshchíín. That is the proper way to introduce and identify myself. I am of the Edgewater clan, and I am born for the Big Water clan. I belong to my mother's clan because we trace our lineage through the female line. Anyone who is *Tóbaahí* is thus part of my family. We don't go strictly by biological descent. That is, my family doesn't just include my nuclear family but comprises everyone who is *Tóbaahí*. Not only that, but everyone who is *Tótsohnii*, my father's clan, is related to me also. What this means is that through the clan's family system my "family" is very large, and chances are that wherever I go on the homeland I will meet someone who is my relative. If I were to be stranded away from home, for example, I could count on my clansmen to help. In turn, I have that obligation too. The most important things is that we are never alone. We are parts of large groups, which are in turn strands in the web making up *Diné* society. Knowing your clan weaves you inextricably into that web. Knowing your clan also ties you directly into the *Diné* creation story, because all the clans are descended from the four original clans that were created by Changing Woman from her body.

My mother is born for *Hanághäahnii.* Our neighbors are also *Hanághäahnii,* related to us through her father's clan. That circumstance is unusual but not unknown. Normally a woman lives near her mother and her sisters, as *Diné* are matrilineal and matrilocal. When my mother's mother died in childbirth, her maternal relatives were obligated by blood and kinship ties to look after her and the six other children. But none of them were in a position at that time to take in extra mouths, so they went to live with their paternal aunt, at a locality called *Nahashch'id hayáázh*, Little Badger. That is where I spent most of my childhood. That tiny old lady was descended from a Zuni captive, and her name was *Bilgííbaa'*, One-Who-Fought-the-Enemy. *Diné* women are given names referring to war. Their stirring sticks, given to them by the Holy People and used to make cornmeal mush, are powerful symbols and weapons against hunger. . . .

SHICHEI BIGHANDI (AT MY GRANDFATHER'S HOUSE)

It is winter. We are living south of my grandfather's house, about two miles west of the stone house. The drought is over finally and we have moved back from the river and the lowlands. We live in a one-room cabin. There is only my mother, my sister, and I. My brothers are away at Stewart Indian School in Nevada. It is a peaceful time. One night, I get a bug in my ear. I hear it scrabbling around inside. My mother borrows a flashlight from grandfather to check. *Choosh léi' át'éélá,* she says. She uses a hairpin to pull out a black, spiderlike thing. I remember it looking like an octopus, though I didn't know that word then.

That summer, my sister and I almost killed our cat. We had placed a rubber band around its neck and forgotten it. The rubber had eaten into tender flesh by the time my mother discovered it. That was Sylvester, a black-and-white *mosí*. I remember the gummy flesh and sharp smell. The hair never grew back on its neck, and as long as he lived he wore a collar of pink skin.

Once in a while we went to see movies at the Chapter House, which is the seat of local government, and sometimes if it was a scary movie, I'd have nightmares. The popcorn and candy the teachers sold lured us too, but there was a big tradeoff. Even the Three Stooges' pranks with a plastic skeleton had me hiding on the floor with my eyes tightly closed and my hands clapped securely over my ears.

One night we are in a *hooghan* for a ceremony. A man wants to know why he is ill and we are gathered there to find out. The *hataalii* prays and sings. When he stops, the lamps are extinguished. We sit in absolute darkness. In the far distance, we hear other voices praying and singing too. Don't say anything, warns the *hataalii.* Listen very closely. See if you can identify the voices. They are the ones causing your sickness. The voices fade and we strain to hear them.

Suddenly there is a noise outside, a thump, and a sudden rush of wind. They know we are doing this, says the *hataalii,* but don't be afraid, pay them no mind. Then there are gasps. An image slowly materializes in the blackness at the center of the room. It is the dim figure of a man, floating in the air. I do not know him, but there are murmurs of recognition from the others in the room.

Years later, I am visiting a relative who accidentally drops some photo negatives and I pick them up. The memory of the image hovering in the darkness inside the *hooghan* flashes back when I see the ghostly reverse images on the film.

A daily terror at that time was a mean wether with one curled horn. It was so spiteful because my older brothers had teased it so much, pricking it with a stick, pulling its tail, but it didn't bother to charge them because they were fast and could easily dodge its attempts or outrun it. Whenever it saw us, however, my sister and I, it tucked its ears back and stamped its feet. We were easy prey, small and timid. It once butted my mother when she was bent over a ewe, helping a lamb to nurse. She whirled around, picked up an enamelware pan that was used as a dog dish, and slammed it over the wether's head. The wether, dazed and shaking its head, backed away and vanished into the flock. It left us alone after that, but we knew it watched us all the time with its yellow slitted eyes. Months later, my grandfather donated the wether to a ceremonial feast and it was carried away, its feet bound with baling wire, in the back of a truck.

My grandfather's favorite dish was *atsiits'iin.* Roasted sheep's head. He would build a fire to singe the wool from the bloody head, tuck the lolling tongue back into the mouth, scoop aside the embers, and bury the head in the heated earth. In a couple hours the feast would be ready. He'd pull out the steaming head, scrape off the dirt, place it on the table, and pour coffee. The tongue was a delicacy, as were the eyes, cartilage, and brains. I was always fearful of the grotesque charred head, especially if it had horns. Years later, that's what I pictured when the missionaries talked about the Devil.

Sometimes I accompanied my brothers when they took the sheep to the artesian well about two miles away near the river. One time, we decided to steal some melons from a field along the way. We snuck down a wash and managed to make it into the melon patch. We thought we had made a successful raid until one of my cousins yelled that someone was coming. We dropped the melons and ran, but the rider caught up with us and easily whipped our legs with her baling-wire crop. She was the daughter of the man in the stone house. Her name was Juanita. She broke horses and never married. Her face was smeared with red ocher and mutton fat, the old-time sunblock.

Every summer we took our sheep to the local sheep dip to rid them of lice and other parasites. It was a community event and for that reason we all looked forward to the day. The people would bring their flocks from miles around. Some of them numbered in the hundreds, and when they moved they raised towering clouds of dust. They came pouring out from between the surrounding hills like frothing rivers of storm water churning and swirling over the brown-and-yellow earth. There was the incessant bleating of lambs and kids, the tinkle of bells, and the barking of sheep dogs. Billy goats and rams made trouble for everyone. People on horseback rode to and fro, keeping the flocks from straying or mixing. Women opened brightly colored umbrellas and gathered for gossip, clustered like blossoms alongside the corrals or beside campfires that filled the air with the delicious smells of boiling coffee and roasting meat. Groups of men gathered in the shade under pines to tell jokes and play cards. An enterprising family would sell pop and ice cream from the back of a truck. Young people affected indifference and tended to food and animals with exaggerated care, all the while sizing each other up. The BIA livestock manager for the local grazing district, a man called *Bijoochii'*—a name referring to his ruddy coloring and similar to the word for a bodily orifice—would dump the medicines into the steaming water. Then the men would throw the panicked sheep and goats into the water, where they would bleat and bawl as they swam from one end of the vat to the other, assisted by women wielding hooked aspen poles. Now and then a lamb or kid would drown and *Bijoochii'* would scoop it out with a hook and throw it aside with a plop. The drenched animals would clamber up the other side, where they would shake themselves and fill the air with flying water.

Every day, my mother would fry potatoes. Red potatoes, white potatoes, brown. We lived on potatoes and flour tortillas because they were cheap and filling. A simple hamburger was a delicacy we enjoyed only on those rare occasions when my aunt's husband, a member of the tribal council, treated us in town. Each morning, I would wake to the sound of my mother stirring the ashes in the stove, and then the roar of the fire as it rose up the stovepipe. Above the crackling of the fire I'd hear her humming to herself or singing along to the radio as she peeled potatoes. Then there'd be the spatter of hot grease as she dumped the slices into the pan. For variety, she sometimes added mutton, onions, canned corn, eggs and bacon, or pork and beans to the potatoes. Sometimes she added flour and water to make a gravy. She could make the potatoes soft and mushy or golden and crisp. She might slice them thick or thin, into cubes, or like hashbrowns. Once in a great while she would buy a can of corned beef or Spam to add to the potatoes. My favorite, though, was potatoes fried in a cast-iron skillet over an open fire. That dish has the power to bring back memories.

My grandfather told of a time when *bilagáanas* drove past on the highway in jalopies piled high with their worldly belongings. They were looking for work in the midst of the Great Depression. They would drive past in their misery and cast glances at our ripening fields. They would sometimes stop to beg or barter for food, trading their meager possessions for corn, squash, and melons. In that way, sewing machines, wedding gowns, coffee grinders, and other artifacts of "civilization" made their way into local homes.

One summer, a truck carrying a load of pigs overturned on the highway and two hundred animals escaped. By fall, many local *Diné* had become pig farmers. Within four years, the pigs were multiplying and the people were tired of pork. The boars began biting people and eating chickens and lambs. That settled the matter. In a while, most of the pigs had been butchered, and only the tusks and stories remained. My grandfather told of the spotted pigs he had once owned, and of the way they tasted in a big steaming dish of posole.

In the summer, my grandfather and brothers would take their rifles and hunt prairie dogs in the afternoon. This wasn't easy because the little rodents were ever alert for danger. A lookout's warning bark would cause a whole colony to disappear for hours. Still, the hunters always seemed to return with a string of fat tawny *dlóó'* dangling from their belts. Grandpa would gut them and stitch the carcasses shut with string, then he'd build a roaring fire to singe the hair off. After the fire died down he'd sweep aside the ashes and dig a pit to cook them. A couple hours later he'd uncover the steaming cache and lay the feast on the table. Their tender and succulent flesh would melt off the bones. Hot coffee, roasted corn, fried squash, fresh chilies, and Grandma's warm tortillas would complete the meal.

My mute aunt would put on her galoshes and go out into the fields after a particularly heavy rain when streams of runoff crisscrossed the land. She'd work for hours, shoveling, making dikes and trenches to divert the water into burrows. After a half-hour or so, the drowned animals would float up. Her specialty was *dlóó'* baked to juicy perfection: moist on the inside, crisp and golden on the outside.

There's a story about two men from the old days when people from the reservation were just beginning to venture into the outside world. In those days it was a common practice to pack a lunch for long journeys. These men were traveling to Window Rock for tribal business. Noon found them at a bordertown café, where they took their bag lunches inside and ordered black coffee. The *bilagáana* waitress was startled to see, when she returned with their cups, that they had unwrapped their lunches and were feasting on roasted *dlóó'*. Horrified, she fled into the kitchen to tell the cooks that those Indians out there were eating puppies! . . .

TSÉHÍLÍ (WHERE IT FLOWS INTO THE CANYON)

South of the Navajo Community College, where I spent a year and a half after coming back, there is a canyon and a lake above it behind a low earthen dam. The lake is relatively new and has become a magnet for fishermen from throughout the Four Corners area. Rainbow trout, which are not native thereabouts, grow to tremendous size in the cold clear water. In summer, in the fleeting shade of a passing cloud, they rise out of the water and stipple the lake surface like raindrops when they fall back. The local people don't fish there because several people have drowned in the lake since the dam was built.

The word and name *Tséhílí* refers simultaneously to the locality and act of the creek entering the canyon there. The language is like that, full of motion. *Diné bizaad* is verb-based, whereas English is noun-based.

Tsaile is the spelling used to designate the small town that has sprung up around the college. NCC, established in 1968, is the oldest tribally controlled junior college in the United States. It is where I learned to read and write my own language. I also learned about *Diné* philosophy and art. It is where my writing career really began. Anna L. Walters, a Pawnee-Otoe woman married into our nation and an accomplished writer herself, teaches creative writing there. She was the very first person to tell me I could write. That was a revelation. I won my first writing contest there with a tale about a young woman named Alana who saved her people from oppression by evil beings with the help of aliens stranded on her world. She overcame great perils in a fantastic journey across a dangerous continent. On the way, she was befriended and aided by an assortment of peoples including Amazons, dwarves, and beings with psychic powers. She learned to vanish at will. And she learned to fly. Unbeknownst to her she'd had those powers to begin with, but she had to discover and learn to use them.

The creek descends from the mountains rising to the east of *Tsaile*—the Lukachukai Mountains, a spur of the Chuskas—and tumbles from the spillway down into the canyon. This is Canyon de Chelly. *Tséghi'*, in *Diné bizaad.* The first Spanish visitors spelled *tséghi'* the way they heard it. Now it's become de Chelly, dee-shay. I had followed the stream for miles, and it seemed like a journey into another world. The silence was astounding. I heard my footsteps echo from the cliffs. Now and then I caught myself jerking my head around to catch a movement. High up on the walls were pictographs, red, yellow, turquoise, and white *Yéi'ii* figures, handprints, animals, symbols and constellations. Where water oozed out of the cliffsides in dark seams, wild grapes thrived. I touched the handprints and was shocked by the cold stone and the recognition.

At its deepest, the canyon walls rise straight up a thousand feet above the sandy floor. In cracks veining the red sandstone walls in alcoves, on ledges, at the base of cliffs, atop rock towers, thousands of *Anaa'sázi* ruins remind one and all of the antiquity of the human presence here. They are all silent, but they are eloquent. Many have been plundered for artifacts, while scores of others repose in pristine condition, as if the occupants had just left for a moment and would return at any time.

My people, too, have stories about that canyon. In 1863 Kit Carson was commanded by the U.S. Army to subdue *Diné*, so he marched onto our homeland with a large force of soldiers and Indian scouts. Over the next two years he relentlessly pursued *Diné* throughout *Diné bikéyah.* Many people took refuge in the canyon, but eventually Kit Carson breached that stronghold. He carried out a "scorched earth" campaign, the systematic destruction of flocks and herds, cornfields and peach orchards, and reduced the nation to a shambles. His unrelenting campaign eventually succeeded, but while they still had the hope and the strength, *Diné* resisted. The canyon was their last refuge.

More than a century earlier, when the Spanish were doing the same thing to *Diné,* hunting them mercilessly across the rugged expanses of their homeland, one band, perhaps relatives, had sought refuge in an alcove high up in the canyon wall. They told children to remain quiet and they might have eluded the soldiers, but a woman could not contain her anger and she stood up and screamed insults. The Spanish soldiers fired on them from the opposite side of the canyon. The bullets ricocheted off the sloping roof of the alcove and all *Diné* hiding there were killed. That alcove is now known as Massacre Cave.

A year later, I am at the University of New Mexico in Albuquerque. I have taken all the available English courses at NCC. I go to Albuquerque because Leslie Silko and Simon Ortiz are teaching there. Also because it is a city. *Bee'edíil dahsinil*, the city named after mission bells.

ESTHER G. BELIN

Credit: Jennaye Derge

ESTHER G. BELIN (b. 1968) is Tł'ógí, born for Tó'dích'ii'nii. Her maternal grandfather is Kinłichii'nii and her paternal grandfather is Táchii'nii. She was born in Gallup, New Mexico, and raised in the Los Angeles area as part of the legacy following the U.S. Indian relocation policy. Her parents completed the Special Navajo Five-Year Program that operated from 1946 to 1961 at Sherman Institute in Riverside, California. Belin has degrees from the University of California, Berkeley (1992), the Institute of American Indian Arts (1995), and Antioch University (2007). Her first publication, in 1991, was a poem titled, "surviving in this place called the united states," in an anthology about Asian American media arts; the poem makes an analogy between Native American relocation and the internment of the Japanese Americans during World War II.

Her 1999 poetry collection, *From the Belly of My Beauty*, won the American Book Award from the Before Columbus Foundation. Her second book, *Of Cartography*, was published in 2017. In addition to writing, Belin is a multimedia artist, and her art is featured on her two book covers.

Her poetry has attracted the attention of readers and literary scholars. Dean Rader, Susan Brill de Ramírez, Mishuana Goeman, and co-editors of this volume—Connie A. Jacobs, Jeff Berglund, and Anthony K. Webster—have all written about her work. In a reflective 2007 essay, "Contemporary Navajo Writers' Relevance to Navajo Society," she recognizes that her voice is one among the many that have come before her: "I realize my voice is not just mine; I speak in a chorus of voices. That is what I like to leave with my Indian audiences, a yearning to search for their place in the Indian diaspora."

Interview

What do you hope readers learn from your writing?

I hope readers see the potential of matching emotion and language as a vehicle for expression. I hope they also see how poetry is a wonderful method for experimentation and useful for metalanguages.

How does the Navajo language influence your work?

Navajo language and thought greatly influence my writing. I find this as one of the coolest things about poetry because, even though Navajo is not my first language, I rely on my experiences growing up with parents who are native speakers to re-create spatial qualities and emotions from the language. Those spatial and emotional qualities of Diné bizaad are integral to how I write and what methods I use to convey the work.

Who or what inspires you?

Images. I often get inspired to write poems when I've seen or imagine a poetic image. These images or scenes often shock me into creativity. Such particular arresting moments are fundamental to any artist's life. Often these moments are signposts I must heed on the road toward an eventual poem.

What advice do you have for beginning writers?

My advice is to read all kinds of books and read books in other languages—do word studies and play around with translation. Doing word studies and translation work can be challenging but it creates an appreciation and fascination with language and placement of words on the page.

Who was the first Diné writer you read?

Nia Francisco.

What was your favorite book in high school? What are you reading now?

There was not a book I kept going back to in high school, but I do remember enjoying adventure-type books like *Watership Down* and *The Call of the Wild*. I did like Walt Whitman, Langston Hughes, and Emily Dickinson during poetry units in English class. Currently I'm reading a nonfiction book about neuroscience and how the human brain manages trauma.

Some of your poems are visually innovative and use placement of text in very specific ways to evoke meaning. Do you "see" the shape of poem before or as you write? If not, when does this come into play?

I do like to use the field of the page as a nonverbal device. I don't really "see" the form beforehand; the form is unique to each poem—again, I consider form as a device.

How do you write or edit differently as a writer now than when you were first starting out?

I give myself more freedom to allow the poem to create itself, rather than craft it.

⩧

Euro-American Womanhood Ceremony

Some say the boarding school experience wasn't that bad
because they learned a trade
at least the men did

The women
they were trained to specialize in domestic household work
to mimic the rituals of Euro-American women
to cook roast beef and not mutton
to eat white bread and not frybread
to start a family and not an education

to be happy servants to doctors' families in Sierra Madre
and then to their own

The young women who never really became women because they
 were taken off the rez before they could go through a
 womanhood ceremony
the young women who adapted to the Euro-American version of a
 womanhood ceremony

Instead of fasting and sweating and praying and running
They set the table and vacuumed and ironed and nursed and fed
and gave birth and birth and birth to a new nation of mixedbloods
and urban Indians
And they were mothers/providers/wives
They were strong and loved and made love and sobered up
and organized weekend road trips back to the rez
Back to the rez where we all came from
and where we need to return
to heal our wounds
from the Euro-American womanhood ceremony.

Ruby's Answer

Sunny day, Southern California restaurant, February 11, 1990. While eating lunch, Ruby is confronted by a blonde woman with frosted hair and gold wire-rimmed Ray-Bans. The woman claims sisterhood with Ruby saying, "I know exactly how you feel because I'm part Indian myself." This is Ruby's response:

If you're Indian
I'm a WASP
White Indians aren't Indians, blondie
Indians survive
You mixed and assimilated and trashed and denied your Indian
blood

You want to claim and regain your Indian identity . . .
maybe in another life
Why all of a sudden do you want to be Indian?
Why do you want to be considered a minority?
An insignificant, inferior piece of red trash?
Why do you want to go from historically supreme to historically oppressed?
Why do you want to be a statistic and a census number and a dropout and a drunk and a savage and a squaw or a princess and a car and a mascot and completely exploited until you no longer want to be Indian?
Are you on crack or did you just get a vision from your great-great-great-Cherokee grandma?
Blondie, this isn't the Girl Scouts
This is religious freedom and unrecognition and Big Mountain and releasing brother Leonard Peltier
Indians don't "come out" like gay people
They are wiped out by the people that gave you most of your blood!

Ruby didn't mind getting kicked out of the restaurant because she got a free lunch.

Sustainability: A Romance in Four Scenes

SCENE I

Of course I love my language. The haughty English phrases I use like a real urban Indian. Not the mythic ones in novels. I am one who loves the language. Moments of nihizaad squashed in my blue jeans back pocket. I love to unfold it gently and tell you how

Indian I am. It was a summer romance that started it all. A wooden spoon from the Chinle flea market. A tentless night among the stars in the Chuska Mountains. I was an eager apprentice, the west coast moisture still supple, padding my fingertips as I read this new landscape.

The Diné man. The ginger touch weaving patchworked love. He must've
felt the loveliness in walking our homeland together. My fascination in
red ant hills, red sandstone canyons, red chííʼ sustained in our bodies.
His lean fingers were tipped with pink shell, carving the tiny star

shapes I speak. That summer we tangled in nihizaad rimmed with
a salty crust, preserved in our damp canyon. The pressure in our breath
sustained. Red dust and fingerprints remain of the summer I declined
to walk one direction, footprints side by side on a rainbow path.

SCENE 2

We redefined Indian. We took hold of the ocean and its glimmering surface.
The Los Angeles ladder of relocation led to an exiled island. I was a child on
a swing in the playground, praying. The sacred L.A. mountains to the north
detracted from the cave dwellers living on the crags of broken ground.

Prayer redefined the recipe. No longer a stripe of softened scar tissue sealing
my womb. Rather a rumination, a glistening gulley, guiding, gushing in song
A metered tug to and fro, mirroring blood, siphoning symphonic, adapting the song.
The water in my womb, that sustenance formed the soil on my tongue, soiling,

salting tóʼdích'ii'nii, the water I hold inside. The L.A. rhetoric formulated the
sassy supermamas. Badass brown girls elbow-deep in hollowed-out internal organs,
thinning the thickness in blood, scrambled bits of nihizaad lost
in the jingle of coin purses, the jingle of the static wires carrying

the rez. Framing us. How we illustrated ourselves into the myths: exile, Indian,
vanishing. The invisibility now a weapon. The American Indian action
figures discounted on a clearance rack and collected by troubadour
scholars studying, positioning, suggestive, disruptive.

SCENE 3

Think that beauty is spilling. Think that beauty is spilling everywhere all the time. When you shower, sing of beauty loudly with a person in mind. That beauty is filling the gap between you and that person. Stop singing when you think the person is cleansed with beauty.

SCENE 4

Imagine all the softwood trees cut and cleared, processed to pulp and fiber, the stripped land exposed, the lost energy, the reversed labor, heating all those winter nights. Our nation, 300,000 strong, recycled and pressed into exiled textured letters, flattened and spiraling, the imprint we love to wail, like the newsprint sustaining the swelling in our speech.

Backbone

I lie on my back
against the ribs

I lie into the sky
against the marrow

I lie listening
the chamber music
of the holy ones
emanate

Lying on my back
sinking into the spine
arching
expanse
breadth
breathing
into

me
balancing

as the female
widens
as the male
extends
as the complements
bind
and grasp
onto footprints
and finger-tipped
spirals
singing deep
and deeper
densely
holding us
all in place

Emergence

I.

She was born out of his cuss words
and spittle
probably urine-matted floors gave essence
to his character
and now to hers
pumped through umbilical blood
her teeth grinding down his bad habits
his laugh
with deceiving smile
a possible caress
right before he guts
Ruby's mother with words
emerging from the bottom of his heel.

When Ruby met her mother

the only roots she could plant
were bitter and twisted and contagious.

From Ruby she wails.

II.

I often wonder
which *Easy Street*
he emerged—
mother only calls him Fast Car
"That's all I remember,"
mother says passively
"It was that kind of love
you know
that some way
kind of connection. That
is how you were created."
My bet is a Caprice
a Chevrolet Caprice
deep, strong blue
not too green
solid blue with maybe some glitter
there was sparkle
from what info I can squeeze out of mother
there was sparkle
perhaps it was his eyes
that mixed-blood blue
sparkling through his eyes
or just maybe
it was his blue jeans
with that just-right fit
sparkling from his highly polished
Pro-Rodeo silver buckle
with real gold trim
I have seen that kind before
with pretty smile to boot

maybe it was the smile
How about a gold-rimmed smile
a front tooth laced with gold trim
sparkling from across
the pow wow arena
I hope he was at least
a lead singer
I hope from up north
I always wanted to go to Canada
perhaps there
I will find him
that Fast Car
that got away
or
ran away
whatever the case
I learned my lesson from that sparkle
that sparkle
so potent and tight
bound into a confined space of beauty
caustic with the least amount of heat
my body still glows from the explosion
Mother and Fast Car
What a sight!

III.

My birth began at thirty-two
from water to water
when mother was ready to birth
a consuming heat rushed her body
being in the middle of winter
folks thought she was crazed
bobbing in and out of the waves on the beach
naked and alive with motion
people snapped photos
"An Indigenous Woman Returns to Ocean Homeland"

one headline read
"Indian Woman Commits Suicide on Beach"
was a popular thought
the salt water
the muse from the waves
were her doulas
all she says is
"Easy Street"
It's as if I just swam out of her womb
into the arms of another
sweet caress
One photo immediately after my birth
mother is just laughing
in bliss
watching me swim
still connected

IV.

I am still haunted
by the voice
or the hand
the one that slams
heads into dresser drawers
shoulders into doorways
hearts into heavy balls of clay
and the pounding pulsed
from the solid mass it created
not a sparkle of life
in sight
just a story
that shivers me
in my boots.

Old Man Jones said
he knew the man
mother called Fast Car

He'd begin
"From up north, I believe . . ."
The year he told me that story
I started to learn "O Canada"
the Canadian national anthem
I sang in the shower
on the school bus
when I was alone
Mother looked at me a bit strange
and I always thought
I pulled one over on her
and she'd just smile
thinking I was working on a school project
I even bought one of those Canadian flags
the kind with the Indian man
covering part of the maple leaf
AIM was big then
so on Independence Day
I sure raised that flag from our front porch
Mother never did budge
on offering any
Fast Car info
so I quit singing
and packed away that flag
by then it occurred to me
mother probably never
understood geography
and my need to locate
myself on someone's map

Morning Song

Only the cat and I are awake
The birds become barely audible with dawn rising
Its white light cleanses our home, tumbling into our thoughts

Like machines that dictate arrivals and departures
I sit here and type—and wonder about Emily Dickinson
About the ink in her wells and the stains on her fingers

The morning song harmonizes as the sun is warming
The appliance hums—heavy, a slothful resonance
Percolating images, wonderfully hopeful petitions
Of daily prayer, piled high like chopped wood, rewarding
And oozing with fresh sap, spiraling from my fingertip pads—
Sometimes, tacky and sharply scented

I keep my language in my back pocket like a special handkerchief that I only display when I want to show my manners in a respectful way

It is always so nice
to hear my language, even if
I don't fully understand it

I know when
someone is telling
someone else off

I know when
someone is telling
a joke, especially if it's about me

I know when
someone is being gentle, or kind
or gossiping and planting barbed seeds
with hushed voices

I know when
I am being reprimanded
"Yádiláh!"
"Doo ja'níí da!"

I know when
people are talking about my children
Don doo Esther biyazhi, bee álchíní
Desbah, Sǫ' Abini, Shandíín doo awéé' yazhi Marie

It is our great
Navajo language, Diné bizaad
that keeps me silent with hózhó, peace, beauty
even if

I am walking in downtown Los Angeles
among the Nakaii dine'é, Bináá'ádaalts'ózí
or Naakai Łizhinii

Their words and language
pass overhead
joining the thin outline of smog

I walk on
mumbling some Spanish, Japanese, Lakota or Crow
leaving them in thought about my origin

In the middle of busy intersections
and energy-efficient street lights
they see a cornfield and canyon walls

X+X+X+X–X–X–X

There are cries between each letter:

The piercing cries of birthing—hot like a mother
The piercing early morning cry of a drunk driver's balding tires
The piercing mid-day cry of an imploding middle-schooler, border-towner, cross-blooder—bloody and invaded—the heavy metals in our blood more bloody than springtime flood waters— can you handle hauling water

for five hundred more years—yes 500 hindered, more sleepless—gaps of memory—can you find me in the cavern between the letters "M" and "E"—the puss-filled gummy sockets of tissue stagnating my voice?

The piercing evening prayers, a penetration of jack hammer pulses pulsating for loveless (un)loving longing for love-filled spaces—quiet spaces of rest, beautified glances . . .

Now I lay me down to sleep, I pray . . .
And what about the coolness of the evening, the tangle of clouds tucking me into bed, trapping me into my nighttime wanderings—my dusky landscapes of rainbow-arced points of entry—seeking shelter—a rest like the shadow from the Most High—a holy mountain retreat

There are seedlings between each letter:

Today I am standing in front of the Creator—I am witness—the slaying of the lambs—the preparation of the meat—fire-roasted with tortillas, green chile, and 'ach'íí—my hands are sore—gutting and cutting—tender around the internal organs, tough and fierce at hip joints—my hands are sore—slapping the bleached, red winter wheat flour into disks—my hands are sore—cedar splinters embedded, cedar smoke infused, cedar sap veneered

Today I am mother in a smothered breakfast burrito—the red chile burning my ass

Today I am peaceful like a river flow—like a river plugged—like a river dried—like a river rivering, a current currenting, a splash spilling and sparkling skyward—like the river used to flow in me—and out—like a soppy addict sitting at the Transfer Station, a transference of laser-scribed CIB, BIA tendril insertions deafening the cries, widening the distance between you, me and home

Today I am emissions of spit swallowed since my birth on a hill down a hall of IHS hospital the window holds oceanic groans, a wave of saliva—I swim in utero—I drown on arrival

There are ________________ between each letter:

Choose the best answer from the list below to fill in the blank—then write a haiku to support your answer

starving Indians	traveling songs
capsules of Discovery Doctrine	mutton ribs
mountain songs	Hollywood Indians
soft goods	tádídíín

Extra Credit: Map your answer on the graph below

east

north dootł'izh

łitso

There are (Jiní)
Other voices (Dishní)
Between each letter (Nisha?)

between each hollow each sigh and forgotten star sayings of and about
and how to hold our map waiting in the heavens high above knowing I
can visit with them whenever I want is good information but not enough
to divert my gaze from the glittering world tragedies—allure allusions
allegations of a better than now existence my shell dented toughened from
mutiny mutilation monstering mothering in a standard-issued shell like
the language I speak and write and cry and plant with a shoveling motion
imploding to make room for more penetration(s) pencil prodders tapping
my flesh testing my urban-smeared blood against the indigenous DNA
tucked into sandstone graves tucked into denim pockets like smashed
noses into ceilings poundings like last night's black eye back door left
open to flee like boarding school runaways in transit to checkerboarded
houses nestled in tar paper reservation wind winding won't stop it

male

female

salt water	1956	Two-Way Inn
1978	bicycle	East LA
popcorn	East Bay	Johnny Shrimp
4 corners	199_	stick-shift truck

assignment 43

1. find the complementary points
2. plot the coordinates at their intersection
3. use the visual text created as a key for diagrams

SHONTO BEGAY

Credit: Dawn Kish

SHONTO BEGAY (b. 1954) is Tódich'ii'nii, born for 'Áshįįhí, and his maternal grandfather is Tł'ízí lání, and his paternal grandfather is Tsi'naajinii. His mother is a traditional weaver, and his father was a medicine man. He grew up herding sheep in Kletha Valley, located near Shonto, Arizona, and today lives in Flagstaff, Arizona. Begay attended Bureau of Indian Affairs boarding schools at different locations on the Navajo Nation and finished high school in Kayenta. He received an Associates of Fine Arts degree from the Institute of American Indian Arts, a BFA from the California College of Arts and Crafts, and, in the 1980s, worked as a National Park Service ranger in the Grand Canyon, the Grand Teton National Park, and the Navajo National Monument. Since 1983 Begay has been a professional artist. His subject matter ranges from the mundane everyday world of Navajo life to desert and natural landscapes to more contemporary and urban settings to scenes of road trips or ceremonial and social gatherings. His work has been shown in major galleries and museums including the Wheelwright Museum of the American Indian in Santa Fe, the American Indian Contemporary Arts Museum in San Francisco, the Phoenix Art Museum, the Museum of Northern Arizona, the Arizona State Museum, and the Utah Museum of Fine Arts.

His first publication featuring his paintings was *The Mud Pony* (1988), the winner of the Owl Award for illustration. As author-illustrator, Begay's first book was *Ma'ii and Cousin Horned Toad: A Traditional Navajo Story* (1992), followed by *Navajo: Visions and Voices Across the Mesa* (1995), from which several of the poems here are excerpted. He has illustrated, among other works, *The Magic of Spider Woman* (1996), the reissue of *Alice Yazzie's Year* (2004), and *Navajo Long Walk: The Tragic Story of a Proud People's Forced March from Their Homeland* (2002). His work has been published in various anthologies, magazines, and newspapers. For many years, his column, "Letter from Home," appeared in the arts weekly *Flagstaff Live!*; "Drawing Life: Delineating My World," included below, first appeared in that series.

Interview

What do you hope viewers find in your paintings?

I hope that they get lost in them, for one thing, to be able to exercise their imagination to see things that I don't even see. And also, there's the sharing of my culture, sharing the vision, and sharing the passion for painting, for doing art, for being a whole human.

What do you hope readers find in your writing?

Maybe a little bit of something, a little bit of words that can guide them to their own prayer. To their own meditation. I like going deep and pulling out things, figuring out feelings and passions, and I hope it gets readers into finding their own voice as well.

I think when I lived in Berkeley, California, I wrote quite a bit for me, nobody's eyes but me. It was a way for me to dispel, at the time, powerful dreams. If a Navajo has powerful, troubling dreams they could talk to a medicine man, find a bit of healing, some smudging, a prayer. But in Berkeley, I didn't have a medicine man, so I became my own. I [thought], I'm going to write it out, I wrote out volumes I have stashed away somewhere. In the late 1970s/early 1980s. It was before I was painting. I was with the National Park Service. I did that for a number of years. So through those times I was writing my dreams, my nightmares.

How does Navajo language or culture influence your work?

Such a big question. I'll just draw from my experience, my childhood, and of course my joys and my pains from the past. I have a lot of coyote stories about all of his antics. But what it is, is this: he plays out all facets of our personality, a mirror back in our face. Of course the whole culture, the language, the stories, the songs and just the connection, the deep connection, with the earth going back home every week, that *feeds* me.

Who or what inspires you, and specifically, what inspired your book Navajo: Visions and Voices Across the Mesa, *which was where two of your works here, "Darkness at Noon" and "Navajo Power Plant," were first published?*

It was all inspired by an image. Sometimes I paint the image. Sometimes I write the image. It goes both ways. I love writing, I love reading. Sometimes it's the image, but they don't turn into visuals, they turn into words.

What advice do you have for beginning writers or beginning painters?

For me it's a little step at a time. I never made the plan to be *here.* It just happened that I love what I do and I want to do the best that I can and that's pretty much the driving force behind me. It isn't so much about the financial gain, although that's a plus, and of course, notoriety is a big thing to deal with as well.

Who was the first Navajo writer you read?

I don't even remember. Maybe it was my sister Florence's letter to me. I think she was in school in Albuquerque and I was back home in Shonto, Arizona. It was a letter written to the family.

Why are books important to you? You have a number of paintings featuring readers. What's your inspiration for the cover painting or the others I see in your studio, including the one you're working on?

It's a portal into imagination, the world that never ends. When I paint people reading, it's also beyond what the picture is, it keeps going on. It's an interpretation of an interpretation of a reader. In fact, my painting *Story Rock* you see hanging in the Phoenix Public Library is just that: that's my magic carpet, that's my time machine, that's also my spaceship, that rock I sat on. I sat there a lot of time, to the point I wore a little hole in the sandstone.

What was your favorite book in high school?

I always liked western writers because they'd describe landscape. It gave me the aroma of sage, the late light over the mesa, the sense of a place I knew well. And, all of the horses, of course, galloping across the pages were fantastic, and all of the cowboys and other people populating these stories, and of course, the dialogue. I bought books at trading posts here and there.

A lot of my friends liked comic books, graphic stuff, which I liked as well. Herding the sheep and reading a book or a comic. And I never left home, while herding sheep, without either an Etch A Sketch or a book. In fact, I used to have what I called "library trees." I had these three trees on my land. One to the northwest, one to the east, and one to, down to the south, kind of far apart, a few miles apart. When the sheep wanders in that direction during the day, I'm always near another branch library. I would have the bundles of books in plastic to keep them protected. And then I'd put them back. Sometimes I still wonder if those books are out there in the tree.

What are you reading now?

I love reading poetry, singer/songwriters, of course. Leonard Cohen and, of course, his latest one, *The Flame*. I really like the writing of Hampton Sides. I just go all over the place now. I feel like I've traveled the world, I've traveled through time and space through reading.

≑

Darkness at Noon

SOLAR ECLIPSE

I was ten years old when the stars came out at noon. After penning the sheep and goats in the corral for their noon rest, I felt a strange sense of uneasiness. The chirping of birds was absent, the buzzing of insects stopped, even the breeze died down.

My toes felt the sand still warm through the holes in my sneakers. The landscape fell under a shadow on this cloudless day. As I hurried through the tumbleweed and rabbitbrush, it got darker. I looked up and saw twinkling stars far above. The dogs were lying in the doorway.

I ran into the darkened hooghaan. Immediately I was told to sit down and remain quiet. I couldn't even eat or drink. My aunt said the sun had died. *The sun had died.* The words hit me like thunder. How could this happen? What did we do? I had only started to live. My brothers sat nearby, silent in their own turmoil. The hooghaan was dark. Only occasional whispers broke the silence.

Outside toward the east, up on the hill, I heard the rising and falling of prayer song. My father was up there boldly standing in the face of darkness, calling back the sun. I prayed silently with him.

As we sat in the darkness for what seemed like eternity, little crescents of light began to appear on the hooghaan floor, faint at first, then brighter. The sun was returning. It was coming back to life. I prayed harder as the stars disappeared and faint blue washed over the sky. The crescents of light on the floor, coming in from the smokehole, started to round themselves out, becoming half circles, then slowly one full, bright hole. The sun had regained its form. The holy cycle. The sacred symbol of all creation was reborn this day for me.

My father came down from the hill exhausted and happy. We ran out to meet him before the elders could contain us.

That day and all the days since, I appreciate even more the sun we thought we'd lost. The colors are richer and the warmth of the sun, more comforting. The days are brighter. The summer heat is welcome.

Each day, I rise just before the sun does, to sprinkle my corn pollen, and to thank the coming day for its gift of light.

Navajo Power Plant

The earth gently releases its roots.
She accepts the gifts of tobacco and corn pollen.

Medicine is plenty upon this plateau.
Reverence is strong, prayers are heard.

Plants to concoct medicine brew, plants to burn for cleansing,
still some to offer in healing to the gods.

My uncle's lips move slightly as silent prayers are passed,
thick brown hands gently placed upon the petals,
arthritic fingers dust the roots.

Carpet of lavender on the vermillion ground
staggers far into the distance between light and shadow.

Concrete fingers stab at the dark summer sky.
Man-made steam clouds rise, white and fragile
against precious black thunderclouds.

Navajo power plant and the powerful healing plant,
they share the same plateau.
One gives us strength and wisdom here and now—
one gives power to strangers somewhere over the horizon—

Drawing Life: Delineating My World

> *Drawing is more than a tool for rendering and capturing likeness. It is a language, with its own syntax, grammar, and urgency. Learning to draw is about learning to see. In this way; it is a metaphor for all art activity. Whatever its form, drawing transforms perception and thought into image and teaches us how to think with our eyes.*
>
> —KIT WHITE, FROM *101 THINGS TO LEARN IN ART SCHOOL*

The very first stirrings of "thinking with my eyes" as a means to create my own world, filled with subjects and symbols of my unconventional and safe reality, came early. My great Diné elders carried in themselves the wisdom and strength born of the act of symbolizing our mythic world through the healing sand painting mandalas. I was intrigued by these ancient templates. I saw magic flowing from their thick and knowing fingers. To my innocent eyes it was as if these existed in another holy place, and were being released from where they already resided. They were the reservoir where magic healing sources awaited.

I saw my uncles and my older brothers and cousins render amazing images on the dirt floor of the hooghaan. The lines were accentuated by the amber light of the kerosene lamp as shadows danced mysteries on the cribbed log walls. I sat in awe of the voices relating ancient stories of heroes and coyotes which they illustrated with stick drawings right there on the floor. I knowingly picked up my own stick and connected my heart and my head to my hands and I drew my first line. In my mind's eye I sketched my horse. The lines were devoid of mass and my brother chuckled. "You cannot call that a horse," he told me before guiding me into that lesson.

My Uncle Harry, from the corner came to my defense. "That is Spirit Horse. Do not mock him." My Uncle Harry, unbeknownst to my brother, had nudged that first hesitant line into one of confidence.

I developed a love for those defining lines and the motion of the hand before I honed the skills to render a horse. My older brother Nelson taught me to draw animals correctly, using circles of varying sizes and connecting them with lines and mass, much as it is taught in art class. Armed with this knowledge, I was a bit ahead of the other boys in school. It was because of their passing interest in a new toy, the Ohio Art Etch A Sketch, that I acquired several of these magnificent toys. It reminded me of the sacred and magical images of the sand mandalas. The boys tossed them after a few attempts, which produced nothing more than straight lines. They went back to their checkers and cap pistols. I cautiously nailed a circle, some curves and then squiggles. For me it was both temporary, and personally healing. The first line that was to be my life was drawn.

"Dii' dashiki' yaazhi' ayoo' na'adjaa'" (This little man can draw) an elder said as I produced another wood fire charcoal drawing on cardboard. I was immediately recruited, and for the next several years I sat hunched over the blessed bed of sand, earth colors spooling from the fingertips of my small untested hand. I felt honored and sacred and it also kept me from harder chores. I learned to stay within the perimeter of that ancient set of templates. I found my chosen place in those days on my knees, face close to the ground, moving to the rhythm of healing chants.

Back in the confines of the boarding school, I continued to create my world away from ceremonial art. I saw that all of my world needed my validation, my vision and meditation within it. I drew superheroes, some existing; others made up in my wild youthful whirlwind of a mind. I drew my cowboy heroes and DC Comics' Sgt. Rock and some of Marvel's bulky characters. I drew Sad Sack, the comic army private that always seemed to end up in a garbage pail with a banana peel as a cover. Turok, the lost Sioux in the land of the dinosaurs was another great inspiration.

Movies shown at school gave me yet more characters to give lines to. Later came various forms of music that set tempo and emotions to draw upon. My world offered up much to meld into constant hand motions. It was during these days that I discovered that I did not need any material to draw. I drew on air with my finger—images only I could see, for as long as I wanted.

"Yee'ya' be'iini ziin" (Be careful, he is a wilding wizard) the uninspired called out among themselves. Bullies kept their distance. In this manner I managed to survive the most brutal years of the government boarding school.

My drawings gave richness and meaning to my life as a young boy. Even my older sister was impressed enough that she coughed up a quarter for me to draw her the face of Elvis. That was not too hard. I made his face a cartoon and she refused to pay. But my passion was never about quarters. When I was at a vulnerable age, drawing helped me survive in a rapidly changing world. It was insulating me with very ancient scripts that carried my story and my fantasy. Drawing gave me more than an immediate contact to that world we call spirit.

My late grandmother confirmed that by telling me the gift of seeing is the power to render within a perimeter of the Diné philosophy of Spirit Break, and to realize you are always creating, and to know what things you can and cannot represent, such as lightning, sacred "Yeii" (deity figures) and serpents. To this day, I never draw them without considering this.

I draw now to record life's thumbnail sketches. I cannot handle a camera so this is my aperture through which my documentations take shape. I draw to keep that channel to the magic world open. I draw my longings, my fears and my little celebrations in living. I want it to be a reservoir of my passion that brings a smile to every face that comes in contact with it. The knowledge of drawing is the armature upon which all other forms of art find its impetus, its aesthetic in form, motion and sound. Just as my very first cry rang off the mesa on that cold winter's night many years ago, my very first line in art gave purity and oxygen to all that is yet to come. Yes, come mar the blank space to define your own first cry. Happy drawing to you.

DELLA FRANK

DELLA FRANK (b. 1949) is of Naakai Dine'é. She was born up in the hills of Aneth, Utah, at her paternal grandparents' place. Frank lived in Aneth until age nine when she was sent away to Intermountain Indian School, a Bureau of Indian Affairs boarding school, in Brigham City, Utah. Since 1965 she has lived in Gallup, New Mexico. Frank has always felt "a sadness because I never grew up at home." She holds a BS in elementary education, an MA in curriculum and reading specialties from the University of New Mexico, and an MA in counseling and guidance from Western New Mexico University. Today, although she is officially retired, Frank works as a home health care worker, assists the older generation with health needs, and works as a GED writing instructor.

Her first poem was published by the University of New Mexico Press in 1989; Frank remembers it was about "how I and my mother went out to the flea-market in Gallup, New Mexico, to try to sell mutton stew and fried bread, but we never really sold anything. We sat there under the hot sun and hoped and prayed that we would sell a portion of our cooked food, but hardly anybody came by." In 1993, she published a short story in *Neon Pow-Wow: New Native Voices of the Southwest*, edited by Anna Lee Walters. Perhaps she is best known for *Storm Pattern: Poems from Two Navajo Women: Poems by Della Frank and Roberta D. Joe*, published by the Navajo Community College Press in 1993.

Interestingly, despite this "collaboration," Roberta Joe and Della Frank have not yet met each other.

Interview

What do you hope readers learn from your writing?

> With my writings, I hope that Diné language readers would "re-capture" their Diné culture in every aspect of the word. For instance, we need to honor our culture, which includes the Diné language and ways of life. We need to re-walk the Long Walk and truly look at what it is they left behind for us to experience—Diné Natives—to appreciate and survive upon. The song "Shií Naashá" was sung by the Diné people as they were walking back to their homeland in the later part of 1800s. They felt freedom upon their faces and they sang this song in joy, I hear.

When you are writing, how does the Navajo language influence your work?

> When I am writing, the Diné language influences my work in several ways. When I am writing, I think about "the way it used to be. . . ." I remember how people used to walk or ride horses a long way just to visit and have coffee with their neighbors. I remember how people used to greet one another in the traditional ways and manners. The Diné people used to treat each other with the utmost respect back in those days. I remember the drums and songs of survival, as well. I remember the four-night ceremony called Ndáá' and how my grandmother used to drag out men and dance with them just to get a quarter. I write to bring back these aspects of Diné way of life. It brings back the goats and sheep that my grandmother used to have back in those days. I remember everything.

Who or what inspires you?

> I have many heroes: you could be one of them. My heroes are all the warriors who fought for our freedom as Diné peoples of today. I envision the canyons of Chinle, Arizona, where our historical heroes fought. Some of the Diné people like my maternal grandmother and grandfather ran towards the canyons of Utah and Colorado, and survived and told their

stories. I feel inspired when our young people talk, dance, and drum, pronouncing their respect of the Diné culture and ways of life! My deceased precious relatives inspire me. I feel their presence in the mornings.

What advice do you have for beginning writers?

My advice to beginning writers would be to believe in themselves as writers, and that they, too, can bring back the Diné culture and ways of life. They need to write about what they feel are important in their lives.

What was your favorite book in high school? What are you reading now?

I loved science. I had a great science teacher, and his name is Mr. Paul Sword. He had compassion for his students, and I felt inspired by him. I have read many books written by different doctors with different issues and concerns. I have read some biographies. I feel inspired by some women writers from all walks of life. I have not really read the latest writings of any Native writers, to tell you the truth. I have been wanting to go to the Navajo Nation Museum in order to look at the latest writings, but I almost work full time now, past my retirement. I love stories that give me strength and purpose in life!

Who was the first Diné writer you read?

I became interested in Diné writings back in the 1980s. I have read some poems written by Luci Tapahonso, Laura Tohe, Rex Lee Jim, and Irvin Morris. I believe I have read some of Esther Belin's writings, as well. My first interaction with a book, and hence, author, was a book of poems called *Beneath My Heart*, by Janice Gould.

Shimasani My Grandmother

For Rose

My grandmother's house is small
It sits on a hill alone
She has a shade-house next to it
She keeps hay for the sheep
Feed for the chickens
Food for the dogs and cats
That wander

Shimasani 'ayǫ́ǫ́'ánííníshníh

When I visit
I sleep in the same room as her
She is small and fits
Into her bed

She chops wood every-night
Lights the fire Before
Beginning her cooking chores

I watch her
As she brings in wood

I watch her
As she begins
to boil the coffee

Shimasani 'ayǫ́ǫ́'ánííníshníh

I watch her
As she throws meat
Into the boiling water

I watch her
Add chunks of potatoes

I watch her
Mix the dough
To make fried bread or tortillas

I watch her
As she tells me about
Her aches and pains

Shimasani 'ayóó'ánííníshníh

I nod carefully
As I listen to her
Talk of misgivings

I help bring in dish water
Careful to not use too much

I help set the table
As I quietly wonder about her

Shimasani 'ayóó'ánííníshníh

She has lived many years
    In the hills and the canyons
She has given birth to many children
She has herded sheep far and wide
She has married many men   Men who went to war
She has walked many canyons   Herding her sheep
She has crossed many rivers   Tears of pain
    Mark her face
    As she holds her stick
    Singing her songs

Shimasani 'ayóó'ánííníshníh

We sit down to eat
Hot mutton stew and crunchy fried bread

She glances shyly across
Light plays on her features

She talks of her generation
How we extend from her   Branching out
And, if she chooses to get mad at us
She has the rights.   To do so . . . .
We had it coming, anyway . . . .

Shimasani 'ayóó'ánííníshníh

We put the dishes up
On cardboard shelves
We settle down for the night
        Stars glitter
        Shadows dance
        Dogs bark in the distance
        Cats meow under the small bed
        Sheep grunt in their corral

I wish my dear grandma   Good-night

Shimasani 'ayóó'ánííníshníh

The Summer I Was 13

I remember clearly the day I arrived at her house.

I was to work for $20.00 a week in the summer.
        I was to   shampoo plush carpets and scrub the big
            roomy house
        And baby-sit whenever possible.

I was 13 years of age then.
Money was difficult to come by back home.

I rang the doorbell
Out she came with curly red hair
And polished red nails.
"You must be the Indian girl that has been assigned to me. . . ."
She took me to the basement.
It was completely bare except for a bunkbed in the corner.
A cardboard "closet" stood upright beside the bed.

A wooden stick was fastened
from one end of the cardboard
to the other.
This was where I was to
Hang my clothes
that summer.

During the nights I felt afraid.
The pipes made "cranking" sounds.
The dim light gave off monstrous shadows,
as imagination played at my mind.

Dread tugged at my heart,
persistent night after night.
I tried to close my eyes, at least pretend to sleep
But it escaped me each time. . . .

(I didn't dare complain to my keeper
For fear I would be dismissed.)

Night after night I closed my eyes in the dark

"Bang Bang Bang"

Went the pipes
And my heart pounded along with the sounds

"Monsters are coming to eat me alive
Witches too!"

Everyday it was the same.
I got up tired, unable to concentrate.

But I tried to pretend that everything was okay
(And I needed the money anyway. . . .)

I vacuumed carpets.
Scrubbed the floors
for the guests expected that night.
I cooked the family meals.
They sniffed at the food
and stood at the stove
to make sure nothing spilled.

That happened the summer I was 13.

I Hate to See . . .

For those who suffer in life

There are certain things I hate to see
By the side of the road
During my many drives

I hate to see
A fattened-up sheep
Caged by the side of the road
A sign near him
Implying that he cost only a little money.
While he walks around under the sun
Hot, thirsty, hungry too!

I hate to see
Scrawny dogs
Listlessly walking by the side of the road
Wondering where the next meal is coming from
If he makes it to the next one!

I hate to see
Poor drunks
Looking lost
Staggering by the side of the road
Holding out dollar bills
To no one in particular
To whoever picks them up. . . .
They're hungry tired and thirsty too!
(Booze should be done away with all over the world!)

I hate to see
Navajo women
Wandering
By the side of the road
Hungry and tired babies
Tucked under their arms
They must be tired of walking—
They're only wearing tennis shoes
No jackets
To keep off the January cold!
(Men should not leave wives over pretty faces!)

I hate to see
Young Navajo people
Hitch-hiking
By the side of the road
"Feeling high"
and trying to go with the "flow"
I wonder
Where they're from
And worry that they need to get home
To their moms, dads
And grandparents too!

Where has the slogan "Walk in Beauty" gone to. . . . ?

And I hate to see
Hand grabbing

For what little money
The Navajos have
Selling them unwanted items
With promises of "Instant Tax Credit"!
I'm sure the Navajos could use money too!

I hate to see these things
By the side of the road. . . .

ROBERTA D. JOE

Credit Roberta D. Joe

ROBERTA D. JOE (b. 1960) is Tódich'ii'nii, born for Kinlichnii'; Bit'ahnii is her maternal grandfather and Hashk'ąą hadzohi is her paternal grandfather. Roberta D. Joe was raised in Arizona and New Mexico. She is an attorney, writer, and artist. After completing high school at Wasatch Academy in Mount Pleasant, Utah, she went on to receive a BA in anthropology modified with Native American studies from Dartmouth College in Hanover, New Hampshire, in 1982 and a juris doctor from the University of New Mexico School of Law in Albuquerque, New Mexico, in 1988. Her law career began as a staff attorney for the Navajo Nation Department of Justice in Window Rock, Arizona; she then worked for fourteen years as an assistant attorney general for the New Mexico attorney general. For six years she served as an Indian probate judge for the U.S. Department of Interior, Office of Hearings and Appeals. Presently she is an assistant county attorney for the Santa Fe county attorney in Santa Fe, New Mexico. Roberta D. Joe lives in the flat country south of Santa Fe, New Mexico, where she spends time in her studio, enjoying walks with her two small yorkies, Dante Marcello Alighieri and Chloe Costanza Manicotti, and cooking. Her work included below is from *Storm Pattern:*

Poems from Two Navajo Women: Poems by Della Frank and Roberta D. Joe, published by Navajo Community College Press in 1993. Her earlier poetry, some of which was later reworked for *Storm Patterns*, was published in *Diné Be'iina': A Journal of Navajo Life*.

Interview

What do you hope readers learn from your writing?

That writing, creative writing, comes from deep inside yourself; that you have to be willing to search inside of yourself to uncover something that you know is emotional in some way for you. Some thing, some smell, some sound, some visual memory, that you can remember clearly. It may be emotions that you've intentionally kept covered for years, but finding them, remembering them, and bringing them out in your writing will result in something creative.

How does the Navajo language influence your work?

Not much, because I, for the most part, do not speak the Diné language.

Who or what inspires you?

My memories inspire me. A desire to be creative inspires me. Nature inspires me, colors in the sky inspire me, and good and bad memories inspire me.

What advice do you have for beginning writers?

Don't be confined by the rules, English grammar. Write what you feel regardless of whether anyone except you likes what you write. Whatever language you choose to write in, make sure you check for typos. I think the most creative art comes from those that don't follow the rules of painting. That's what writers should do. Learn the rules, but once you know what the rules are you do not have to follow them to write something good.

What was your first published work?

Storm Pattern, published by Navajo Community College Press, 1993.

Who was the first Diné writer you read?

Luci Tapahonso.

What was your favorite book in high school? What are you reading now?

This makes me chuckle and smile because I don't remember a favorite book in high school. What does come to mind is a poet our English teacher brought to the school to do a reading. Don Stap's chapbook *Kristine* (1971). It's a small paperback book of poems. That was the first time I remember being inspired to write poems. I like going back to reread parts of *Zen and the Art of Motorcycle Maintenance*. To me, it's about passion. These days I read a lot of cookbooks. I like to cook.

÷

Emotional Illness

dry senseless anger
possesses her
whirling grey
confusion
poisons her bloodstream
a dark intrusion
disorients her
days occupied by crowded dreams
force her into small uncomfortable places
the smell is ugly
strange lights
annoy
the
periphery of her
vision
those witchpeople
sent the foggy
sickness
on a hot Lukachukai day
lightning
struck the ground
into her being
she inhaled the smoky cloud

Storm Pattern

Bobby has a standing wooden wardrobe
filled with rainbow waving
Yeibichei.

She rolled them up

stored them in the wardrobe

because they would not

lie quietly

in a row

on the bare floor.

Thursday night

The Yeibichei chanted
a celebration.

Rainbows were strewn everywhere.

North colors were in the East.

West colors were on the wrong hangers.

South colors were inside out on the floor.

The doors of the wooden wardrobe shook.

The wardrobe could not contain

the enormous noise

of the rainbow waving

Yeibichei.

The wooden doors flew open!

Neighbors called the police.

Bobby answered the door when the police arrived.

She invited them inside

out of a restless cloudburst

and whirling lightning.

They found no evidence of the reported disturbance.

The storm pattern dispersed.

Friday morning was quiet.

Bobby picked up

the sacred prayer sticks

to carefully rewrap them in rainbows.

The first spring thunderstorm was over.

Sunset Woman's Ivy League Escape

Sunset Woman figured it this way:
If she climbed the granite hill
she could rest
smile
on top
pleased to
have
flagged down
just one sunset
on its way back
to New Mexico

Her feet slid over dull layers of thick, decaying leaves.
She smelled Fall, a heavy autumn blanket with unfamiliar folds.
She could not feel the earth.

Her heart stung and hurt in dry alien snow.
She tasted Winter, choking wetness, bitter with prejudice.
She could not cleanse with this water.

Her hands missed texture in the pungent green.
She felt Spring, an unbearable forest watching with disapproval.
She could not touch her history.

Her eyes saw no orange horizon fire in the saturated days.
She saw Summer, an evaporating mist without shape.
She could not see The West.

She figured it this way:
New England
is no place
for a hitch-hiking Sunset Woman.

Coyote Shuffle Romance

Last night
trying to teach you the two-step
with those silly rabbit stars in my eyes

We bumped
into the door
elbowed the wall
We tripped
on the carpet
became entangled
in the weave of a Navajo rug

our coyote shuffle romance

To control our dance,
I counted the steps for you
Tried to lead
thrown off by heartbeats
distracted by the
heavy breathing
I lost count
Passion took my "one-two's"
Threw them on the dance floor
like
sawdust
I closed my eyes

Dust from those silly rabbit stars
covered our feet

Our coyote shuffle romance continued into the night

HERSHMAN JOHN

Credit: James Montang

HERSHMAN JOHN (b. 1972) is both a poet and a short fiction writer. He is born to Bį́įh bitoodnii and for the Tódich'ii'nii. He was born in California and raised on the Navajo Reservation, near Sand Springs. He enjoys reading poetic theory and comic books. John received his BA in English and MFA in creative writing, both from Arizona State University. Before attending Arizona State University he was accepted to attend the Oxbridge Program, an international educational immersion program of courses at Oxford University, United Kingdom, after he graduated high school. There, he took classes in poetry and art history; both courses had profound effects on him. According to John, as he read more poetry and studied classical art from ancient Greece, Egypt, and the British Isles, he learned the techniques of line breaks, forms, tone, intent, imagery, and rhyme schemes. Having returned to Arizona, he began his studies at ASU in the engineering program, but that program left him uninspired. Only after he switched majors—at the suggestion of his former high school English teacher—did college, in John's words, "became fun." Since then he has pursued the writing of poetry and teaching as well.

Many of his words reflect his Navajo heritage, growing up as he did on and off the Navajo reservation. In 1995, the same year he started his MFA program, John published his first two poems, "Coyote's Eyes" and "Grandmother Moon," in *Expedition Magazine*, published by the University of Pennsylvania Museum of Archaeology and Anthropology. His works have been widely published by anthologies and literary journals: *Arizona Highways*, *National*

Geographic, *Water Stone Review*, *Arizona Republic*, *Yellow Medicine Review*, *Nuclear Impact: Broken Atoms in Our Hands*, *Hayden's Ferry Review*, *Journal of Navajo Education*, *Puerto del Sol*, and *Red Indian Road West*. In 2007, the University of Arizona Press published his first collection of poems, *I Swallow Turquoise for Courage*.

John has been teaching for the past twenty years. As a full-time faculty member at Phoenix College, he teaches composition, poetry, comic book writing, and American Indian studies courses.

Interview

What do you hope readers learn from your writing?

I write to tell my stories and to show I am a poet. In high school, I took a poetry class where I was exposed to meter and rhyme. I read a little on poetics, and explicated a poem. I hope readers can take a little bit about who I am, where I am from. Also, to learn about my journey as a writer, learning from high school to college to writing on my own.

How does the Navajo language influence your work?

The Diné language in my writing echoes my grandmother, Susie Worker. To communicate with my grandmother, one had to know Diné. In my first manuscript, there are two predominant voices (besides my own), that of my grandmother and Ma'ii. When Diné words are used, it's the only word that fits the poem. Language is like poetry, and the use of other language is important in writing, whether it's Navajo, Hopi, Crow, Hawaiian, French, Japanese, it's all holy, it's the basic units of sound.

Who or what inspires you?

I am inspired by my family, my family stories, my traditional stories, my friends' stories, and so on. I am inspired by the different poets I read. I am inspired by my travels halfway around the world. I am inspired by other Native writers, from Diné writers to Hawaiian writers to Inuit writers. . . . I love watching films, sci-fi, fantasy, action, to name a few. I am inspired by other worlds like Narnia, Metropolis, Mordor, Hogwarts.

. . . I once thought, and have heard some students say, "I don't want to be jaded by other books and writings, or cultures, or faiths, or films." That is wholeheartedly not true, and lazy. To breathe, to learn, to read is important to any writer.

What advice do you have for beginning writers?

Always write: write everything down, from ideas to dreams, because once you don't, it's gone forever. Education is an important way to become inspired. I am inspired by all my teachers and my lessons I learned. Always read, write, and learn, is my advice for a beginning writer. Once you stop reading and writing, you're really not a writer.

Who was the first Diné writer you read?

The first poem I remember was by Luci Tapahonso, "Come into the Shade." I remember her describing Shiprock, a place I've been many times. It was in college when I first encountered the poem, in the book *A Breeze Swept Through*. I remember it was a great exercise on sensory description, what does something look, smell, taste, feel, and sound like . . .

What was your favorite book in high school? What are you reading now?

I remember Holden Caulfield's story vividly, by J. D. Salinger, *Catcher in the Rye*, along with Franz Kafka's *The Metamorphosis*. I remember reading Marvel's *Secret Wars*, and witnessing the first superhero crossover event. The books I study today are Sylvia Plath's *Ariel*, Nazim Hikmet's *The Poems of Nazim Hikmet*, and Gertrude Stein's *Tender Buttons*.

≑

My Feminist Grandmother

Grandma didn't have to march on
Washington, D.C., or resist
Politicians. Bras, she did not
Own. Feminism does not exist.

Grandma owns all the land, cows, corn.
Her words are final; we listen.
Arguments end. And the word
Feminism does not exist.

Our clans are passed through our mothers.
What's his clan? Always make sure he's
Different. Grandma will always know.
Feminism does not exist.

Her daughters never move from home—
Grandma can arrange marriages
And bargains for her son-in-law.

However, a male in-law may
Never look upon Grandmother's
Beautiful face—know this is very taboo.

Our creator, Changing Woman,
Made all that there is: Earth,
Squash blossoms, sheep, stars, life, men . . . .
Feminism does not exist.

Divorce is rare, when it happens—
Her sons will protect their sister.
Put all his belongings outside.

I tell Grandma of Eve, dark veils,
Patriarchy. I go on to say
Many women have no voice, can
Be beaten, and wait on their men.

Grandma, did you know you have to
Take on Grandpa's name? *Quit telling*
Jokes like Coyote.

But, she does love my tales
Of Amazons, warrior women.
She replies, *they're just like Navajos*.

Storm Patterns

after the Tuba City stylized Navajo rug

Black Black Black Black Clouds Edges
Clouds Black Edges Beauty Red Edges
Spiderwoman Underground Weaves Together Edges
Loom Weft Wool Lazy-lines First Woman
Stumbles Into Her Home Webs Edges
Wefts Looms Black Sky Above Rain
First Drops Fall Black Spirit Edges
Ants Run More More Dark Lines
Spinning Wool Into Clouds Rain Thunder
Enter Her Home Learn Weaving Edges

Center

Lightning Black Clouds West Wind Edges
East Mountain North Thunder South Edges
Mountain Red Wind White Thunder Strike
Water Earth First Woman Learns Edges
Wool Dyeing Black Red White Mixing
Edges Waterbugs Sing Spiderwoman Teaches Edges
Falling Arrows Falling Feathers Falling Clouds
Ending Winter Calling Spring Thunder Edges
Four Lightning Bolts Strike Center Edges
Navajos Learn Black Edges Black Black

The Dark World

Ałk'idídą́ą́' jiní

Listen and remember.

The wind blows from all directions.
Look at the skin on your fingertips. Can you see the trails
The wind left?

When we were created, the wind blew.
It is the wind that comes out of our mouths.
It gives us life.

Grandma Spider Woman's voice drifted off . . .
The wind took her story—

Sitting alone in neither day nor night,
I am called *Áltsé Hastiin*, First Man.
Sitting alone in neither despair nor hope,
I am part being, part nothing, part man, part alive.

Outside someone escaped his dark world.
He ran with awkward steps away from the officer's heels
Which sounded like dull spurs. With slurred speech, he yelled,
"It was magic that set me free! Magic! Magic!"
The sound of breaking beer bottles also ran after him
With the night wind, who whispered this story to me.

In the far reaches of my mind, Thought Woman appeared.
She spoke and I thought . . .
I wonder if the cop caught that wino.
She spoke and I thought . . .
I hope he didn't; I don't need no company tonight.

This cell which has no people or furry animals
It is the First World again.
This cell which has no sun, moon or stars
It is the Black World again.

First Woman lives here
She is trying to build a fire
Made of turquoise and coral logs
To guide me home.

But I can't see any fires to lead me back.

Earlier, I saw a star made of cheap brass.
It shone bright from the captured lightning
In the ceiling. Tamed and broken like a painted war pony,
The lights buzzed with a soft purr.
The star
Was pinned to Dan Begay's pressed blue uniform.
The tribal officer walked the barred halls
Where he inspected other drunks and some wife-beaters
In the Navajo Tribe's Tuba City jail.

Then he commanded the cells to become the First World:

"Lights Out!"

The Mist People live here
I can't see their bodies made
Of singing water in this dark.

The lights went out as fast as lightning could run.

Dan Begay's voice was like Spider Woman's own power of creation.
She wove storm rugs together with long strands
Made of time, dark clouds, rain, mud, thunder.

When each rug was done, it was as beautiful as
The storm's last drops summoning the Rainbow Priest's blessings.
But it meant that someone was complete.
So we die.

The cornfields yellow.
Someone's grandfather falls into a deep sleep.
The wind ceases to blow.
An elk steps onto the Interstate.

And it all becomes dark again.

The Insect People live here I can feel her sharp steps.
A black widow climbs
The length of my brown chest.

I touched the cold wall and tried to scratch my way through,
Into the next world, the Blue World, like Locust did.

Locust freed the holy beings from darkness by digging his way through
The different layers of sky, to the world where all birds exist.

Swallows, Crows, Macaws, Penguins, Turkeys . . . .

The tribal cop caught me driving a car in this glittering world,
Unknown to me, I was weaving the road like a swimming salmon.

I was drinking cold beer.
I didn't have a license.
I didn't know who I was.
I was drinking hot wine.
And the tribal cop sent me back to the Underworld.

Why did I do this?

As Áłtsé Hastiin, they didn't know who I was.
They forgot where they came from; they forgot their language.
Now I sit with the taste of urine, vomit and whiskey mints.

After each story told, Grandma Spider Woman
Always warned me to never forget: Remember and know—
She said a person without story isn't a person at all.
He is lost.

Dead men and dead women.

Coyote lives here somewhere   Out there in the night, his tracks
                                                                      Lead away from many quarrels.

After the beings emerged from the First World,
Coyote threw a rock into a deep lake.
The beings watched it sink with a splash,
And each ripple shook the beings' anger.

The people were mad because of Coyote's words:
    "If the rock floats, people live forever.
    If the rock sinks, people will die . . . ."

A Strong Male Rain

The air dances with wet sand off golden dunes.
The horse begins to get excited
From the whispers of rolling thunder in the distance.
A tidal wave of dust swallows the sky.
A heavy rainstorm is coming.

Slowly he crawls across the sky, angry.
He's large and bumpy with thick, strapping gray muscles.
This storm cloud is male, that's what Grandma says.
"When the clouds gather anger, they cry thunder and rain.
    This is the Male Rain."

The sudden winds kick up sand into my eyes. I blink.
In a drying puddle from yesterday's storm, I see Darcy's face.
Darcy, a Jewish girl from Phoenix—
A friend also afraid of the Male Rain.
Her brother Ean brought on her fears.

Grandma brought on mine.
She told us kids to sit still and don't talk during a storm
Or we'd get struck by lightning.
When Darcy was young, she used to sit at the window
And watch the lightning show during monsoon season.

Ean walked to his sister by the window.
He grinned his teen-age teeth and said,
"You know, if you stand too close to the window,
    A *Kugelblitz* will get you."
"A Kugelblitz?" she questioned.

"Yeah, a ball of lightning to chase you."
She never watched the light show again.
Instead during stormy nights, she silently cried in bed.
Little Jewish tears added to the monsoon's rain.
She told me this story one rainy night.

I told her about the Male Rain and what not to do during a storm.
She told me about Ean and his tale of Kugelblitz.
I guess Jews and Navajos aren't all that different.
We were both afraid of thunderstorms.
We have other past storms we were afraid of too.
She had the Holocaust
And I had America.

Lightning flashes. . . Thunder follows. . .
I begin whipping my horse, trying to escape the storms.

NORLA CHEE

Credit: Norla Chee

NORLA CHEE (b. 1963) was born to the Turtle Clan of the Oneida Tribe and born for the Kinyaa'áanii in Brigham City, Utah; she currently resides in White Rock, New Mexico. She completed a BA degree and an MA degree in English from Northern Arizona University with her thesis, *Voices*.

During her undergraduate and graduate studies, Chee published poetry and short fiction and was featured several times in the journal *Studies in American Indian Literatures*. In 1995, she received a best of issues honor from *Highlights Magazine* editors for her story, "Shoo Sheep," which focused on the experience of a herd of sheep appearing on the playground of a school one day, a not-uncommon experience on the Navajo Nation. *Highlights*, with more than three million subscribers in 1995, had the largest circulation of any children's periodical in the country. In 2001, Chee published *Cedar Smoke on Abalone Mountain*, from which the following poems are excerpted. About this book, poet Jim Simmerman comments, Chee "seamlessly weaves the spiritual with the daily, the present with the past. . . . [The poems] eschew sentimentality for clarity of vision such that their overarching tone of respect—for tradition, for event, for place, for people—is earned again and again." Her new book, *White Shell Woman*, is looking for a publisher. Kenneth Lincoln mentions Chee alongside other Navajo writers in *Speak Like Singing: Classics of Native American Literature* (2009) in a section on Indigenous writers who continue to use their tribal languages. Anthony K. Webster, linguistic anthropologist and co-editor of this anthology, also references some of Chee's work in his discussions of the use of "Navlish," or Navajo English.

Interview

What do you hope readers learn from your writing?

Native Americans are not just beads and feathers. Even if we are not wearing beads and feathers, we are still Native. *Cedar Smoke* reflects the part of my life where I was most influenced by the beads and feathers attitude. My new project, *White Shell Woman,* is evolving past that.

How does the Navajo language influence your work?

When I use Navajo in my writing I am emphasizing the meaning of words. [For example,] "Cheii," as a Navajo, means more than just the title of grandfather. In Navajo any elderly person is a grandfather or grandmother, but for white people it is limited to immediate family. The Navajo emphasizes respect.

Who or what inspires you?

Music, pictures, new stories. Sometimes I might pick out a word or two from a song and build something different around it. [For my poem] "An Exhibit Tells the History of Diné Women Weaving," it was exactly that. There was an exhibit at the museum in Window Rock.

What advice do you have for beginning writers?

Take criticism constructively, not personally.

Who was the first Navajo writer you read?

Nia Francisco's *Blue Horses for Navajo Women.* I came across the book in college. I think a teacher mentioned it. I just remember thinking I didn't know there were any modern Navajo writers. I'm sure I read Luci

Tapahonso. Like I said, we're not all beads and feathers. I don't go out of my way to read Navajos just because I am Navajo.

What was your favorite book in high school? What are you reading now?

High school was forty years ago! I don't recall being "inspired" by any books growing up. Reading was just to escape. Right now, I am reading *Decision for Disaster: Betrayal at the Bay of Pigs*, by Grayston L. Lynch.

Several of your poems included here ("Wagon Ride"; "Far Ahead in the Past"; "An Exhibit Tells the History of Diné Women Weaving") focus on time and the intersection of the past, present, and future. What inspires you to write about personal or cultural memory in your poetry?

History is important to Native Americans. It also has a lot of bearing on how we live today. With everything we do, there's always a story of the way things used to be. The fascinating thing it is still that way for some.

Good-bye Honey, Hello Silver and Dust

(for nicole)

Sister let out the new lamb and kicked the old cat.
She swept up the ash and scattered the rats.
She heated the lard and fried the dough
early on the morning of the All Indian Rodeo.
She donned all her turquoise and tied up her hair
locked the door and strode off to the Window Rock Fair;
From there she run off to find her own fleece.
Meanwhile, her cat yawns in the window facing the east.

Wagon Ride

Some of the People have memories
about the ride in early dawn.
The day had the heart of a young boy and his first horse.
The day had the heart of a family gathering pinon,
the heart of going into the Chuskas for firewood,
the heart of women's gossip from the wagon.
When the People rode the day had the sharp sound
of wagon wheels across white rock.
It smelled like sweaty horses, and
salted fat wrapped in a cold tortilla.
From these rides, my father says,
they named the last hill,
before it was a power station, Where Coyote Sits.
He tells of memories that happened
before the highway
when the ride into town had the heart of storytelling.

Far Ahead in the Past

We talk our women's stories for awhile by the
fire,
sitting on sheep's wool, whispering
Spider Woman's yarns deep in the night.
        A cloudy, starless night
when the monsoon has passed through
and left the grass green
        and the air alive.
Some one of us is spinning old cultures,
when I am struggling to know this one in which we are
living now.
                Beyond the fire *ma'ii* sheds his coyote skin
        and appears as the moral of our story.
        We re-discover emergence from there,

having heard the fables of Coyote in First World,
Coyote First Being, Coyote Who Made the Constellations.
It wakes us to our prayers.
        But we find none of us have come with corn pollen.
So we pour a Budweiser to the Four Directions
and pass a joint around.
                The Spirit Trickster dances naked
        between the children sleeping nearby
        clutching Game Boys and Walkman stereos.
When they grow up, they'll herd sheep
and spin yarns around ma'ii.
I think for awhile it should be this way.

An Exhibit Tells the History of Diné Women Weaving

The train came in
bringing over one hundred years
home in the last boxcar.
The tapestries hung on the wall
were skeletons from the treasury
of US war closets.
Each was identified
if only by a question mark.
Silhouette was used to camouflage
and fill in decay.

Scenes of plateau land breathed in the weaving
Color   Warp
                Scheme   Weft
The rhythm is of the women
telling each other survival stories
even after surrender.

Suffering was a place in their hearts
and when they'd no voice left their hands wove

what they could never give up hoping for.
At their loom the rhythm was for peace
swift as eagles' wings
to return them home.

The train came in filled with possibilities
of the connection behind human will.

Winter brought cold.
Cold was a threat.
Everything about her was numb. Her dreaming raw.
Her heart blue with cold.
Even her weaving was numb, the final design lost,
but it kept her warm.
She was not a visionist, to see some day the value
of her weaving.
The cold was a threat.

In spring her weaving diversified.
She was homesick for olden days, forgotten ways
and was inspired to weave rain clouds
and skybands into her blankets, also
weaving in the enduring stories
it takes to fill out a life.

The tapestry hung on the wall
Told the history of Diné women weaving,
Told from grandmother to granddaughter.
The rhythm is a place in their heart.

SHERWIN BITSUI

Credit: Ungelbah Davila

SHERWIN BITSUI (b. 1975) is Tódích'íi'nii, born for the Tłízíłání. Originally from White Cone, Arizona, Bitsui is currently an assistant professor of English at Northern Arizona University in Flagstaff. He earned an AFA from the Institute of American Indian Arts Creative Writing Program, where he has since taught in the Low Rez MFA program, and a BA from the University of Arizona. Bitsui is the recipient of numerous honors and awards: a grant from the Witter Bynner Foundation for Poetry, a Truman Capote Creative Writing Fellowship, a Native Arts and Cultures Foundation Artists Fellowship, an American Book Award, a PEN Open Book Award, a Whiting Award, and a Lannan Literary Fellowship. In a *Superstition Review* interview, Bitsui shared his thoughts on his affinity for poetry: "I've come to realize that my Navajo worldview is what makes my poems possible. The movement, the extended visual interplay and sharpness of the images all rely on the motion and movement my language captures in daily speech. . . . I want my work to feel alive at the moment of the reading—I want people to sense they are in the poem with me, witnessing these events as they unfold. Verbs are helpful in making such gestures, they make my poems feel like a landscape—a landscape is never still."

Bitsui's poems are published widely, and he is the author of three poetry collections: *Shapeshift* (2003), *Flood Song* (2009), and *Dissolve* (2018). Bitsui's imagery originates from Dinétah and is rearranged in ways to disrupt or hyper-locate perspective. His poems reveal the intersection of Diné traditions especially in his use of language as sonical landscape. When asked about his mentors in an interview with *Ploughshares*, Bitsui explained, "I am fortunate to have had many professional mentors in my life. . . . Often in Diné culture we say 'doo aasa'hó si'zįįda,' which translates to 'I don't stand alone'; this aphorism speaks volumes to how I became a poet. I came to poetry alone, but in time, many others came to stand with me."

Interview

What do you hope readers learn from your writing?

I hope they learn to be drawn into a body of work that makes them experience their world differently; that it challenges them to see things anew. I hope my work gives them permission to seek out their own idiosyncratic ways of writing poems.

How does the Navajo language influence your work?

Yes. I love moving between languages, and losing myself between modes of thought and perspectives. I still have a long way to go in terms of learning the most intricate dimensions of Navajo language and thought—it's a vastly complex system of knowledge, one that continues to create areas within language that influence how I may structure an English sentence or poetic line. Navajo thought is always at the source of my poems.

What advice do you have for beginning writers?

Read widely. It's important for young writers to always have some sense of what is happening in the literary world. I'm always interested in poets who challenge me to think and absorb their work, even though at first their poems may seem difficult to read. I learn much by discovering how my mind must reshape itself to understand what the poem is truly saying.

Who was the first Diné writer you read?

Luci Tapahonso.

What was your favorite book in high school? What are you reading now?

I don't know if I've had a favorite book in high school. I often was drawn toward the book by its cover. My friends were metalheads, so often we read horror fiction. I read all the time, mostly student work. I teach poetry for Northern Arizona University and the Institute of American Indian Art's MFA Low Residency Program in Santa Fe, New Mexico.

Asterisk

Fourteen ninety-something,
        something happened
and no one can pick it out of the lineup,
its rising action photographed
        when the sign said: *do not look*
                irises planted inside here.

But look—
        something lurking in the mineshaft—
            a message, ice in his cup,
                third leg uprooted but still walking.
It peers over his shoulder at the dirt road dug into the mesa's skirt,
  where the saguaro blossoms bloom nightfall at the tip of its dark snout,
    and motor oil seeps through the broken white line of the teacher's loom.

Something,
can't loop this needle into it,
occurs and writes over their lips with thread;
        barnacles on their swings;
        fleas hyphened between their noses;
            eels asphyxiating in the fruit salad.

Remember, every wrist of *theirs* acclimates to bruises.

Twigs from their family tree flank the glove's aura
and asterisk water towers invisible,
while fragrant rocks in the snout remain
unnoticed in the bedroom,
because the bridegroom wanted in,
Pioneers wanted in,
and the ends of our feet yellowed to uranium at the edge of fear.

The Northern Sun

I find it necessary to breathe the morning air, to smell the potatoes frying, and watch the ceiling smoke into soft, white abalone dreadlocks, when I wake up abandoned, inscribed with *never open, look into, or stash in the backseat of your car.* I wear a mask made from the map of Asia.

Search for me in a ravine, on a cliff's edge reaching for the sun. Find me on the hood of a car racing through the stars, on the velvet nose of a horse seeking its dead master waiting with saddle and bridle.

It is necessary to see the reflections of birds on the temporary ponds of melting snow. Grandfather, you named each mesa: sister, brother, friend, and I steered onto the pavement not knowing that inside our houses, the rain would clear and our fragrance would leap from our pores and into the canyons to be covered by crumbling black rocks.

Sometimes the mud on my boot breaks over fresh carpet, the payroll forgets our names, while the insects on our lips find our hidden names inscribed on their wings, and we roll through thorns to find the patterns of our loneliness scribbled on our bodies like images of dragons tattooed on rocks in a Route 66 mineral shop.

After this, you will reach to scratch your back and feel nothing but a black hole, spiraling like the agitator in an empty washing machine. You will bend backwards with your mouth pressed on the linoleum, whispering, *sister, I need a sister*, but you will not be able to reach her. You will be ten inches away, and never have you knelt low enough to hear the undercurrent of a breeze lost to twilight summers.

The cigarette ignites the bedsheets, and I write my last sentence. Lamp shades cover me; my eyelashes wriggle in my pants pockets. *Your vocabulary is like the breakfast menu of a science convention.* Bricks ripple underfoot, the moon reveals her daughter for the first time in 28 days, born with fists instead of hands.

A writer breaks every pen he can steal from the henhouse; disappointed, he returns to the hospital and informs the nurses that he should be pulled from the flames immediately. He sweats, points at his right foot, and says that he regrets flying back to earth obscenely underdressed to witness what he calls a malnourished theater eating its legs for dinner.

Is this what I deserve: a white anthropologist sitting beside me at a winter ceremony? *Listen. Your people speak like weeping Mongolians.* Perhaps it is because we have been staring at airplanes too long, I tell him, that our throats have turned into hollowed-out spider legs extending over the rough wings of a salivating moth, who rejected its cocoon as a child, saying how ugly it made him feel to be in a bed that resembled an anchor rusting in the shadow of a feeble cloud.

This time we feel the padlocks snap. Prison inmates untie their imaginations, which can sometimes be seen in the high desert of Arizona, lukewarm magma flowing through the sky at a 90-degree angle. The last time I saw the sun reflected red, I was pulling a screaming baby from her clutching, drunk mother on Highway 77 at noon. As the mother bounced off the pavement, I shut the baby's eyes and kicked the dead driver's foot from the gas pedal. The rear tires spun backwards.

The beer in my refrigerator still smells like bread in the morning. My mother's goose bumps continue to make me shiver when she tells me to scratch her back.

The IHS doctors gave her some lotion, but it doesn't help, so we scratch and scratch and scratch . . .

I just wanted a decent cup of coffee and a cheaper view of the Washington Monument, which loomed like a bright sun stream in a forest where the dark holds you like the wind holds you in a desert canyon. The cab driver asked if I was American Indian. I said, *No, I'm of the Bitter Water People.*

The glittering world, this place that we fly into where traffic lights play tag with our eyes when we lay back singeing our faces with the light of passing freight trains. What's there but rum and Coke? Bottle walls standing knee-deep in confusion and rat traps disguised as dreamcatchers?

Five years ago, my language hit me like saw-toothed birds reaching to pull my tongue from my mouth. I didn't know what to expect when my grandmother poured gasoline on the leaves and then fired it, saying, *This is the last time I'll ever harvest.* It was the way the sunset caught her cracked lips, the way her lips folded inward, which made me realize that there were still stories within her that needed to be told, stories of when we still wove daylight onto our bones and did not live like we do now, as night people.

Somewhere in here, our minds glow like fog lights, a Coke can bleeds sugar, and the eyes of a turtle ooze from a high school water fountain. Somewhere in Chinle, Arizona, a blender is surrounded and pelted with gravel and cement stones by children whose parents drift through cheap wine bottles like steam rising from the necks of hemorrhaging antelopes.

Frogs smell rainstorms against a shield of ocher clouds. Two A.M., the first flakes of ash surround a family of beetles dining in the cracks of the *hooghan*'s fading walls, the flashlight of a policeman siphons dark waters from the spit can of an old medicine man singing the last four songs of his life. Inward, I can feel the gravel in my veins soften.

Chrysalis

It wasn't the leaves that descended upon you
or the horse that knelt on the river's edge,
pushing his nose through mist,
    a root that wanted to peel itself into a flower.

It was ash,
dry as the skeletons of drained soup cans
on the river front
where a man's coarse throat bleeds
because the language is a dying thing,
covered in blankets,
    beaten with forks and spoons.

These baskets have become graves,
    a shot glass of tears tucked between the legs of a veteran,
a wristwatch pulled tightly around his tongue
so that he may savor this hour
when death drags its tail across the necks of hunted children,
who are shivering again under the sun's sharp chin,
half awake in a boat on a shore of gray gulls,
pressing grapes into their eyes,
drinking the wine that leaks from their shadows.

Cities break into sand before the approaching shovel;
their windows glisten in the soft light of the Milky Way
as I remember it.
    How young I was to read passages of the Bible,
my wings caked in earth,
mud forming in my footsteps,
water seeping from my lips when he came to drink.
He came to drink and would not stop.
He was a bee pollinating the milky surface of the moon reflected in the rearview mirror.

The deer blinked and all was well again,
calm as the breeze blowing though prison gates.
I shave the edges of my mustache and imagine cutting the policeman's
  arm from
his flashlight.
But still it did not stop the lions from sniffing the snouts of dying bulls,
or the red squaw from selling her jewelry in aisles of restaurants serving
  leaves
and grass.

And no, there is no one here.
This casket: the seed of a blood clot.

Bread dipped in gunpowder is to be fed to the first graders in that moment
when their hair is cut
    and a ruler is snapped,
and their whispers metamorphose into a new chrysalis of thought.
A new wing emerging from the lips of these Indians,
who are no longer passing thoughts in the paragraphs of an oil-soaked
  dictionary
but hooves carved into talons,
hilltops from which light is transformed into the laughter of crickets.

I want to remain here
where he doesn't drink my lips
or remove the cocoon my eyes have become.

Rattles erupt on the north horizon.
The harvester unties her shoelaces.
I see the sun, eclipse it with my outstretched palm,
and dig away my reddening skin.
    "It wasn't like this before," I tell myself.
When I am thrown into a florescent room where the sink hunches
like an eagle claw,
it stops,
pulls the wind to a breathing space the size of a mouse's lung,
and I am drowning in the air around my feet again.

Antelope are gnawing into the walls of the city.
And *those* Indians are braiding yucca roots into the skin of their scalps again.

I want to fall beside them,
count their fingers:
        five hundred and five rows of spilled blood marking the trail home.
The trail will not be followed again,
because there in the ears of the Indians
are echoes of the hissing belt
and the laughter of thieves
measuring the length of the treaty
with the teeth of the jury that is seduced by the glimmers of gold.

It is ash, all of it!
Fruit flies buried in the skin of onions,
canyons seeking the river that has left them orphaned,
cars cruising their velvet wheels over teeth and beaks,
eyeless dogs barking in hailstorms,
and owls, two of them coming from the east,
carrying the night between them: a wet blanket designed by a woman who dreams of
        lightning,
saying that we have finally become mountains
rising above a valley of weeping dishrags that cling to the ground below,
raising fences and crosses and houses.

And no, this is not about sadness:
the gasp of a mute who buries his legs in the arroyo bottom
when the first drops of rain pepper his forehead,
who earlier that morning brought a leaf into the front yard,
saying that we may grow from this,
we may inch into the next world
and rummage for nectar in the thinning bones of shadowless thieves.

This plate before me is made from broken tusk; this fork, the fingers of a rat,
and we eat leather in caves behind train tracks.
These caves where our hair breaks into ash when washed
are a place of birth;

the first cry echoing from the amphitheater
was a song sung in thinning air.

This is not about the rejection of our skin;
the mud dries as it is poured into our ears.
But the linguist still runs his hands up the length of our tongues,
perplexed that we even have a tongue at all.

from *Flood Song*

tó

tó

tó

tó

tó

tó

tó

I bite my eyes shut between these songs.

They are the sounds of blackened insect husks
folded over elk teeth in a tin can,

they are gull wings fattening on cold air
flapping in a paper sack on the chlorine-stained floor.

They curl in corners, spiked and black-thatched,
stomp across the living-room ceiling,
pull our hair one strand at a time from electric sockets
and paint our stems with sand in the kitchen sink.

They speak a double helix,
zigzag a tree trunk,
bark the tips of its leaves with cracked amber—

they plant whispers where shouts incinerate into hisses.

Stepping through a drum's vibration,
I hear gasoline
                    trickle alongside the fenced-in panorama
of the reed we climb in from
and slide my hands into shoes of ocean water.

I step onto the gravel path of swans paved across lake scent,
wrap this blank page around the exclamation point slammed between us.

The storm lying outside its fetal shell
folds back its antelope ears
and hears its heart pounding through powdery earth
underneath dancers flecking dust from their ankles to thunder into rain.

I am unable to pry my fingers from the ax,
unable to utter a word
without Grandfather's accent rippling
around the stone flung into his thinning mattress.

Years before, he would have named this season
by flattening a field where grasshoppers jumped into black smoke.

A crow snaps beak over and over again:
the past is a blurry splotch of red crosshatched with neon light;
    on the drive south,
            windows pushed down,
        you scoop pellets of canned air
    and ocean across sand dunes,
        across the waning lick of moonlight on the dashboard
        to crease the horizon
            between petals of carved snow.

Bluebirds chirp icy rocks from their stomachs
and crash,
        wings caked heavy
with the dark mud of a gunmetal sky,
to the earth's bandages
        shivering with cold spells and convulsions
                in the market
                        underneath an avalanche of apples.

A redtail hawk scrapes the sandstone wall with its beak.

A shower of sparks skate across the morning sky.

You think this bottle will open a canyon wall
and light a trail
trampled by gloved hands
as you inhale earth, wind, water,
through the gasoline nozzle
at trail's end,
a flint spear driven into the key switch.

You think you can return to that place
where your mother held her sleeves above the rising tides
saying, "We are here again
on the road covered with television snow;
we are here again
the song has thudded."

Bison horns twist into the sides of trains
    winding through the broth-filled eyes of hens
        squawking from the icebox;

shock-coils from the jet engine's roar
        erupt from the memory of splintered eagle-wing bone.

Pinned down with icicles on the loosening floor,
    an alarm clock wails from speaker box to speaker box
        probing for hornet nests inside the tourmaline seeds of dawn;

its scalp *scalpeled* alongside what is "ours";
    its memory of bone axes x-ed out with chrome engine paint.

Flicking off the light switch.
Lichen buds the curved creases of a mind
pondering the mesquite tree's dull ache
        as it gathers its leaves around clouds of spotted doves—
                calling them in rows of twelve back from their winter sleep.

Doves' eyes black as nightfall
shiver on the foam coast of an arctic dream
        where whale ribs
                clasp and fasten you to a language of shifting ice.

Seeing into those eyes
you uncoil their telephone wires,
gather their inaudible lions with plastic forks,
tongue their salty ribbons,
        and untie their weedy stems from your prickly fingers.

You stop to wonder what *like* sounds like
when held under glacier water,
how *Ná ho kos* feels
under the weight of all that loss.

I cover my eyes with electrical wires,
see yellow dawn eclipse Stop signs,
        turn green and screech into phosphorescence.

Each flickering finger:
a memory of a flashing yellow sign,
blinks between charcoal sheets of monsoon rain
then slices through the thawing of our hunger
with the cracked eaves of a shattered house.

Its autobiographical muscle—
stringing trees into a forest, convulses,
only to be flattened under its metallic leaves
and sold as bricks for its basement of fire.

What land have you cast from the blotted-out region of your face?

What nation stung by watermarks was filmed out of extinction and brought forth resembling frost?

What offspring must jump through the eye of birth to be winked at when covered with brick sweat?

What ache piled its planks on the corner pier, now crumbles onto motionless water, sniffed at by forest smoke?

What makes this song a string of beads seized by cement cracks when the camera climbs through the basement window—winter clouds coiling through its speckled lens?

What season cannot locate an eye in the dark of the sound of the sun gyrating into red ocher after I thought you noticed my language was half wren, half pigeon and, together, we spoke a wing pattern on the wall that was raised to keep "us" out, there where "calling" became "culling," "distance" distanced, in a mere scrape of enamel on yellow teeth?

What father woke, turned over his wife, she didn't want to, but he pushed until the baby leapt through, now, now, now, strummed into a chorus of burn marks on ceilings where police sirens fruit magpie skulls on trees of monsoon lightning?

What, what, what—is how the song chimed in wilderness.

I wanted to swallow the song's flowers, swim diagonally its arched back, its shadow
stinging my hands with black pollen.

We were on the same surgical table waiting for the surgeons to carve us back into shape.

The drum pulsed somewhere in the dark and I heard a woman unbraiding her hair.

I felt morning songs leap from the *hooghan*'s smoke-hole and curl outward from the
roof of the sky, gliding through us like rain.

I sang, sang until the sun rose.

The shadows of my face grew into a swallow with folded wings and darted into the fire.

A cloud became a skull and crashed to the earth above Black Mesa.

The cloud wanted to slip through the coal mines and unleash its horses.

It wanted to crack open bulldozers and spray their yolk over the hills so that a new
birth cry would awaken the people who had fallen asleep.

It wanted to push their asymmetrical ramblings into the weft of the storm blanket, dye it
hazel and sink it into the rising waters.

A city dragged its bridges behind it and finally collapsed in a supermarket asking for
the first apple that was ever bitten.

No one questioned the sand anymore.

No one untucked themselves from their bodies and wandered the streets without knowing their clans.

Everyone planted corn in their bellies and became sunlight washing down plateaus with deer running out of them.

The phone was ringing through it all.

The line was busy when I picked the ax
and chose the first tree   to chop down.

DWAYNE MARTINE

Credit: Dwayne Martine

DWAYNE MARTINE (b. 1975) is a poet and writer living in Scottsdale, Arizona. He is Jicarilla Apache and Navajo of the Naashashi, born for the Haltsooí. He grew up in Gallup, New Mexico, and has an undergraduate degree in English from Stanford University. He works as a professional technical writer in the financial services industry.

His first published poem, "Indian Birth," was published in *Red Ink* in 2002. His short story about the DAPL protests of 2016, "The Receding Dark," is included in *First Came Fear: New Tales of Horror*. Martine's poetry chapbook, *Azee' Nitsáhákeesi: Thought Medicines*, winner of the 2018 Sequoyah Chapbook Award, was published in 2019 by the Sequoyah National Research Center at the University of Arkansas at Little Rock. His work has appeared in national and regional print and online journals, including *Kweli*, *American Indian Culture and Research Journal*, *Yellow Medicine Review*, *Hawai'i Review*, and others.

His work is influenced by being born and raised in a border town of the Navajo reservation and encompasses the paradoxes and ironies of growing up in an occupied homeland. As a third-generation English-educated Indigenous person and the first generation of his family to attend college, he writes for family and friends, both bilingual and monolingual, on reservation and off reservation, and all those Indigenous people whose complexities cannot be reduced into a simple dialectic. He writes, "I want my parents, my siblings and all my relatives, as well as my college friends who have become college professors, to see themselves in my work. I want to make a place in literature for us all. And to not leave anyone out."

Interview

What do you hope readers learn from your writing?

I have two ideal readers in mind. One is based on my family. I want them to see themselves, to recognize the depth of character and feeling that mark their lives, and to see that depth fully rendered on the page. My other reader is all other people. And I want them to understand that depth, if not to recognize themselves in my writing.

When you are writing, how does the Navajo language influence your work?

My mother is Jicarilla Apache and was raised with Jicarilla as her first language. My father is Navajo and was raised with Navajo as his first language. They didn't teach myself or my siblings either language. But I always grew up with both sets of relatives speaking Apache and Navajo with my parents. I know my parents think in their languages. When they explain something someone else said, they always give attribution in every sentence like one would in Athabaskan grammar. That grammar is missing in my mind. I know words, I can conjugate verbs and can even have short conversations. But complex thought is missing from my mind. That absence informs my work, but it does not delineate it.

Who or what inspires you?

My grandmothers inspire me. My Masani and my Nali were both very different women, yet also very typical of who I have come to understand Navajo women to be. My Masani went to boarding school. She adopted non-Navajo ways. She was a community health representative. She spoke multiple languages. She divorced my grandfather. She lived in many different places, including off the reservation. But she was also a weaver and made her living in her later years from her weaving. She also, after all her journeys, returned to her birth land to live her old age. She was a remarkable woman. My Nali, by contrast, lived where she was born most of her life. The farthest I think she ever traveled from Pinehill was Albuquerque. She was a sheepherder all her life. It was said, she could lift hay bales like a man in her youth. The only English word I ever heard her speak was "Jesus." She considered herself a good Christian. She married and divorced and raised her children with help from her mother. She lived a very long life. She also was a remarkable woman.

What advice do you have for beginning writers?

Don't be afraid. Make mistakes. Learn. Understand criticism can be taken or not taken. But that effective criticism will make you a better writer. Be humble and thankful others will read your work and offer help. And above all else: read! Read everything. Never stop reading.

Who was the first Diné writer you read?

Luci Tapahonso.

What was your favorite book in high school? What are you reading now?

Beloved by Toni Morrison. I am currently reading about quantitative regression models for work. The last book I read was *Citizen* by Claudia Rankine.

÷

Parsing

The thought
was of a spider weaving

intricacy into intricacy,
a lace code,

a raised leg joining
catch to catch,

terminal to terminus,
the noctilucent filaments

that spark,
crackle from

the black screen,
a concatenation proper

for an all too breakable
cypher. Understanding.

Each silken length
held with the delicacy

of an old woman
holding a noose

or, hand over hand, a line
straight up out of night,

building a capture
for each word here.

Thought Knife

The pollen of my mind
gathers on the floor in a heap,

Thrush yellow,
it glows with unknowing.

I question meaning making
yet still use language

To do so, engendering doubt
is the same as fomenting belief

when the characters you use
are still the same alphabet.

Take this: an *other* understanding and make a fever,

a weakening pulse, or
a white knot on reason's x-ray.

Béésh Nitsíkeesi = *Thinking*
metal, Thought Knife, the Metal

That Thinks, Navajo for
"computer," that from which to

excise English. Use the idea
itself to cut around the mass,

remove the uncontrollably
expanding whiteness.

Thinking metal, Thought
Knife, Béésh Nitsíkeesi.

Hwééldi

We walk the lengths of this land.
We walk and walk, as movement is life,

as breath is proof of the body's heartbeat,
proof the towering red cliffs,

the verdant snow covered mountains are real
in this light, those that rise up whole around us,

complete against the dark sky,
complete in their beginnings and endings.

We walk and drink in the night,
listen to the horsemen charging behind us,

in front of us, in the sky above us,
listen to the cries of those who have fallen behind,

who were never meant to have gotten even this far.
We bleed out stars in the moonlight,

chilled blood, clothing frozen blood,
falling like stars from the sky's open palms over us.

We walk and walk, as movement is life,
is proof of the body's breath,

proof the ashen ground underfoot is real,
that the night we drink will not end or tear us open.

We walk and vomit out this walk,
listen to the cries of those who have fallen behind

and were never meant to have gotten even this far.
We walk and walk and drink in the night,

bleed out the stars complete in our beginnings
and endings on the frozen, stilled and stilling earth.

TACEY ATSITTY

Credit: Dorothy Grandbois

TACEY M. ATSITTY (b. 1982) is Tsénahabiłnii and born for Ta'neeszahnii. Her maternal grandfather is Tábąąhí and Hashk'ą́ą́'hadzóhí from Cove, Arizona. She currently lives in Tallahassee, attending Florida State University as a PhD creative writing student. Through her father, Atsitty has links to the Indian Placement Program, overseen by the Church of Jesus Christ of Latter-Day Saints. She is a graduate of Navajo Preparatory School and holds BA degrees from Brigham Young University and the Institute of American Indian Arts. She earned an MFA in creative writing from Cornell University. Atsitty serves as the director of the Navajo Film Festival and on numerous community boards in the Salt Lake City region. She is an advocate of culture and language revitalization.

Atsitty embraces both her faith and her love for Diné culture by uniquely braiding into her poetry strands of Diné story and empathy for the grief and losses experienced by Indigenous people, especially women, as well as her lived experiences. "Song of a Great Nat'áanii—Shimásáni," Atsitty's first published work, appeared in 1999's *Eagle's Eye Magazine*. Her work has also appeared in *POETRY*, *Crab Orchard Review*, *Kenyon Review Online*, *Prairie*

Schooner, *Crazyhorse*, *New Poets of Native Nations*, and other publications. In 2018, her first book, *Rain Scald*, was published by the University of New Mexico Press. In 2020, along with Laura Furlan and Toni Jensen, Atsitty guest edited the *Massachusetts Review* special issue of new Native-authored works of fiction, poetry, and nonfiction responding to the four hundredth anniversary of the Plymouth landing. Atsitty has been a recipient of the Truman Capote Creative Writing Fellowship, the Corson-Browning Poetry Prize, the Morning Star Creative Writing Award, and the Philip Freund Prize.

Interview

You quote a slogan from the National High School Poetry Slam Competition in San Francisco, which says, "The poems are waiting." How has this phrase influenced your work?

Poems manifest themselves when they want to. If I try and put a poem a certain way, it won't work. I need to see what the poem wants to be.

Describe the process you used to assemble the poems for your first book of poetry, Rain Scald, ***published by University of New Mexico Press.***

Half of the poems are from my homeland, the canyons around Cove, Arizona, which hold many stories. The second half of the book describes gorges and their importance to Native people in that area. When I was studying at Cornell for my MFA, there was a series of deaths from students jumping into the gorges, and for me they represent death and loss. Writing these poems was my way of healing from these tragedies.

Talk about your writing, the genre you favor, how the Navajo language influences your work, and the main audience for whom you write.

Poetry is the genre I favor, and I find the way Navajos speak English makes its way into my work in words and phrases. I like to use the sonnet form, and in my chapbook, I have fifteen sonnets where the last line in a poem becomes the first line of the next poem. This took a long time to write. As far as my audience, I write for an academic group or anyone who appreciates beauty.

Who do you go to for poetry advice?

A few friends, the Rock Canyon Poetry Society in Utah, the Four Corners Poets Society (some), Arthur Sze at IAIA because he is a great craftsman, and self-editing.

What Indigenous writers have influenced your work?

Luci Tapahonso, Laura Tohe, and Esther Belin. I met Luci and Laura at a 2000 Native Writers workshop in Rough Rock organized by Monty Roessel, and they encouraged me.

Who was the first Diné writer you read?

Luci Tapahonso.

Ach'íí'

I.

In my pocket: intestines
wrap fat, and it's so stiff
when cold. It looks like—

we shouldn't speak
so young. Instead, knead salt,
flour, and water.

Our toys, I've tasted them:
sheepherders or soldiers.
Should they harden

and be painted, or should
a hole be blown from the insides.
All that salt.

II.

Dad's baby brother, his intestines

broke, and he couldn't pee.

He died because he was so full.

Just like his grandmother,

the day she walked out of the hogan,

dropped to her knees, holding her

stomach—so mixed up inside

when it exploded.

III.

After all those explosions in Vietnam, it must've messed my uncle up pretty good. He could never eat ach'íí' again. He had to have three Enemy Ways done. We had to haul so many sheep. It's a long ride in the back of a jeep all the way to Farmington to be baptized. I stood next to that wall of bricks at the Apache Building, wearing my squash blossom: a line of females v'ing down to the male, and there rested his tongue, almost between my breasts.

IV.

I remember She Who Wasn't Spoken Of—
each Red Vine costed a nickel, that easy twine

across the street from our little red-bricked
house—They say she drove so fast

she whorled into a puff of smoke
behind Table Mesa the day she died.

Dad says he remembers the first time he died,
that long bus ride when they took him

to Utah for school. He had been memorizing
land formations: an angel the size of his hand

disappeared, and after that he was so empty
from crying and so full of remembering

rocks, he just fell asleep. He remembers
stealing pennies from his foster sister

to buy red licorice. He was always in trouble
for that or for sling-shotting chickens.

Only three survived the morning massacre.
Only one sheep was taken from the flock.

They stole it, all those Navajo boys,
led it to the mountain edge, where
they built a fire and slit its throat:

laughing into the dry
night, fat dripping
from their mouths.

In Strips

I.

fingertip knead	neck, stitch issue	sentence tear
this rickrack struggle	line by blossom	rest on fault
in the spread	wrap, sat on	my wrist, the roundup
crosswire threads	warp-and-weft effect	when we gather
muscle like crevice	bless, us up-stitch	song, yeah
nose of mountain	collar, yeah	or ugly

II.

bark, take care	the language we use	push it around
or or or	beyond that	gather the hip
or wrinkle	rub flower	or compass
or smear nickels	into clavicle	pick moments—
settle into letters	clipped them	break rickrack
word at the bottom	these are elbows	says, either page
zhiins, over the i	like stars, skin	quilt, look up

III.

let me respond, stick	out our ribs:	tiering course
private as armpit	I am sorry, say	that again, sip
where the skin	gather, let me	swing, storytell
of land keeps	in our strife	pass by pass
know there's infant	within the rocks	within the guts
lava rock is not lava	rock, but blood—	know of monsters
leap in all	fury, from ridge	to fall, water trace
forehead, nose	chin to breasts	tummy to knees

IV.

but this, this	is not a mountain	is seam rip seam
stress on the fold	is not a gorge, align	is walls in back stitch
bark of wrinkle	what binds the raw	edge, the sashing
and piecing	of built up or collapse	of create, appliqué
hills to sky, land	altogether, words	like clouds, sentence
like mountain sack	gone with the grain	in strides of bark

Calico Prints

It was morning when she left, her pockets filled with bones. A small stack of round flat bread steamed beneath cloth. After she stoked the fire, she stepped toward the hogan exit. At the sides of aspen, she staggered northeast, barefoot, toward the tree line. Her hands dripped yucca-root foam. One hand gripped her stomach, the other reached to where the mountain flats break the blue contour. She was on her knees when it exploded, her skirt muddied. Her clay fingers held ghost beads. It was the water she drank, soaked in tailings. Many nights she had lain in sheepskin, damped. That morning the firmament unraveled into a bolt of aqua calico. She stepped into yards of apricot blooms, carried herself in her skirt, steps and steps. *Stemless blossoms*. She followed patterns of earth and saw how they matched the floral sky:

her children tracked staggered footprints to the wash's edge.

VENAYA YAZZIE

Credit: Venaya Yazzie

VENAYA JAY YAZZIE (b. 1972) is Diné (Navajo)/Hopi from the San Juan Valley in northwestern New Mexico. Her heritage is rooted in eastern Dinétáh at Huerfano and Chaco Canyon, New Mexico, yet she also carries her father's Hopi heritage from northern Arizona. Her clan affiliations are Hooghanłání, Tódích'ii'nii, Tó'aheedlíinii, and Kisani (Hopi). Yazzie is an alumna of University of New Mexico (MA), Fort Lewis College (BA), Institute of American Indian Arts, and Alaska Native Arts (AA) in Santa Fe, New Mexico.

She is a member of the Northwest New Mexico Arts Council and serves on the Navajo Heritage Cultural Center Board. In 2014 Yazzie was awarded the Mesa Verde Artist-In-Residence at Mesa Verde National Park and has previously worked with the Bisti Writing Project. In 2015 Yazzie was invited to participate in the Narrative Witness, Indigenous Peoples: Australia–United States artist-in-residence project as a photographer. She is a cultural educator and works to promote art, culture, and literacy in Navajo reservation schools and border town communities. She is a practicing artist, poet, and photographer in the Four Corners communities. Through her work in the arts, and as a researcher, Yazzie engages in decolonizing acts by reclaiming the truth about the history of Indigenous Southwest people and by telling the modern stories and experiences of twenty-first-century Indigenous peoples.

Interview

How has your work as a visual artist influenced your poetry, and/or how has your art influenced your poetry?

My art and my poetry complement and feed each other. They appreciate each other's work. In a poem, there is an image and story behind it, and my photography is a form of storytelling as I collect, restore, and reimagine history. In my paintings I am intersecting both of these art forms (poetry/photography) and this is where the *hózhó* dwells for my life—this is how I keep my culture and modern life intact and in a good balance.

We're interested in your cultural work in the Farmington, Bloomfield, Aztec, and reservation schools. What have been your challenges? Your successes?

All of these schools (BIA, parochial, and border town) need more cultural/art teachers. There is a need for more Native teachers who are artistic, flexible, and patient. Working within the art methods and theories I have witnessed how these tools can help children excel and to heal from that genetic trauma they are carrying. Though they are not conscious of these inherited traumas (via Long Walk exodus of their ancestors), these children carry great burdens. Teachers express their gratitude for helping students "heal." I stand steadfast in how vital the Artway is for our children, especially our young generations of Diné (and other Indigenous) students.

Tell us more about your participation as a photographer in the Narrative Witness, Indigenous Peoples: Australia–United States artist-in-residence project.

I worked with the Aboriginal people of Australia and other Indigenous people across American and Canada, which included poets, writers, and visual artists. In our collaboration and experience, my eyes were opened to find that we collectively have the same problems concerning colonization and oppression in our tribal communities. The great commonality with the Diné was evident through their art. The project involved no travel, and for my contribution, I used my photography to tell a story as witness to the San Juan River's contamination in August 2016. My project evolved into a photo essay that highlighted the importance of place and historical memory. I envisioned the river as an archetype and connected to the land and to the feminine principle. The title of my work is *Woman of Water: Baa.*

What projects are you working on now?

I am still working on images that tell the story of the Gold King Mine Spill, which contaminated the San Juan River not only in Durango but also downstream through the Navajo reservation and on out to Lake Powell. I want to present my art on this topic around the Four Corners area. I am also gathering an oral history of my family. I have a blog, *Indigenous Adornment*.

I have been able to gain more art/activism collaborations with strong women from the western Navajo region, on the issue of uranium and related issues of American industry and oppression of people and land, especially on the Navajo Nation, where there is still so much uranium contamination, via abandoned mines and open pits.

My current research, concerning "Be Matriarch, Not Feminist," comes from my constant immersion of life with my family matriarch, my late grandmother, Jane Werito Yazzie, who passed away on February 4, 2020. It was within her narrative that she shared the female expression and female jargon, which are centered in gendered language asdzáá bízaad. It was through such constant language and historical references that I was inspired to focus on the concept of what American society defines as "feminism." I realize that feminism cannot have any suitable connections to Diné (female) culture, the reasoning being that we are a matriarchal society, which is rooted in the traditions and philosophies of our ways of knowing, our epistemologies. As an adult Diné being, I want Diné girls and young women to understand that our rich history of the female being as matriarch is sufficient for a well-balanced life mentally, spiritually, physically.

Who was the first Diné author you read?

The Native author I became really conscious of was N. Scott Momaday. I read his work in my early junior college days at San Juan College in Tótá (Farmington), New Mexico. I remember being drawn to his use of a Navajo prayer he had in the beginning of his novel. From that read, I got to know what Native writers were writing about.

The first Diné writer I read was Luci Tapahonso.

≑

gathering early dawn

níl'i

graying cedars grab the horizon
dawn. sky pulls it closer
and then the desert beetles
sing the songs
each
gathering blue. moving
the stillness loud in the arroyo.
above,

below, behind, in front.
orange sky wraps us. the space
you find in the shawl of matriarchs,
or in the crevices of
warm mesas as you walk in shadows.
and the
quarter moon above your crown swirl
follows.

gathering at early dawn

géé'.

alá ashdla'íí

reflects the shine in female eyes
in all directions. horizon follows
you inside the Hogan to breathe your prayer
when you sleep. horizon at
the fire stove—draped over brown shoulders.

yaa.

arriving nighttime wanders
at desert feet where echoes
move in blue light
and the second world hummingbirds gather
talking our clans.

hayokaał

The Pine Nut Eaters

You've seen them.
Sitting still. Sitting peaceful.

Sitting with chízi fingers pinched at their desert mouths.
Desert tastebuds
waiting for that earth taste.
Pine nut taste.
Nutty taste of desert earth mingled with
pine
nut
shell.

Navajos have scurried to and fro.
Navajos from Teesto, AZ traveled east
in the direction of Sisnaajiní—
white shell mountain.

Packed into shiny double-cab trucks, Navajos
from Tuba speed down Interstate 40 east.
After pit stops in Gallup, they exit at Bernalillo
and drive north to Cuba area.
Where they got word
that the pinõn nuts are huge!

They doze in and out sitting side by side in route.
Auntie has cloud dreams
of salted, roasted pinõns dancing
above the children and cheii. Just like the night before Christmas
story, but instead of visions of sugarplums,
only deep brown pinõn nuts are dancing.

Huge, monster brown pine nuts
dancing circles around their chooshii bed heads.

Just last weekend
in Hopi the women shouted in song,
"Bring us pinõns. We want pine nut taste on our mesa tongues.
The trees 'round here don't have pinõn on them. We want to eat pinõns
too!"

You've seen them.
Sitting. Standing. Kneeling. Picking.
You've seen them
sitting with empty pinõn nut shells all around their feet.

Translations:
chízi—rough, dry skin
Teesto—AZ community in western Navajo reservation
pinõn—nut from high desert pinõn trees
Sisnaajiní—Navajo sacred mountain to the east located in SW Colorado
cheii—maternal grandfather
chooshii—loose, messy, unkept hair

No Español

I don't speak
Sp-a-n-ish
No Habla Español

Irony smirks at me,
a light skinned woman
watches expressionless.
I smile Spanish less.

Shi'ei Diné nishlí.
I'm Navajo.
A nomad ancestor
of those Na Dene from the icy northlands
and the Pacific Hupa on
the misty west coast.

Navajos from
eastern rez dirt washes and hills
and checkerboard boundaries.
My relatives, shi'ké
tromped in Chaco wash
danced in early dawn
imitating yei grandfathers
singing morning songs.
I don't speak
Navajo
so easily.
Life situations can be
hazardous
cause when I turned five
I entered McCormick elementary
on the south side of town.

Grandmother said,
I will allow her to speak English
I will allow her to learn English ABC's

I will allow her to learn
My Country Tis of Thee
I will allow her to be urban Navajo.
I acquired my ABC's and 123's
and
an acquired,
foreign Saxon dialect that
grade by grade
ambushed and
trampled my Diné tongue
in Mrs. Smith's
kindergarten stage room.

I don't speak
Spanish.
I am Diné.
A Navajo
who can read it
write it
and speak in a urban
modified version of it.
It's choppy,
unrehearsed Navajo
and it's mine
and grandmother
and grandfather get it.

grandma loves SOBE

Grandma likes SOBE
she drinks it
at early dawn
while grandpa
dips yesterday's tortillas
in
hot goat's milk.
KNDN
All Navajo all the time
blasts
from cheii's ancient AM radio—
stirring week old
dead rez flies
on the blue windowsill.
45 minute plus drive
to town:
Naat'áaniinéez, Tséghánoodzání
or to Tota', the water place
where great, great grandmother
Asdzáán bizałani'
gathered ripe
green harvest:
ch'ééjiyáán do naayízí
ayoo łikaan.

great grandma hunts
for pallets of SOBE
nestled on slab concrete
walkways at SAMS.
Her hunt parallels nature;
complicated
but, simple
like stepping into dirt puddles
when
dry ground doesn't allow water

to soak in,
and it keeps it on surface awhile—
making sure it understands
the ritual;
the honor of entering
organic elements
on a spinning universe
deep and wide during spring—
when female rain
mingles with mesa ridges
and when grandma buys her
cases of SOBE Herbal life.
Shima'sani SOBE ayoo biłikaan.

ORLANDO WHITE

Credit: Arash Saedinia

ORLANDO WHITE (b. 1976) is from Tólikan, Arizona. He is of the Naaneesht'ézhi Tábaahí and born for the Naakai Dine'é. White earned a BFA from the Institute of American Indian Arts and an MFA from Brown University. He is a faculty member at Diné College in Tsaile, Arizona, and produces the Saad Na'ach'aah Reading Series. White was once in a punk band, Unofficial, and appeared as a musician in Blackhorse Lowe's film *The Fifth World* (2005).

White's work has appeared in numerous journals, including *Ploughshares*, the *Kenyon Review*, *Salt Hill Journal*, *Sentence: A Journal of Prose Poetics*, *Red Ink*, and *Superstition Review*. He is the author of two books of poetry, *Bone Light* (Red Hen Press, 2009) and LETT*ERR*S (Nightboat Books, 2015), which received the Poetry Center Book Award. He has been a recipient of a Breadloaf Fellowship and a Lannan Foundation residency.

White's interest in sound, in letters, in language, and their connection to reality and human understanding of it, is linked to Diné bizaad. In an interview with Matthew Ryan Smith for *First American Art Magazine*, White discusses this line of influence in detail: "Objects in our language are personified or described through an action. This means an object, like a computer, is a noun in English, but in Diné we say *béésh nitséskees*, which loosely translates to 'the metal is thinking.' So, when we talk about things, it's always in phrases, in lines, and animate. The phrase is not limited to just a couple of meanings either, like in a dictionary. Rather, it opens up our thoughts to the possibilities of what *béésh nitséskees* could be. It opens up our imagination." White is a literal revisionist, masterfully crafting studies that are visually beautiful on the page and meditatively dense. He creates intimate connections using line, image, and the letter itself, utilizing very specific Diné constructs of viewing and interacting with the world.

÷

Sentence

Look:

paper screen

blank;

the color white,

a zero,

hollow light bulb,

the O   not yet typed.

This means

no imagination
without
its *imagery*.

Letters   can appear

as bones

(*Do not forget the image*)

if you write with calcium.

Because a subject

can be half of a skeleton,

the verb, the other half

and the skull,

a period.

The i is a Cricket

The book is open.

Can you hear

and see

the cricket?

Listen.

It sounds as if

someone is rubbing

the bristles

of two combs together.

Look closer.

Legs are struggling

like an upside down fly,

like a blinking eyelash.

Touch it.

And you will feel

its tiny hairs.

There is a letter

on the page

that has bent legs.

Before you close

the book

let it leap off the paper.

Fill in the Blank

1.

Ink: proof of existence.

2.

Bones

shattered

on   black:

subject   and   verb.

3.

If you

break a skeleton

in half;

put   it back

together:

a complete   thought.

4.

Use   a pen

to puncture

a skull;

seeps   into comma.

5.

The sentence,

a structure

of two parts.

6.

Punctuation: use it

to connect the bones.

Meditation

I listen to the dark zero in my skull. It sounds like ink filling a white dot on a black sheet of paper. Sometimes it is a punctuation mark with little dark wings; it does not fly, blinks like an eyelash. I always wait for the first letter to appear on the page. And when it does, it shakes its fist up at me. At times, language wants to be dressed in a suit, white necktie. But I prefer a pause between ink and letter when words are silent, unclothed. The clock on the wall swallows a fly, and I see tiny legs struggle between the teeth of a number. Somewhere inside the dark, a shadow tries to lighten the dot on the letter i. He rubs it against the paper; it smears instead. This is what I like about language. The way one folds sentences and feels the bones of words, letters crack, then unfolds them, tiny dark pieces that reconnect again on the page. I do not like to go past the period, because language resists death. Because underneath, bones, subject and verb wait to be revealed. The way one can erase milk to find calcium; the way an erased letter on the page dries into white. The top of the letter i is not *a tiny round mark made by or as if by a pointed instrument.* It can be a rounded letter, a blank zero, or an unwritten circle. Imagination is an equation: x and y can be added, subtracted, multiplied, and divided. *You were an unnatural birth*, she said. I was a letter in the center of an o, born, and pulled out, head shaped like a punctuation mark at the sentence's end.

PAPER MILK

Newborn alphabet cries its vowels and the page nourishes them: *a* opens into a *u*, it becomes a tiny cup, fills with paper milk; the *e*, too, unfurls to an *o* and nurses on the colostrum of pulp-thought attaches sound from *motherese* to thin sheet of white. Form, a structure of feeling, an instrument of print means to foster—the verso and recto will be caretakers of our infant text, as writing develops calcium to bring like to ink, letters become collagen of thoughts.

n

undulates

between

page,   ink: a language

blood vessel.

Oxygenates   cadence.

Without it   *being*

will not have breath.

Write, means to

place life

into   book.

Letters live,

reaffirm   self

within   it.

An ink vein

funnels

plasma thought

through   word

in moment   one

pens it.

DISSOCIATE

Rip vertebral column from *q*

snap the ribs off *x*

from its ink skin pull out the skull of *e*.

This is why we disembody form from flesh,

we divest.

How does a letter disjoin itself

when it imprisons its self?

The persistence of composition means

nothing without the shapes of letters.

Because they must wear dark fabrics,

pale neck cloths—but now *j*

dressed in black scrubs,

surgical mask, grasps a dark scalpel.

She will dissect the disposable head,

so next time you see *i*,

only the body, dotless.

BYRON F. ASPAAS

Credit: Byron Aspaas

BYRON F. ASPAAS (b. 1976) is Táchii'nii, born for Tódich'iinii. Raised within the four sacred mountains of Dinétah, Aspaas holds BA and MA degrees in creative writing from the Institute of American Indian Arts. Aspaas's writing revisits the destruction of sacred land and engages his readers in a dialogue about preserving Diné culture and land. In a 2017 essay, "Nádleehí: One Who Changes," Aspaas explains how these elements are interconnected and under continuing threat: "Diné people have been fighting the ecological destructions of sacred lands for many, many years. In stories, the land is what provides us with beauty. Hózhó. The land feeds, nourishes us, but I fear it is being scraped away by our own people. As Indigenous peoples, we forget reciprocity should be taking place. . . . As Indigenous children, this direction towards becoming America's adopted children has forced many of us to forget. As descendants of those who walked in fear and in shame, by way of forced concentration camps, we remembered hózhó, hózhó nahaasdlii'. As surviving descendants, we must recall their dissidence and relearn our stories as Diné."

Aspaas's first published work, "CoG," was included in *Yellow Medicine Review* in 2010, and since then his writing has appeared in numerous journals and anthologies. Among those are *RedInk*, *200 New Mexico Poems*, *Weber:*

The Contemporary West, *As/Us: A Space for Women of the World*, *Semicolon*, *Denver Quarterly*, *International Writing Program Collections*, *Rumpus*, *Cloudthroat*, and *Akashic Books*. He is working on a collection of essays and poems as well as a fiction project. He uses imagery and persona to present explorations of language, landscape, and identity. Currently, Aspaas resides with his partner, Seth Browder, their three cats, and six dogs in Colorado Springs, Colorado.

Interview

What do you hope readers learn from your writing?

For years, I wanted to write something for my family, which is the reason why I began to write. Before my mom passed away, I wanted to harvest the stories for my nieces and nephews that were my teachings as a child. Sometimes I feel like the ma'ii—my life is filled with so many wrongs.

How does the Navajo language influence your work?

In high school, I took a Navajo language class. I picked up the language sounds quickly; my mom was amazed at my progress. She said it was probably because they taught Navajo in preschool.

It dawned on me, much later in life, that Navajo had always been a part of me. Those words have made their appearances within my work. I am not fluent, but my memories of Mom and Dad speaking to one another at the dinner table lives inside me. What words, phrases, and dialogue I know are beginning to leave me. My wish is to return home soon before I forget.

Who or what inspires you?

I speak about my mom quite often, as she is the reason, I began to write at age thirty-two. I am forty-three now. Each family member is an important character to me. Each person in my life is a life lesson. Each reflection is important and becomes valuable growth to me and my writing. My personal story is seeded by curiosity of family and heritage and land. My people are inspiration.

What advice do you have for beginning writers?

Continue to read. I read constantly, now, since finishing graduate school. To the beginner writer: remember, your craft is never the same when you complete reading a book. As a reader, you will begin to notice and borrow and evolve into the writer you will become. Keep a journal. Write everything down.

What was your favorite book in high school? What are you reading now?

I was twenty-four when I read my first book, *The Color Purple,* without instruction, and I cried because it was a beautiful book, and it moved me emotionally. I did not know writing could do that. Recently, I finished *The Tao of Raven* by Ernestine Hayes. Hayes is a great influence in my work. She inspires craft and narrative.

Your piece in this reader is a memoir. What other types of genres have you been working in, and which genre(s) best suits your creative voice?

I once sat in a craft talk in graduate school where a lyric essayist said, If your audience thinks you are reading poetry, you're doing your job as a lyric essayist. I write lyric prose. It braids poetics into story and weaves a beautiful voice that sings.

My first fiction short story was published in March 2020. It is part of a collection by Akashic Books, called Santa Fe Noir, that includes writers like Ana Castillo, Jimmy Santiago Baca, Elizabeth Lee, plus many more amazing writers.

My first publications are in poetry. Poetry is in the foundation of all writing. Lyricism is in Diné creation story. It's in Diné bizaad. It's Diné.

Who was the first Diné author you read?

Easy. Luci Tapahonso. Dr. Connie Jacobs's class.

⩧

Interstate Badlands

I don't know how to begin my story. Initially, I wanted to share this experience that included a tale of the coyote. As a child, my first introduction to the character was in a book I plagiarized. In seventh grade, my version was placed high upon the wall, with other great stories that my science teacher asked for: *How do you think the stars were created?*

Guilt has sat high on the walls of my heart because I felt like coyote.

"How do I begin this story?" fumbles in my mind. With a new laptop in front of me, I sometimes wonder how did I ever get through school? At thirty-three years old, I placed myself into a class that evolved into a creative writing degree and then an MFA in Creative Writing.

I do feel the beginning of this story should call for an exposition—an interjection, a small fact about me—explaining how writing was my worst subject as a child. My first book was a read-a-long where I followed the words of the *Tawny Scrawny Lion.* I never read anything else in book form, thereafter. My first diary was a small booklet of papers that I wrote in for a few days explaining how I missed my family while I spent six weeks in Champaign-Urbana, Illinois, in 1993. I was sixteen.

Might I add, I never wanted to write. My spelling was embarrassingly corrected in seventh grade during a spelling bee. My English courses were remedial until tenth grade. And my stutter continued to follow me when I was asked to read aloud in front of my peers.

In college, I learned a story has three parts: a beginning, middle, and an end.

In graduate school, I fumbled with the narrative arc. *Where is the conflict, inner-conflict, the climatic point? Why are you not writing a linear story?* These were phrases I heard constantly—and anxieties resurfaced.

In March of 2016, I drove home to visit family members of the Four Corners region. They lived in New Mexico. I lost my best friend the month before, so my car had driven this path a few times—probably more than it had in the past ten years. It seemed with this visit, my car swerved automatically around familiar dips and fumbled on new ones. Tóta' is where my story begins, a reservation border town, where some of my earliest memories have spun themselves into reflections of my personal journey. . . .

My childhood community had shifted. What were once dirt roads are now paved with loose gravel; the elementary school I attended is no longer standing—a sandy mound of ghost-memory remains. In the dark, a new school stands erected, tall, like a double-layered cake decorated with concrete. Its bright lights flicker upon a once darkened neighborhood.

My dad was not home when I opened the door. Since Mom died, I am told he is never home, but the porch light remained on and I sat in silence, listening to the refrigerator speak. As usual, it hummed and echoed down the hallway where I laid, in Mom's room—wrapped, awaiting slumber. . . .

For thirteen years, my dad worked as a heavy equipment operator for the Pittsburg Midway Coal Company. For thirteen years, I watched Dad leave on Sunday evening and return Friday afternoon—sometime before school ended—and each weekend began with a surprise, but then it ended with sadness in goodbyes. For thirteen years, my dad traveled one hundred miles away to live on a dragline, as big as our house. He operated the crane for money, scooping coal for the home we occupied in New Mexico. For thirteen years, he worked the nightshift and Mom became our dad while Dad became a creature of the night—working the twelve to eight shift—his eyes red with no sleep. For thirteen years, Mom began to show age while Dad remained ageless.

Because of nightmares and fear of sleeping at home, I began to travel with Dad to his worksite. Once, he snuck me into the coal pits and I watched the crane move slowly like a brontosaurus dipping into a lake of rock. I slept in the back of my sister's car, wrapped in Dad's blankets, listening to the moan of the machinery. I was nine years old.

Upon driving home one morning, I watched the sun color the desert bright yellow and brown, then noticed the white lines drift to the middle of the car. *Dad,* I screamed. Dad's eyes opened as he directed our vessel to the side of the road. We were fifty miles away from home on a two-lane highway, located between Gallup and Shiprock. Highway 666 was known for its head-on collisions—maybe all those who crashed were just as tired as Dad.

Do you think you can drive, son? Dad asked.

I can try, I said.

It's almost like the motorcycles at home. All you need to do is steer. I'll have my foot on the pedal, he said, *Sit on my lap, son.*

Okay, I said.

For fifty miles, my dad held his foot on the pedal. My foot rested upon his foot to add pressure to the gas, if needed. With one eye closed, he kept watch on the asphalt river, ahead. With me positioned at the helms, my guidance was trusted as I led us home, down the highway and through the windy dirt roads of the Burnham Badlands.

At age ten, my foot reached the pedals of my sister's car. No longer a pirate with one eye closed, my Dad began to sleep comfortably. As I aged, landscape became present when purple mounds of clay turned mile-markers and the badlands of Burnham became a map for story. Scattered rocks, red from fire, revealed truths of a story I heard when Monster Slayer and his sibling fought evil.

Pittsburg Midway Coal Company devoured mountains while Dad remained employed with them. Behind our home, the Navajo Coal Mine has nibbled at the Burnham Badlands for thirty years, since I began driving, and nibbled at my memory because those stories are now gone.

I was not innocent, remember?

I was like the coyote.

Our cars needed food, our homes needed food, and our appliances needed power, which was like food.

We consumed like monsters.

K'é was introduced to me by Dr. Benally in my Navajo Culture class where my older sister and I took this course as an "elective" at San Juan College. I was twenty-three years old when I asked my parents about K'é and what it meant to each of them.

Mom said K'é was like family. Dad had a similar translation leaning towards clans.

"What about Sa'ah Naagháí Bik'eh Hózhóón," I asked.

For a moment, I think my mom almost fell over when the phrase flowed from my mouth.

"Ha'át'íí?" Mom said.

Both she and Dad looked upon each other in disbelief and smiled.

"Where are you learning this?" she asked.

"Navajo Culture," I said.

Sa'ah Naagháí Bik'eh Hózhóón is said to be the duality within each of us—both male and female counterparts nestled into one another, wrapped and swirled inside *us*, awaiting to present themselves if needed. Sa'ah Naagháí, the male presence, becomes recognizable as protector and aggressor of the two forces; Bik'eh Hózhóón, the female equivalent, nourishes and heals with health, strength, and sustenance. They are considered negative and positive entities (not in the literal sense), energies complementing one another, existing wholly, never separately. "Without one entity, one would never be balanced," jíní. Together, they become the power of creation.

"We are made of male and female," Dr. Benally said to the class.

Sa'ah Naaghái Bik'eh Hózhóón is a harmonious action between male and female, therefore, becomes balanced within each of us. It should be performed throughout one's life and used within the universe as both positive and negative (male and female) energies establish serenity within all beings, and not just humans, *all* things. To achieve Sa'ah Naaghái Bik'eh Hózhóón, one needs to practice it and find beauty within their life because Sa'ah Naaghái Bik'eh Hózhóón will transpose them towards peace of mind, establish an emotional stability, promote physical strength, and create ecological awareness.

This process begins with K'é—family.

Standing before two monolithic sandstones, memories of Monument Valley, of Chaco Canyon, of the Burnham Badlands flooded bits of me like monsoon rains—rushing through caverns of emotion where pinks are flushed with reds and grays are colored purple, with moisture, and silver clouds are sewn to the hems of the horizons, pillowed above desert reflection—southern Utah has been painted as home, my home—Diné bikéyah.

While I sat inside my parents' home, thinking of a question posed to me on Facebook: *Byron what is your view on this?* Attached was a post by the Heritage Foundation. It stated: "Under the president's power plan, certain Indian territories are especially singled out." The link was titled: Obama's Clean Power Plan Will Destroy Navajo Nation Jobs.

A YouTube video presented itself.

In this video, a young Diné girl shared her story of a castle with three chimneys. She said the castle was visible from her window. This castle is near Page, Arizona, I believe. She continued to say a warrior needed armor to enter the castle. Her voice seemed innocent and inviting.

> Ałkidą́ą́—it was ritual to watch Dad prepare each Sunday as he placed armor onto his worn body. When Dad returned on Friday afternoon, the scent of Dad returned, as well. The combination of coal mixed with sweat, splashed with coffee, presented itself when he staggered into our home, drunk-like—eyes red with fatigue—and slumped onto Mom's bed, exhausted from the week's beating. I used to think my dad never aged when I was a boy. His hair was always black like mine until the day my brother died, from leukemia, and the coal mine stripped him of his armor and the valiant dragline he used to dip into the earth. Not long after, Dad could not sleep. He roamed our house until four each morning, reading or watching TV or probably overthinking *why?* His hair began to wither with color and silver began to set in. Sadness overwhelmed him and the scent of coal mixed with sweat, splashed with coffee, stained Mom's room for a very long time.

In this video, a young Navajo man said he wanted to give back to the community. He said he wanted to follow in his father and grandfather's footsteps while working at the power plant. As this is spoken, landscapes of the red desert panned to wild horses running wildly, as Horse Shoe Bend reflected the beauty of sky—tranquility is released in flute-played song.

> Ałkidą́ą́—like my father, my dad, Shizhé'é, I wanted to give back. I wanted to give back because that's what we were taught as children. Like my father, my dad, Shizhé'é, I wanted to work and make money as an engineer, so I can be someone of stature of dignity of respect, but my degree was never completed. I left school in 2003. It was my second attempt at college. I was a junior with credits in civil engineering. But before leaving, I was an intern at the Bureau of Land Management. I spent two summers in Rawlins, Wyoming. I was nothing like my father, my dad, Shizhé'é, who was only drunk on tiredness—and unlike my father, my dad, Shizhé'é, I learned to be drunk and became overweight and squawked "Cowboy Take Me Away" at a shithole bar that smelled of piss while my tiredness was mixed with beer and bad karaoke.

In the video, Arizona State Senator Carlyle Begay said the natural resources of the Navajo Nation were a blessing—namely coal. With well-spoken English and a voice of an educated man, Begay sat situated with a mauve-collared shirt and a fuchsia polka-dotted tie. He unfolded the truths about coal and revealed its integral connection to the community. The tone of Begay's voice was sincere, and his face looked somber. As the video continued, Speaker of the Arizona House of Representatives, David M. Gowan, Sr., exhibited the relationship between Arizona and the Navajo Nation, talking about the importance of the Colorado River and the role it played in creating energy. As the video came to an end, employees stated their experience with the power plant. An elder Navajo man spoke truths and how smoke is not smoke, but the smoke those see was *only* generated steam, *only* water. He said, those who *do not* understand power plants should ask questions, not assume. The last employee was, maybe, thirty who spoke of concern. He stated his situation of sadness. It was displayed in his eyes before video faded to black.

> Ałkidą́ą́—as children, we were raised to believe coal benefited us. Yes, financially, we were given the security our grandfathers and grandmothers, our fathers and mothers, worked for as coalminers. As children, we were raised and taught to buy and spend and buy more, never asking where money came from, and we wanted more. As childrén, we were given securities within our homes our cars our belongings and we were fed to believe coal mines lived forever. As children, we were given the security of benefits, benefits that aided those who spent time in hospitals with diseases, like leukemia, that pulled families away from school, a school system that taught Diné children to devour and consume and take and eat and throw away—but never question: *What if it all goes away?*

The little girl in the video was told the power plant was the heart of the land. Its heartbeat can be heard by many, she said. It's been beating for a long time, she said, more likely longer than hers. It will probably live to be, at least, one hundred and twenty, she said.

> Ałkidą́ą́—I grew up in a house where two castles with multiple chimneys stood outside my bedroom window. At night, I watched lights sparkle like orange stars that blipped with a timed cadence. Sometimes, I sat upon my parent's HUD home, and watched a milky way of lights brighten the valley below. Sometimes, the natural gas company's torch would light up the cloudy desert sky and I would pretend Lady Liberty stood below while I stood in New York—but there was no Lady Liberty, no New York, just dirty air, and my hand over heart.

What happens in one hundred and twenty years when all is gone and scraped away?

Ałkidą̨ą̨—I grew up in a house where two castles with multiple chimneys stood outside my bedroom window and I watched their eyes glow with bellows of clouds weaving its story of gloom into the sky while the land rumbled from its hunger. . . .

Ałkidą̨ą̨—actually, not that long ago—I was asked to consider writing at age twenty-two, a semester before Navajo Culture class. My instructor said my stories had essence of adventure. It reminded her of Luci Tapahonso, she said. I said no to her when she mentioned the word "editor" to me. I explained to her my dreams of being an engineer.

Honestly, I feared the English language. I still do. But, that kernel was planted.

I did not grow up speaking the Diné language. I don't know what my first words were, but Mom told me preschool taught our class Diné bizaad. She said she tried to continue speaking with me, but it faded.

"Maybe that's why you picked up the language so easily," she said, "because it lives in you."

My dad was more blunt when I tried to blame him for our lack of Diné bizaad. The hurt in his eyes retaliated, "It's not my fault you were too damn stubborn to listen."

He was right. We were taught to consume, not appreciate.

Dr. Benally sparked my interest when K'é was introduced to me. Story began to culminate within itself when Náadleehí was mentioned and the importance of Child Born for Water—who was a twin, a Monster Slayer, a child born with fluidity. It was mentioned that people *assumed* Child Born for Water was a boy only because he was a twin to Monster Slayer, the older brother, the powerful one, probably the bigger of the two—and when colonized thinking and Christianity was introduced; Diné thought changed and the people became Navajo.

When I drove through southern Utah, I noticed the landscape. I noticed Twins appear in different areas after [my friend] Hannah pointed out The Temple of the Sun and Temple of the Moon. What I told her later, when we walked through the cathedral of rocks, "They remind me of Naayéé' Neizghání áádóó Tóbájíshchíní, son of Jóhonaa'éí and child of Tóneinilí—the Monster Slayers of the Diné." What I had noticed, while driving through southern Utah, were the mislabeled names like the cheesebox, a cheesy label for a product, when hoghaan presented itself instead—the female home known to nourish, heal, and provide strength for those within her—Bik'eh Hózhóón. As I drove through southern Utah, I noticed Twins guide me as my car became thirsty for gas, bitoo' ádin, and my heart pounded with fear because I didn't know where we were. Yes, *we*, my car and I. Months later, I learned where we drove, in southern Utah, we were near what the bilagáanas called the area Bears Ears, not the Twin Warriors I thought them to be.

Where are the Indigenous place names? Where are the Indigenous stories of these locations? Where are the people who remember them? Where are the Monster Slayers?

It wasn't long ago that I began to write. Because my mom was nearing the end of her life, I enrolled myself into a school that crafted me into a master of creative writing. Every day, I questioned my ability to convey story: *Am I really a master?* With my grammar and spelling as the villains of this story, I began to rewrite my narrative arc by introducing inner-conflict with sources of weaknesses. I presented new characters by developing a voice for a brother I lost, which also included a segment of a grandma that my nieces and nephews will never know—namely, my six-year-old nephew. I began to write for Shizhé'é because his narrative included me—I am a child born of two waters: Táchíínii áádóó Tódich'íinii nishłį. I began to write through the memories of my sisters and brothers who are part of me. I began to write for the landscape and lost stories scraped away by those who colonized the people, the land, the language, and the story. I began to write to help rewrite a literary landscape chosen by those who educated our ancestors. I began to write to reclaim voice. I began to write, so I can heal.

I wanted to begin this story with a coyote tale, but I figured this whole story is filled with coyotes and multiple tales. I am a coyote who's learned from the mistakes put along his trail. Every day, reverberations of coyote pulse inside each of us, whether we like it or not; we are all tricksters. We are survivors. We learned from story, our past mistakes.

In Diné stories, there were monsters, jíní. Those monsters destroyed the people and shook the land from within. In Diné stories, the people were misguided by a powerful gambler, who lied and cheated and stole people, making them slaves—the gambler has returned. In old Diné stories, we prevailed and banished and celebrated by giving back to the land. Jíní, that which is said.

JAKE SKEETS

Credit: Jake Skeets

JAKE SKEETS (b. 1991) is Tsi'naajinii, born to Tábąąhá, and Táchii'nii, and Tódik'ǫzhi. Born in Gallup, New Mexico, he grew up in Vanderwagen, New Mexico, and has lived in Albuquerque, New Mexico, and Phoenix and Window Rock, Arizona. He holds an MFA in poetry from the Institute of American Indian Arts and, before that, earned a BA in English and a BA in Native studies at the University of New Mexico. Skeets is currently faculty at Diné College on the Navajo Nation. "Techno Beats," written between 2006 and 2009, while Skeets was in high school, was the winner of a Gallup Public Library contest and led to his first publication in the *Gallup Journey*.

In a 2012 blog post, "Matthew Jake Skeets Writes Because . . . ," he offers the following insights about his creative vision: "I write because there is story in me, in my parents, aunts, uncles, and in my people. I write because there is story Navajo people have carried with them and were so shockingly shattered by that one C-word I refuse to say. . . . I write because my mom can't tell me how she feels. I write because my grandfather can't tell us how he fell in love. I write because Navajos are too afraid to speak. I write for them. . . . I write because brown people are too afraid to truly speak what they live. I write for them. I write because I need to make my people human."

His poems have appeared in *Boston Review*, *Waxwing*, *Yellow Medicine Review*, *Red Ink Magazine*, *James Franco Review*, and elsewhere. His community work includes organizing Pollentongue, a poetry salon and reading series, and acting as a faculty mentor for the annual Emerging Diné Writers' Institute. Skeets is the founding editor of *Cloudthroat*, an online publication for Native, First Nations, and Indigenous writing and art, and a founding member of Saad Bee Hózhǫ́: A Diné Writers' Collective. Jake is a winner of the 2018 Discovery/Boston Review Poetry Prize. His first collection, *Eyes Bottle Dark with a Mouthful of Flowers*, was selected as a 2018 winner for the prestigious National Poetry Series for Milkweed Editions and received the 2020 American Book Award. He is also a 2020 Whiting Award winner.

Interview

What do you hope readers learn from your writing?

I hope they learn a new way to position themselves within the world. My role as a poet, student, thinker, and Diné man has always been about critically thinking about my positionality in relation to everything else. It's an important step to truly protecting land and language because when we learn to position ourselves, we unlearn the types of violences we were conditioned to act upon and enable from a Western, colonized way of thinking. I also hope once they learn their positions, they can start to listen. Listening is always the first step. As newborns, we listen to the wind in order to take our first breaths. As children, we listen to our parents or people around us. As young adults and adults, we should listen to everything. Then, as elders, after we've listened for a lifetime, we learn how to tell stories, sing, and pray.

How does the Navajo language influence your work?

Diné words are poems on their own. They spark so much imagery and action. If you walk through the flea market or listen to your aunts as they make stew before a ceremony, you hear poetry. A poem is often heard before it's written. For me, learning Diné as a second language has helped me with process. Diné is a language of energy, an attempt to mimic or transcribe or translate natural occurrences in an attempt to communicate. Like in Orlando White's poem "Nascent," to convey a horse, Diné attempts to describe the sound a horse makes. Diné forces the person to become the horse. That process of communication has taught me the process of making poetry.

Who or what inspires you?

I think inspiration is a falsehood. However, if I were to describe the feeling of inspiration, I would say I feel most in sync with energies when I am listening to my family tell stories or my mind is repeating a memory in my head. So basically, storytelling inspires me. The act of creating moving images that replay in your head in speech, writing, or film inspires me. I often find the urge to write a poem when I'm in a movie theater or listening to someone else read their work.

What advice do you have for beginning writers?

My advice would be learn to listen and listen well. I don't think we all know how to truly listen until we've actively practiced it for some time. Part of listening is reading and reading as many things as possible. Another part is remaining silent as the world moves around you.

Who was the first Diné writer you read?

The first Diné writer I read was in my junior year of high school at Window Rock High School. My college prep eleventh grade English teacher, Ms. Chee, gave us a scanned packet of Native American poets. I came across poems by Luci Tapahonso and Laura Tohe. Specifically, "Hills Brothers Coffee" by Luci Tapahonso was the first poem to which I remember responding. I do not remember much about high school but I remember that day completely.

What was your favorite book in high school? What are you reading now?

My favorite book in high school was *In Cold Blood* by Truman Capote. I carried that book around with me everywhere. Today, I am currently reading *There There* by Tommy Orange and *Not Here* by Hieu Minh

Nguyen. I still carry books around with me daily but the list has grown.

Let There Be Coal

I.

A father hands a sledge hammer to two boys outside Window Rock.
The older goes first, rams a rail spike into the core, it sparks—

no light comes, just dust cloud
glitterblack.

The boys load the coal. Inside them, a generator station opens its eye.
A father sips on coal slurry from a Styrofoam cup, careful not to burn.

II.

train
tracks
and
mines
split
Gallup
in two

Men
spit
coal
tracks rise
like a spine
when Drunktown
kneels to the east

III.

Spider Woman cries her stories coiled in warp and wool. The rug now hung
in a San Francisco or Swedish hotel.

We bring in the coal that dyes our hands black not like ash
but like the thing that makes a black sheep black.

IV.

This is a retelling of the creation story where Navajo people journeyed four worlds
and God declared, "Let there be coal." Some Navajo people say there are actually five worlds.
Some say six.

A boy busting up coal in Window Rock asks his dad, "When do we leave
for the next one?"
His dad sits his coffee down to hit the boy. "Coal doesn't bust itself."

From Under His Cover

I tell them at noon in a damp hooghan. The sun whispers
in from the eastern door. My father keeps low in prayer.
Tobacco too vibrant in my teeth. The peyote root
hangs too heavy to stomach. The ground unsmooths

beneath me and I feel the confession swell like bile.
My older sister cries with me. I still smell the stove coffee
and dawn rain. My mother digs cold into the sand. Smoke
curls between my lips as I shudder through dry heaves.

Words come, searing my tongue. I tell them I've kissed
boys. I tell them about my boyfriend and how he's Arizona,
Tsé Nitsaa Deez'áhí. His clan is Coyote Pass, born for Zuni
People, from Under His Cover and Black Sheep. He holds

his hair like Born of Water. I tell them about his singing
and how he ate dinner with us during the Navajo Fair.
My brother places his arm around my shoulder. "It means
you're holy," my aunt weeps. "It means you're holy."

My father hands me an eagle feather, puffy at the plume.
"For protection," he hymns. The smell of ceremony
in my hair will never truly leave. I tell them at noon in a damp
hooghan. I tell them I am able to love without them

Thieving Ceremony

You've come for me twice before. Body swollen
with booze. Fires for eyes. Each time, I let you have me
and let you cry. Let me
heal you. It is your hands
that touch me. We become the black wool of a night sky
every time. Slide out of our clothes in a backseat,
in a back room,
black as a ye'ii mask.
We kiss, caesura to ensure the blackening. We are First Man
and Turquoise Boy ash-married in a ceremony that is ours now.
Make charcoal
of the boys before us
who have only come to make love to the mass graves
in our teeth. To them our flesh is still soot, still furnace,
still jet, still a cornstalk
and juniper tree
left burning.

Blue Edge Cord

loom   beam
hogan   beam
rainbow   beam
sun   beam

the
          panel
                    of
          sheep
corral

blue edge   cord
cliff ridge   cord
braided   cord
rain   cord

stripes of black and white

thousand dawns
thousand eves

thousand years of a sunlight beam
thousand more to twill its cord

seeds in
          turkey
                    feathers
          set
free

thousand lives bloom through
thousand lives come on back

hear them sing along edge   cord
see them step along beaming   beam

BOJAN LOUIS

Credit: Sara Sams

BOJAN LOUIS (b. 1980) is Naakai Dine'é and born for 'Áshįįhí; his maternal grandfather is Ta'neeszahnii and his paternal grandfather is Bilagáana. He was born in Gallup, New Mexico, and grew up in Flagstaff, Arizona. He earned his MFA in creative writing from Arizona State University in 2009 and BA in English from Northern Arizona University in 2003. For more than fifteen years, he was employed as an electrician and construction worker. Louis was the inaugural Virginia G. Piper Fellow-in-Residence at Arizona State University and in fall 2019 became an assistant professor of English and American Indian studies at the University of Arizona.

He is a poet, fiction writer, and essayist. His first publication was a flash fiction piece, "Askii łchii (Red Boy)," published in *Red Ink* in 2005. He has been a resident at MacDowell. His writing has appeared in *Kenyon Review*, *Platte Valley Review*, *Hinchas de Poesía*, *American Indian Research and Culture Journal*, and *Black Renaissance Noire*, *Alaska Quarterly Review*, *Yellow Medicine Review*, *As/Us* journal, *Mud City Journal*, and *Off the Path: An Anthology of 21st Century American Indian Writers, Volume 2*. He is the author of the nonfiction chapbook *Troubleshooting Silence in Arizona* (Guillotine Series, 2012). His first poetry collection is *Currents* (BkMk Press 2017), which received a prestigious 2018 American Book Award from the Before Columbus Foundation. In an interview with *Superstition Review*, Louis discusses the influence of music on his creative process: "I listen to music all day, every genre, though I generally write to metal, noise, or doom. . . . Coil, Earth, Aphex Twin, Mayhem, Neurosis, Chopin, Bach, Brujeria, Sepultura, Behemoth, Slayer, Converge, Satyricon . . . I really could go on and on. Music where I don't readily discern the lyrics, where the vocals are more percussive, pure guttural emotion. Poetry, for me, is percussive. It can be noise, acoustics and sonic qualities."

Interview

What do you hope readers learn from your writing?

I suppose my hope is that readers recognize the chorus of voices and multilayered, nonlinear experiences occurring within my poetry collection. That time isn't linear or necessarily cyclical but happening all at once. Past, present, and future occurring within each moment of daily life, which manifests as one being attuned and attentive to all beings and things around them. In regards to my fiction, that one can be both working class and literary and that one can certainly survive trauma and remake a family.

How does the Navajo language influence your work?

For me, it's reclamation. I'm not yet fluent and my comfort using Diné sways drastically from month to month, year to year. It makes me feel fucking crazy: both connected and grasping within a void of my inability. As a result of both of my parents' traumatic experiences in boarding school, where they were beaten and reprimanded for speaking Diné, they didn't actively teach me or my sister the language. It's a scar and decision they regret, but that's how trauma and the stripping of culture works.

Who or what inspires you?

Everything. The strength and resilience of my parents; my ancestors and their struggle to survive. Music. Art. Traveling and putting myself in new and uncomfortable situations. The unfamiliar. Nice pens and paper. Craftsmanship. Electricity. Food. Running. Food.

What advice do you have for beginning writers?

Read, read, read, and get a job. Work early and work late. Refrain from punishing yourself. Avoid careerism and competition, unless you're hopelessly as such, then: good luck.

Who was the first Diné writer you read?

Probably Luci Tapahonso, then Sherwin Bitsui and Laura Tohe. Rex Lee Jim and Irvin Morris.

What was your favorite book in high school? What are you reading now?

At this point, high school is a blur to me. I read through the majority of William S. Burroughs's work. Haven't touched it since. *Invisible Man* by Ralph Ellison, *Crime and Punishment* by Fyodor Dostoevsky, and *Lolita* by Vladimir Nabokov were my favorite in high school. All read during my senior year. Currently, I'm reading *World Light* by Halldór Laxness; *Lanark* by Alasdair Gray; *Another Country* by James Baldwin.

What gave you the strength or courage or audacity to write about the complicated truths in "Beauty & Memory & Abuse & Love"?

Anger. Frustration with the therapist I was seeing. Anger. Self-hatred. Pain. Self-medicating. Metal. Anger. The want to be "better" for my partner, parents, and community. Anger. The beauty in all that.

Currents

Phoenix, Arizona

I.

Each new sun asks: be
no thing more than me,

have nothing beyond need

—send opened your whole
being, lifted face, arms spread.
Though only part of me

is blessed, a body exerted
after long hours, responsibility,
and the need to ease tremors.

———

The last of March's
welfare won't go past
the eighteenth, hunger pains

dull month to month.
We've burned the final
log from February's half-

cord; son's schoolbooks,
claimed lost, are enough
to get the fire going.

———

My youth wasn't warm enough
to stone prairie dogs,
skin and eat.

The drive past the flats
no longer makes instant
noodles cheaper.

Mornings blind when throats throw
heat—stutter steps skid linoleum.
Untouched eggs feed me, forget me.

II.

Mom's a woman with
red skin and long receipts,
an aluminum façade

of sparkle-talk and sheen.
Measuring steps: easy win,
sudden guess.

Sissy boys
tear and candy don't
take care.

———

There isn't a nickel
in any cushion—
skeletal-hair remains

collect all over.
Red drips redder
than my skin,

redder than swallowed
embarrassment,
than slap—freezing feet.

———

A dark hall's corner,
a damask of lines,
the call-to mom uses,

telling me I don't add up.
I penguin-walk and cross
feet. In grass I pull

my knees up;
still, the grass
grows toward me.

III.

The coin-fare for
a crosstown bus a rosary
for time on my own.

Slow approach on
the upcoming stop, a heavy
let, a stiffened step

on concrete
right-angled silhouettes
the butane flame dawn.

———

The water's
hot and
there is light:

the home
encloses a
son lost

until 6:30 brings
noise of traffic
delays and brewing.

———

I get
little out
of this,

pay is ungrateful,
I eat little—
my eyes bulge.

I don't know
the woman
letting time slip.

Nizhoní dóó 'a'ani' dóó até'él'í dóó ayoo'o'oni (Beauty & Memory & Abuse & Love)

7 April 2014. Over the weekend I attended the thirty-first Annual Tucson Poetry Festival as a representative for a literary magazine of which I will be an editorial staff member. Aside from manning a display table of past issues I conducted a writing workshop with the mighty Simon J. Ortiz—Acoma intellectual, writer, and poet—aimed at youth and young adult writers, though anyone, of any age, was welcomed to attend. After the workshop, I had lunch with Orlando White, a Diné poet, and he and I attended another workshop facilitated by poet Harryette Mullen. The focus, or at least what began as the focus (we didn't stay for the duration of the workshop), was childhood memories. We, the some forty to fifty workshop participants, were asked to think of our childhoods and engage our five senses, for children remember and associate concrete connections through tactile sensations. We were asked to free write and to describe three to five distinct memories from each one of our individual childhoods.

Colonization and decolonization connote and denote violence. Colonized people are murdered, raped, silenced, dehumanized, removed, extracted, have had their tongues and eyes cut out, have been fed to dogs, are made to hate themselves and their community members, assimilated, lied to, and on and on and on. A decolonized person seeks to shout, scream, relinquish their hurt and hatred, become the navigator of their self-image, obtain productive and healthy positions in and for the greater good of their communities; they look toward the future while continually waking up to the past. Their sleep is disquieted by night terrors. Their patience stilted by exhaustion.

The workshop prompt proved to be difficult, if not impossible. I'm often adverse to friends inquiring about what I was like as child and even more adverse to my parent's recollections of specific events or stories from and of my childhood. Do I remember lying beneath a black Chevy truck (or perhaps it was a GMC) with my dad while he fixed it and pretended that I was helping? Or, being ornery on a trip back from visiting my mom's foster parents in Provo, Utah, and pulling over at some nursery where, among the plants, I was in someway calmed? The time at the Navajo Nation Fair, fishing trips to Wheatfields Lake, the birth and growth of my sister from an infant to a toddler? No, I remember nothing and respond to these stories with lies about my remembering them because my mom has pictures of most of these moments, and because there are pictures, and because I'm a writer, I can say *yes* there are memories.

In Susan Sontag's essay, "An Argument About Beauty," from the posthumous, somewhat unfinished, collection *At the Same Time: Essays and Speeches* published in 2007, she begins with the Catholic Church and Vatican's 2002 scandal of covering up the sexual molestation of adolescents by their priests. Sontag quotes Pope John Paul II as telling American cardinals summoned to the Vatican: "A great work of art may be blemished, but its beauty remains; and this is a truth which an intellectually honest critic will recognize." The Church as art, as Beauty beyond fault. I believe Sontag thought as much, agreed that beauty equals consolation. Her son, David Rieff, writes in his forward: "Did she write to console herself? I believe so, though this is more intuition than grounded judgment." I certainly write to console myself, though I've come to realize, and more importantly acknowledge, that through writing and the striving to make art I more often than not re-traumatize myself by engaging and going to the dark and ugly memories, which I more easily access than the happy ones that my parents recall. The beautiful notion of childhood; the Diné ideal of hozhó, which can be translated roughly as *the balance of walking and living in harmony, in conjunction with all beings and all things, that each element of the universe has its place and purpose in the* machination *of existence*. Now, *machination* is my word though I'm fairly certain that it's apt for the translation. Diné bizaad (the Navajo language) directly reflects this ideal in its specificity and precision in regards to who is speaking, your familial and clan relationship to the speaker, when and where they are speaking, in physical relation to whom they are speaking, and in relation to the world, the universe. Essentially, you can't just say shit, as is the case with the absolute beauty and frustration of English (Bilagáana bizaad). Similarly, the Diné idea of balance can be thought of in relation to William Carlos Williams' thoughts on poems being *small machinations*. Every word, space, punctuation, and interaction with the page is intentional, of the utmost importance. One poorly casted cog or wheel and the entire process falls apart, becomes simple thoughts on paper rather than art. Can beauty, then, be all things: the damned, the holy, the sacred, the sacrilegious, the wrecked, the reconstructed, the artificial, and the natural?

We were asked to write for fifteen to twenty minutes, at least that's how long I think it was. For a few minutes nothing came to mind, I envisioned a literal blackness, a room and darkness—someone flipping a switch. When I finally wrote, I put this on the page reluctantly:

1. Body blue and your limbs
   taste harsh like rotten kale.
   Not fresh, so there's no sound,
   no crunch but only squish, which
   is word for a sound, but in this
   instance it's a feeling, a verb.
   The idea of pressure upon you.

2. You remember husky, a stolen
   jug of pennies. You remember the
   inability to decipher the noise
   of the dog being poisoned, the
   depth of the burial, and if there
   was even grass.

3. Don't be an idiot, your parents
   didn't make enough to water grass.

Nothing really useful or impressive, though that's what first drafts or free writing become for me, for any writer aware of their consistent and constant failures. There are obvious issues in the above free write. First, I'd already written a poem about my neighbor poisoning our dog and robbing our house, although I didn't include the part about the jug of pennies. Second, being sexually molested/physically abused/abused sexually/molested physically doesn't sound like squish. More like *rip* and *thud*, slow hands clapping. Third, I never ate kale as a child. I didn't eat kale until my late twenties, after I lived in a city, fell in love, and discovered Whole Foods.

In the first chapter of *The Wretched of the Earth* Frantz Fanon writes, in regards to the colonized, "As soon as they are born it is obvious to them that their cramped world, riddled with taboos, can only be challenged by out and out violence." I first read this text in high school after seeing it pictured among a pile of other texts in the liner notes of Rage Against the Machine's newly released CD, at the time, *Evil Empire*. I misunderstood Fanon's thoughts completely, as many younger readers do and as many older, "educated" readers still do. Anger is nothing to turn one's head at, to disregard, or to use as an excuse to criticize. Jamaica Kincaid, in her conversation with the *American Reader*, tells her interviewer, in response to a question regarding the mixture of humor and anger in her writing: "There are all sorts of reasons not to like my writing. But that's not one of them. Saying something is angry is not a criticism. It's not valid. It's not a valid observation in terms of criticism. You can list it as something that's true. But it's not critical." As we say, and others say, on and off the reservation, past and present, *fuckin' A right*. Anger has long been, and used to be, my response to the circumstances of my childhood, ethnic demographic, and creative voice. Always more anger than love, though there was for me, or might have been, an obsession with violence—daggers protruding out of my skull, barbed wire wrapped around my body. My every response was anger, often misdirected, but always refocused upon myself. I sought to understand not only my mental and physical trauma but also historical trauma, both of which I still seek to understand. Love, I believed, to be associated with weakness. Pussy ass motherfuckers fell in love. Strong, stoic, the not-giving-a-shit types refused love, refused ideas of heaven, denied the ability of happiness to last. I drank/drink, popped/pop pills, snorted/snort cocaine and crushed pills, smoked/smoke bud, and tried desperately to fuck away the anger, depression, guilt, and suicidal thoughts brewing in my psyche, in my entire being. I've existed in all and in a variety of these fashions from thirteen to thirty-three. I have not found a definite answer, know no absolute. Rather, I've taken the view that my life, my existence is a job; making the continual attentiveness to my partner's emotions and well-being a priority, not solely for her, but for myself as well. I would never have voiced this in my life previously (though that may be inaccurate): I have learned that it's possible to love myself. To say, all right violence, you've had your limelight, now it's time for you to take the backseat and observe for the remainder of the trip. As for anger, it can always take the helm while I watch the passing landscape.

The excuse that I used in order to leave the "childhood writing" workshop early was my adverse reaction to the strange and unfamiliar patty-cake sort of activity that ensued after the timed writing exercise. I won't recount the details of the activity because I didn't understand the activity and have no ken of it. I was unable to access anything after the prompt about childhood because it had triggered my non-responsiveness, my retreat. Here is why, which some may have already inferred up to this point, I retreated. Beginning with my early childhood on the Navajo Nation in Window Rock, Arizona, I was sexually and physically abused at the age of three or four by a neighbor who babysat me and her cousin, and by an older boy at a Catholic School I attended. After moving to Flagstaff, Arizona, at the age of five or six my abuse continued with another babysitter whose eldest son welcomed me into his gang (though I wasn't ever actually a gang member aside from his kicking my ass; he was a sixth grader and I in preschool), and finally by two older cousins, first by a female, then a male; all of this until eight, nine, or ten. These years are all blurred to me. And not every instance was of a single occurrence, some lasted summers, some lasted years. I prayed to Jesus, to the Virgin Mary, to God, to the archangels Michael and Gabriel, to the Hopi Kachinas I'd memorized for some reason, and not one answered. So I prayed to Satan, or darkness, the idea and story of being cast out, of being the knower of a knowledge that was poison or a different kind of light. Eventually, I stopped praying, "believing." Christianity, Catholicism, organized religion are systems of colonization. I felt/feel that they made the colonized feel guilty, evil, yearn for forgiveness, judge one another, and base their ideals on an existence that is greater than this earth. Did I mention that I stopped praying, stopped believing? Nowadays, I wake before or with the sun and I pray to it, to the sky, to the earth. I don't always know what I'm saying, but at least I know what each hasn't done to me.

Decolonization and love seem like unlikely partners or unique inner demons. But that, too, is erroneous. Since that workshop, that trigger, I've read and read and read, which is one of the ways that I've taught myself empathy, that and thousands of dollars worth of counseling, EMDR, failed prescriptions by a clinical psychologist (I was prescribed an experimental delivery system, meaning pill, of Risperdal and a shitload of Xanax after expressing a history of addiction to pharmaceuticals that culminated in my trying to shoot myself at twenty-seven and my gun stovepipe jammed, and having worked up the nerve to transcend the fear of it, shit and vomited all over myself and laid in my kitchen alone for a couple days), and finally cognitive and behavioral therapy.

I've learned to forgive myself or to let play that scene in *Good Will Hunting* where Matt Damon's character is having a sort of breakdown and Robin Williams, as the school-of-hard-knocks doctor, consoles Damon's character, telling him something along the lines of *It's not your fault, it's not your fault*. A scene that one of my first girlfriends in high school played for me, as if the simple act of viewing it would dispel the hallucinations, both visual and auditory, that I developed as a result of the years of repressed memories and trauma. Hallucinations that lasted for years, that caused night terrors I still deal with (though significantly less frequently), that helped me hate, that compounded my anger, that led me to two suicide attempts (the first at twenty with Jack Daniels and Demerol, a trip in an ambulance to the ER, stomach pumps, IVs, rehydrating suppositories, and my first required visit to a counselor), that led me to live my life in parentheticals and footnotes, though there are no footnotes here because footnotes are another colonizer, as Junot Díaz illumed to us in *The Brief and Wondrous Life of Oscar Wao*. Decolonization is violent, it is spiritual unrest, it is for me the other side of the river, the western lands. William S. Burroughs, in what is regarded as his finest work since *Naked Lunch* (though this can be argued heatedly), writes in the culminating sections of *The Western Lands* (published 1987 by Penguin Books):

> I want to reach the Western Lands—right in front of you, across the bubbling brook. It's a frozen sewer. It's known as the Duad, remember? All the filth and horror, fear, hate, disease and death of human history flows between you and the Western Lands. Let it flow! My cat Fletch stretches behind me on the bed. A tree like black lace against a gray sky. A flash of joy.
>
> How long does it take a man to learn that he does not, cannot want what he "wants"?
>
> You have to be in Hell to see Heaven. Glimpses from the Land of the Dead, flashes of serene timeless joy, a joy as old as suffering and despair. (257–58)

In a way, and even more so for others, decolonization can be the recognition, the recovering of a time between "filth and horror," "disease and death of human history"; a bold way to say this would be, a time before Columbus, the Slave Trade, the sugar trade, Christianity, Thanksgiving, Manifest Destiny, massacres, forced walks, displacement, reservations, scorched earth campaigns, boarding schools, oil and coal companies, uranium, superpower, the Washington Redskins and Chief Wahoo, the KXL pipeline, the femicide of Indigenous women, and on and on and on. A time when we were able to kill one another fashionably, with "honor" because fuck all that noble savage bullshit. Humans have a beef, sure, but the greater evil will always be greed and "power." "You have to be in Hell to see Heaven." You have to know the devil before you know the savior, and sometimes vice versa, but you have to know the colonizer before comprehending the destruction of angels and the angelic; the acceptance that there's no reward after this life, only this life.

After completely ditching the workshop and opting for a drink outside on the patio of the Hotel Congress, haunted by the myths of John Dillinger, some of us poets sat, talked shit, and negotiated the events for the evening that remained. A writer, not Diné, but Blackfeet from Montana said something along the lines of *you never ask a Native to talk about their childhood. That's Indigenous 101. You think life on the reservation is pretty? Fuck that. Natives never talk about their childhoods*. In the days that I've been composing this, erratically and with disregard to other life obligations, thanks to all the literary-triggers, I've thought of two things. The first was triggered by the workshop, of course, and Orlando White himself, though not at that specific moment, but by the memory of the words and images from the first poem, "To See Letters," from his debut collection *Bone Light*. The speaker's stepfather calling him by his middle name so as to dehumanize him, the speaker's fascination with letters, his physical abuse at the hands of his stepfather, his adolescent ability to forgive, and the final stanza: "When David hit me in the head, I saw stars in the shape of the // Alphabet. Years later, my fascination for letters resulted in poems." This is decolonization. The violence we mirror on ourselves and others nulled.

The second is the hardcore band Converge, whose discography I've listened to exclusively in writing this, but more specifically the song "All We Love We Leave Behind" from their latest album of the same name. It's about the singer Jacob Bannon's loss of one of his dogs, which he had for the majority of its life. What's important about this for me is that dogs have always been one of the few solaces I've had. I think of protection, love, family. Not property or accessory. I think of the days of sleeplessness and exhaustion. I think that one day I'll figure out how all this happened.

NATANYA ANN PULLEY

Credit: Natanya Ann Pulley

NATANYA ANN PULLEY (b. 1976) is Kinyaa'áani and born for bilagáana; her maternal grandfather is Táchii'nii and her paternal grandfather is bilagáana. She is an assistant professor of English at Colorado College in Colorado Springs and earned her PhD in creative writing from the University of Utah in 2013. Her first published work in 1998 was a lyrical nonfiction piece, "Earth Body," selected by *Scribendi*, an undergraduate journal at the University of New Mexico. Pulley has published fiction and nonfiction in numerous journals including the *Collagist*, *Drunken Boat*, the *Offing*, *McSweeney's*, *Waxwing*, and *As/Us*. Her work has been anthologized in *#NotYourPrincess: Voices of Native American Women*, *Exquisite Vessel*, *Shapes of Native Nonfiction*, *Women Write Resistance*, and more. Pulley is a former editor of *Quarterly West* and *South Dakota Review* and a guest editor of the horror journal *Black Candies: Gross and Unlikeable* (a special issue with all female writers and artists). She is the founding editor of Colorado College's online literary journal *Hairstreak Butterfly Review*. Her short story collection *With Teeth* was selected as a winner of the 2017 Many Voices Project competition and was published in 2019 by New Rivers Press.

In an interview after the announcement of this award, Pulley discussed her influences: "I engage in a tradition of storytelling, in which the narrators are teasing out the idea of what it means to be part of a story. I believe this comes from hearing my Diné mom's stories, which were a lovely mess of Navajo traditions woven through family histories and her assimilation experience as part of a program that removed young Navajo children from the reservation to live with LDS families in Utah. . . . Time was never linear in any of these stories and in the Diné way, there were no explicit morals or endings to these stories. Instead, she would gather her perspective of the world through these patchwork tellings."

Interview

What do you hope readers learn from your writing?

I'm not sure a reader learns from *my* writing as much as they learn *to listen to themselves*. As readers, we listen to when a sentence is striking or an image feels alive. Listen for when an idea resonates. Writing is never just writing, but also listening. I feel we—writers and readers—share this space.

How does the Navajo language influence your work?

I didn't grow up in a Navajo-speaking household or area. It was something that came when we were visiting family and when my mother would find the words at times. She was shamed for speaking it, so I didn't hear it often. I did though pick up on her intonations and inflections and the syntax and flow of language she used. I see that in my work. I also grew up knowing there was a different word for things—a word that spoke to a people and culture in ways that English cannot and does not. So, I still wonder when I choose a word—if there is another that captures my idea not just more completely, but through a philosophy of what a word is and can create one's reality. And I imagine how I can stretch the English language to a breaking point or turn a word around on itself so many times that it becomes useless unless grounded in a people and place.

Who or what inspires you?

Sound more than anything else inspires me. Even when I think it is quiet, there is the sound of air and vibration. When I give in to the sound, it becomes easier to allow all things to inspire me because all the images and sensations and story ideas respond to the sound or rhythm or pattern I am experiencing. There's a lawnmower outside. My dog shuddering in his sleep. The clicking of my keyboard. A small squeak in my chair. There's a story here, but it starts with sensing these vibrations. There is no other inspiration than opening up so willingly to our own senses.

What advice do you have for beginning writers?

Read a lot. Read widely. Read and listen. Then read your own work aloud and listen for your voice. Grow your voice as you would anything else: with time, practice, failures and successes, guesswork and expertise, with fear, love, and patience. And wonder.

Who was the first Diné writer you read?

Shimasani's letters to shima.

What was your favorite book in high school? What are you reading now?

The *Sandman* graphic novel series in high school. I liked a lot of fantasy too (*Dragonlance!*), but I had a hard time reading the books assigned and the classics. It took a lot of concentration and I didn't always understand what I was reading. It wasn't just that I didn't relate, the language was hard to understand. So, I liked graphic novels best. I try to read a few books at a time: *Where the Dead Sit Talking* (Brandon Hobson); *New Poets of Native Nations* (Heid E. Erdrich); *Loteria: A Novel* (Mario Alberto Zambrano); *The Lost Daughter Collective* (Lindsay Drager).

⩧

In This Dream of Waking, a Weaver

None of Klea's limbs or bones answered her. She lay like a stone being demanding her spine to obey. The ceiling, a new coldness threatening to fall on top of her. The shadows of the commemorative military plates and the clay-horned toads mounted on her wall sank into the same darkness of the corners of the room. She didn't know where the soft light was coming from, but only that it must have been behind the figures surrounding her. They grew and shrank as she tried to form sounds and cries. Nothing. A self un-mouthed. Numb tongue.

Klea thought she was accustomed to her reoccurring sleep paralysis. She'd experienced it nearly every night since she could remember. She thought the dream intruders in her room were familiar by now. Familiar like the presence of bodies hustling around bus stations and grocery stores. There was always a space made in her half-sleep for some form to come to being. After breaking from her paralysis, she would remember it as if she were on the slab, an autopsy, and the intruder: a cataloguer of flesh and organ and the data offerings of bone.

Tonight's occurrence was different. The figures morphed and duplicated into a murky halo around her, instead of their usual dark errand of stillness and observance. She could not make out the faces or clothes, but they seemed to her to be shades of all the same family members from earlier that day. And instead of the tidal noise of storytellers, the figures were silent—voices held. A veil of quiet holding back a planet of sound—for now.

Klea could only whimper at them. No answering limbs or circuitry to help her jump from her bed and put the family figures back in a line. Back in a brightly lit room—that conference room in a hotel in Shiprock. A place for all the Tohonnie family members to gather. Four days, she had been there. Video recorders. Laptops. Papers and pens. Anything to help document. Not for any agency or foundation, but for herself. She wanted to pull her people and their stories and connections, like streamers into one giant well-planned party. Many times she'd sped through Navajoland listening to her mother's stories. Her mom never took a break from talking at her. "Back there is your auntie Bess's first hogan with Rodge Cowboy," and "Your grandfather walked me through this field, corn and watermelon before the easement," and "Cousin Rita lived here but not for long, not long, I think." Those stories crowding Klea for hours—never hearing one specific family member's life story and no resting places between time, people, or events. She had stepped on the gas harder hoping to speed through the area. Speed to a destination with only one story: she at her Uncle's with her mom. The new puppy litter, sandy and talkative. The cousin's baby boy quiet with a wide reach and strong hands for pulling hair.

No more winding and racing through her mom's stories. No more asking again which of her grandfather's sixteen brothers a cousin belonged. No more sensing of rifts and bit lips and mental walkouts when other members of the family were mentioned or spotted near town as if they had stepped out of an ether of shame or past slights or lost journeys. Her mother's explanations were a barbed wire warping and tightening along the washboard, red-dirt roads between Flagstaff and Shiprock.

But this family conference! This gathering! This "Stop by for a picture!" The great documentation! She would write down the names and dates of the sprawled and rising family. Would set up the laptop for those ready to record their own lines and connections. Would help the elderlies to softer chairs, warm cups of coffee, and would be patient—take in the sounds and smells of bodies busy with living, before she would point to pictures and ask who was who, and the wheres, and the whens.

To Klea this thing was an escape from trying to soak up all the stories. She could remember some moments here and there, but she could never remember the names, the areas, the faces. It was as if she was never built for stories that weren't on a screen, played out in front of her. As if the only stories she wrote were some one hundred-ish characters long or heavy with texting shorthand. Bits. Her notions of family scared her. Relatives would morph into giant immortals, too full of a presence to relate to—like the ones surrounding her bed, as she didn't yet sleep, but could not move or scream or seem to breathe. Her nightly ritual of horror: sleep paralysis. She entered a sleeping world as a waking being.

Today had been the last of the four days. She'd lost sight of the project and stumbled throughout the room. Talked out, she checked recording devices and took pictures. At first she'd captured as many relatives in a shot as possible, then walked over and wrote down everyone's name. Some she recognized from visits prior. Others from Facebook. One or two seemed like faces that were always around her in one way or another. A trace of family, a possibility space culled together from what must have been memory and resemblance.

In the corner of the conference room was a type of prison. It was her idea and no one—not her mother, not her closest aunt or most outspoken cousin—suggested she not do it. She was resentful when she looked at the corner—with its long blue sheet hanging from the wall and to the side of it, a slouching table with her newly purchased clipboard. She wanted everyone's pictures. One at a time. Facing forward. Name on the clipboard, all the names: given, assumed, teased, and changed. Corralling the data, the dates and places of birth, when available.

No one went to the corner. No one asked about it. All Klea knew was that it was, somehow, a place of shadow. Why had no one said anything? Why do they let her do these criminal things that to her seem to put the world into clearer spaces with borders and definitions? Facts. She just wanted to click on each relative's picture and understand immediately their place and therefore her place in this world. Her grandfather had sixteen brothers. Her grandmother sixteen sisters. This family, a jumble of yarn, didn't have to exhaust her the way it did. If only she could document—

When Klea could not sneak outside or to the bathroom, she drummed a line in her head: "At least we have plenty recorded. Plenty recorded. Plenty recorded." The drumming came at the height of her anxiety—when her hands felt like shaking and when she began to notice too many things, like the smell of horses and peppermint or the gang tattoos she could only assume made sense in another type of family—one pulled together through blood ritual and world-dreams. When she began vibrating into a panic, she was drawn to the crushed red velvet of her great-great auntie's blouse. Wanted to hold it between her fingers and think of bimá sání and how easy it was to just sit near her silently. Never needing to know anything, but what it felt like to take up a space next to grandma and to smell of coffee and flour. To rush to the barrel of water outside the hogan and fill a tin mug with cool water. Shoo away the kitten at her foot.

Great-Great auntie isn't correct. The terminology, that is. *What am I to her?* Klea thought and tugged her jeans back up from falling off her hips.

Auntie Evie squeezed her hand and leaned in close. When Evie spoke, Klea's vowels took a new shape. Some ended more abruptly. She paused more when speaking. Threaded words and dragging sounds disappeared and instead, she found her language slowed to plateauing formations. She spoke with the shape of the mesas surrounding her grandmother's home, flat and even, then a slow rising to a new type of flat and even—one closer to the sky. Evie's lips and chin clenched briefly as she motioned to the elderly woman. Her voice dropped. She said the woman told another cousin yesterday that Uncle Tyrone Jr. was not really one of the brothers. Evie's voice trailed off and she mumbled and giggled while still squeezing Klea's hand.

The last group of people to leave took the rest of the food with them. Klea and her mother helped carry the sandwich meats and breads, the muffins, soda, and uncut watermelon to their car and piled it all in next to a bag of dog food and some school supplies. Just moments before when Klea could no longer remember the name of anyone she met that day and was wishing for the firm squeeze of her aunt Evie's hand, Klea's mom had rushed up to her still talking to herself. Mid-story. Something about a playfriend her mother remembered, if only slightly. A girl she would call "big sister" and a corral with a billy goat that wouldn't stop yelling and bucking. They called the goat Shideezhí after the girl's younger sister whom they would hide from until she was so mad she'd yell and throw rocks at them as soon as she found them.

She met the new "big sister" and her daughters and a young boy that was in the care of one of the daughters though it was unclear to Klea why or how. As her mom chattered away at the woman and her daughters, Klea smiled politely and wrote down the names of each person in the group, but the letters were caught up in one another and she knew she wouldn't be able to read her own handwriting later. When the young boy began tugging at one of the daughters and pleading to her that it was time to go, Klea mentally began doing the same to her own mother. The group was nice, but for Klea she had long since hid inside her a self that welcomed new friends and new family. Instead, she simply wanted some factual reality. Who was who. Where was where. When was when. The young boy's hand was sticky from a gumball and Klea opted to kiss the little fellow on the cheek instead of shake his hand. A brief moment with her lips close to his face, his cheeks plump and fresh, his skin smelling a little sweat-stained, but also wind-worn: like he'd stuck his head out the window during the drive for whatever reason the young seek a wind that drowns out all else but the blood of the working body. Klea's instinct was to scoop up the child and run off with him for more trading post fire gumballs and to nap in the shade. The sound of bimá sání spitting sunflower seed shells pulled fresh from the past to the now.

As Klea and her mom gathered up the disposable cameras, they counted two missing, but found two neon pink hair clips. They also found a scarf—not the soft and lustrous kind bought from a trendy corner of the internet, but the sheer and itchy gauze ones that her grandmother tucked between her mattress and the wall of the hogan—the ones she had thrown around her head and tied under the chin in a whip of a moment.

When it came time to take down the corner photo area, Klea stumbled over there alone; she swore and sweated and tugged at the sheet when it caught here and there on the generic framed prints of mesas and sand dunes that adorned the hotel wall. She was clumsy as she tried to silence the still-too-loud whisper of cotton sheet against the hardwood floor. She folded the paper from the clipboard and tucked it into her back pocket, not wanting to throw it away, fearful someone might spot it in the trash.

Klea's mom found the event to be a success. She gushed as she listed the people and interrupted herself with branches of stories or notes of interest. An uncle was unable to come, but he sent a list of people he remembered to be his cousins when he was younger and before his mother died and his stepmother died and the woman that lived with his father for several years unmarried died.

The list was buried in the backseat next to notebooks and folders and her mom's last-minute road trip kit of bandages and safety pins and homemade round neck pillows for all the grandmothers. They buckled up slowly, arms exhausted and distracted by the sudden end of sound and movement and sugared pastries.

"Can you believe it?" her mom repeated. "I just can't believe it."

Klea didn't stop nodding, cracked the window and took in the dry road air, held it in her chest until it burned. She used her turning signal longer than she needed to and she snapped at her mother each time she was told where to turn or how fast to go when Klea already knew the way and could read the signs.

Back at her mother's house, Klea was grateful (and only somewhat ashamed by it) when her mother finally mentioned having a headache from the excitement and Klea set a small cup of Diet Coke and some ibuprofen next to her mother's bed. She turned the TV on low and closed the drapes. "I'm glad we didn't have the family here," her mother said. "I told you there wasn't enough room here. And now we can rest." As Klea closed the bedroom door behind her, she could hear her mother's cell phone whistle and woo and her mom's winged voice start once again, mid-story, mid-life, mid-whisk.

I'm horrible. Klea knew and repeated this as she changed into her PJs, as she flew through TV stations, recognizing almost every show by just one character or the music or the setting. And she certainly knew she was still a horrible person later that night when she lay paralyzed in bed with the morphing beings around her. They didn't move closer to her on their own, but the room began to shrink and soon they seemed almost on top of her. She couldn't stop the space around her from retreating. Instead she whimpered and found her throat full of wool.

Klea jerked awake and scared off the small long-haired chihuahua that was nestled up against her thigh. She could hear the click click of the creature's claws as he skidded out of the guest room and around a corner and nudged at the bedroom door where her mother was (hopefully) asleep. She turned on the bedroom light, urging the disappointed and waiting figures from the room.

She could use a site like ancestry.com or perhaps build her own family chart through any one of her design programs. She could write it all out on a large piece of paper. But the idea of compressing her family history into data or lines on a page felt cheap and easy. Klea did not want to feel cheap nor did she want to be the kind that takes the easy road. She wanted to be the sort of person to go to a four-day gathering with her own blood and not so much flit about like her mother, but perhaps sidle up to people and smile and make them feel at ease. Her older brother could always do such things, but could never get time off of work, and actually if he had been there, Klea would have felt even more incompetent than she already did.

No, she wanted something organic. Some way of remembering that her mother seemed to have. Some way of grasping these histories and planting them inside her to let them grow and show their own signs of genus and pollination. Klea wanted to be an earth thing, something of soil and water. Of coded and bursting cells. And of light-made, force-made trembling, growing branches.

"Like a fucking family tree," she said aloud.

Klea slumped and cried. She felt like she was five and crying over nothing in particular, like she wanted to drop the thing she was crying over and let it crack against the floor when it fell . . . only to cry harder. The kind of tears only another child would have: a fresh, heavy wetness to them that comes from nearing an absence in one's life, a space not yet ready to be filled with alcohol or work or gossip or feel-good and horror movies or even an addiction to serving others. Perhaps that adopted or foster-care boy would recognize such crying as his own. His black hair and skin the color of pinon shells reflected in those around him, but tugging at the adult nearest. His forced inclusion into the room of voices murmuring and sometimes a singer. Sometimes a singer out of nowhere like her grandmother's blind and half-paralyzed sister would sing. The middle of a conversation. The middle of a car-ride. A tremble song. The young boy and Klea never knowing what is going to happen next—do they shut up and listen? Do they sing along? Should her younger sister stop giggling? And instead looking out the car window, heads pressed to the cold glass, watching the long song of sand and blushing pink rock, the occasional curious horse looking back at them. And the way Klea would yank at the old Wagoneer's window handle and stick her head out as they neared her grandmother's home. Yell at the dogs to stay clear from the tires and hop out before the car came to a complete stop. She and that now-and-always family boy sharing a planet, sharing a sun.

In the dining room of her mom's house, Klea scribbled the young boy's name and the names of the people he was with on a notecard and tacked it to the wall. This, her mother's "I call her big sister" family. She included Shideezhí the goat on the corner of the card. She began shuffling the rest of the note cards until another name came to her. Klea wrote it down and tacked it to the wall. As the names started piling up and more details from the last four days popped into her head here and there, she wrote everything on cards and tacked them close to a name or in another section of unknowns. Someone had new shoes the color of asphalt and pink neon. Another had dimples that threatened to swallow the rest of the young girl's face. On a note card: the types of smiles: smirks, full and lipped, the smells: hay, coffee, the distinct smell of freshly printed paper, tobacco, rose perfume, flour, and cedar. The overheard words and phrases, the woman that always nodded, the man that was always leaning, the other man that would take her hand, but instead of shaking it, would hold it with both of his as if to hold her rather than greet her. All the partial-handshakes, the soft hellos. The names, so many boarding school names: Luther, Jermaine, Dorothea, Erwin, Neil, Laverne. And then Many-Goats, Nez, Yazzie, Tapaha, Singer.

Her purple marker ran out of thick ink-soaked lines and Klea rushed to find a red one. A black permanent one. And string. Yes, string. Before she could forget, Klea fastened the end of the string from one name to another. Sometimes pulling the string taut, sometimes too much and cursing while she re-fastened the string to the first card. Sometimes the string had to arc over other strings or droop down to the floor when she couldn't recall much more about the person. She used white string and blue. Sometimes yellow and black. As she moved around the room, she'd glimpse a pattern and lose it again. She'd feel a momentum building and lose it to a long battle of weaving strings and cue cards and repositioning. No no no, Vince is related to the Chinle area people though he came from Red Lake. No no, this sister is really the mother someone said. But too young, so too young to be a mother then. She is only mother here on this wall and along the hushed conversation of the four-day gathering. As if the side talk and the hints and questions had tumbled from the great gathering into these threads of Klea's made graceful, but solid. Soft, but structural.

In this dream of making—this surge after her paralysis—the sun did not rise, and when Klea felt done enough to sit back into the archway to the dining room, she could not help but imagine herself a clever, spinning thing. An ancient thread-generating incarnation. As if she did have eight legs to smooth these lines throughout the room. As if she was blessed with many eyes, small and large, light-absorbing rows of them to take in the work of the room. With more practice, with more time, with more blessing ways, she could learn to weave this thing into funnels, orbs or sheets. Pull the loose bits tighter and adjust the corners.

A family tree, she thought. How absurd. How unnatural. As if a branch of her bloodline could ever end. As if a tree was still a tree without sensing a forest. As if there could never be family in the treeless parts of the desert. Rather, this web. Stronger than steel, but slight and delicate. A ballooning thing. A thing made and remade and recovered and made new throughout generations. Split generations, lost ones, folded ones, brightening ones, all. And the only thing prey to this pulsing system was that version of Klea who built a photo ID area—an internment, that cold preservation of letters and numbers and attempts to capture the surface of a person. That fly. The resurrected census, a nothing process compared to this heavy dance of thread.

DANIELLE GELLER

Credit: Marie Hathaway

DANIELLE GELLER (b. 1986) is Tsi'naajinii, born for the bilagáana. She was born in West Palm Beach, Florida, and has lived in Florida, Pennsylvania, Massachusetts, and Arizona, where she completed her MFA in nonfiction at the University of Arizona in 2017. She is an assistant professor of writing at the University of Victoria, in British Columbia, Canada, as well as a faculty mentor at the Institute of American Indian Arts. Her first published work, in 2013, was an essay titled "Ya'at'eeh, I Say," in *Silk Road Review*, a project first begun in 2007 as an undergraduate at Shippensburg University, about her disconnection from the Navajo language and culture and her dissatisfaction with her mother's answers when she tried to ask her questions about both. A thread in that essay inspired what became "Blood; Quantum." Her work has also appeared in *Brevity* and the anthology *This Is the Place* (Seal Press, 2017); "Annotating the First Page of the First Navajo-English Dictionary" was published in the *New Yorker* in 2017, and her essay "The Origin of My Laugh" was published in a 2020 issue of the *Paris Review*. She is a recipient of the prestigious 2016 Rona Jaffe Foundation Writers' Award.

Geller's *Dog Flowers* (2021) is a memoir of her return to the Navajo reservation after the death of her mother. In an interview, Geller notes, "She left us when we were really little and she didn't like talking about her childhood or growing up on the reservation. . . . After she died, I inherited her diaries. . . . She was not the person I thought she was and [I] started understanding why she left the reservation, why she left me and my sister, why she couldn't stay and take care of us. I learned more about her and I am like my mother, I am this person, I can see her in me." Geller's memoir deconstructs family myths and honors the complexities and truths of her past and her personal and cultural heritage.

Interview

What do you hope readers learn from your writing?

Because I feel like I still have so much to learn—about my mother's family, culture, and history—I often try to shift the authority in my essays. This might be a holdover from my brief life as a librarian. In my essays, I'm always pointing to other storytellers, writers, and teachers, like: Look! Read Kim TallBear! Admire this Heid Erdrich poem! I want to share the places I am looking with my reader and teach them how to look.

How does the Navajo language influence your work?

Because I was raised on the East Coast by my white grandmother, I come to the Navajo language as an outsider. My mother was never taught to speak the language, either, but you could always hear an echo of it in her voice: the way she structured sentences, the cadence of her speech. I loved to listen to my mother talk. But I don't have an affinity for learning language, and I doubt I will ever be fluent in Navajo, so I use it sparingly in my work. The language becomes sound and texture because my understanding of words' meanings is so incomplete.

Who or what inspires you?

If the question is what inspires me to write, the answer is "a question." When I write, I am usually trying to solve a puzzle about a memory; a conversation; a pattern of behavior I or someone I love has fallen into. Human behavior is life's biggest mystery to me.

What advice do you have for beginning writers?

Be aware of the frame. Even if what you are writing feels like a standard narrative, a story that follows Aristotle's inciting, rising, and falling arc, pay attention to the historical, cultural, political, religious forces that influence your perspective and, thereby, shape the story you tell. What have you chosen to leave out, and what have you chosen to include? What information about yourself have you given to the reader, and what don't they know about you? Especially in creative nonfiction, where the distance between the writer and the writing is smaller, these questions are important to ask.

Who was the first Diné writer you read?

Laura Tohe's *No Parole Today*!

What was your favorite book in high school? What are you reading now?

My favorite book in high school was Gabriel García Márquez's *One Hundred Years of Solitude*, which led me to writers like Isabel Allende and Salman Rushdie. I have a deep love and appreciation for speculative writing, including science fiction! The book I'm reading right now is Jordy Rosenberg's *Confessions of the Fox*, which combines my love of alternative historical fictions and footnotes.

Blood; Quantum

A few days before I turned three years old, my mother and my father packed my younger sister, my cat, and me into a car to drive from Florida to Window Rock, Arizona, to visit my mother's family on the reservation, and to register me and my sister with the Navajo Nation. The cat jumped out of the car somewhere in Texas, and my father was bitten on the leg by a brown recluse spider, and he was arrested on an old warrant and did a stint in jail, but we made it to the reservation otherwise intact. My few memories of that visit have been pieced together from stories I've been told, but I do have two lasting artifacts from our only trip home: a photograph of my mother, my grandfather, her two brothers, and me, standing in the yard behind my mother's childhood home, and my Certificate of Indian Blood.

What the certificate proves is that I have 1/2 degree Navajo Indian blood, and my Census Roll Number is 636,234. If the records were public information, you could find my name on page 557 of the Southern Navajo Indian Census Roll, and below it, my sister's. The only thing the Census Roll got wrong was my birthdate: not July 29th but the 28th, though it's unclear if the mistake was the technician's or my mother's.

What the certificate proves is almost nothing.

Nearly two years later, on May 3, 1991, Florida's Office of Vital Statistics issued me a new birth certificate, forty days after the courts granted my white grandmother legal custody of my sister and me. It wasn't much of a court battle—my parents, separated and alcoholics both, agreed to surrender their parental rights before the case ever saw a judge. The only thing Florida's vital statistic clerk got wrong was my name: not Danielle April Geller but Danielle Geller, though I know for certain it was my grandmother who forgot the name my mother gave me.

When people asked me, over the years, if I had a secret Indian name, I should have given them my middle: April, T'ááchil, when wind blows life back into the desert.

But a few years after the adoption, my grandmother moved us to a little town called Yoe, in central Pennsylvania, the whitest place on earth. My mother was hundreds of miles away, and her family even farther.

I did not know my blood clans; I did not know my family, not by name or by sight or by laugh; I did not know their traditions; I did not know their language; I did not know what portion of history to call my own.

But once, as I sat in the empty hallway of my middle school, an older man stopped in front of me and said: Are you Native American? I'd bet anything you are. When I said yes, he just smiled and moved on. And once, when I was fifteen and cleaning tables at Hardee's, a white-haired man in a baseball cap looked up from his biscuits and gravy and said hello in my mother's language, in words I didn't recognize. I stared at him in confusion until he told me he had worked on the reservation and married a Navajo woman many years back. And once, when I was sixteen and cleaning the snow off my grandmother's car, my Hopi neighbor walked down the driveway and announced: You must be a Navajo woman. Weeks later, as he showed me through his two-bedroom apartment, he confided that he had always wanted an Indian mother for his sons. And once, when I told the Mexican man on the bus that I was not Latina but Native American, he asked me to what degree, and when I said half, he said:

Good. That means the blood isn't too thick. But once, when I came home with a barbell through my tongue and a ring through my nose, my white grandmother said, in disgust, "It must be the *Indian* in you," which was always cheerlessly funny to me because I never felt Indian at all.

RACHEL HEATHER JOHNSON

Credit: @HeatherJohnson

RACHEL HEATHER JOHNSON (b. 1986) is from Sheep Springs, New Mexico, located in the juniper-studded eastern foothills of the Chuska Mountains. She is a mother, daughter, sister, niece, aunt, granddaughter, and great-granddaughter. She belongs to the Táchii'nii clan and is born for Kinyaa'àanii; her maternal grandfather is Tsenabahi ł nii and her paternal grandfather is Bit'ahnii. She writes poetry, fiction, and nonfiction and won *Prairie Schooner*'s 2017 Summer Nonfiction Contest. She is working on a memoir that investigates the intersection between Western psychology and Diné spirituality. She is also writing a literary murder mystery, tentatively titled *Ash*, which is dedicated to missing and murdered Indigenous peoples. Johnson's work grapples with issues of identity, surviving personal and historical trauma, systemic inequalities, the complexities of mental health and well-being, and the land as sacred. Her experiences as a sociology research assistant, sexual assault victim advocate, and child protective services social worker also inform her writing. Her first published poem, "Skin Like Mine," appeared in Sigma Tau Delta's *Rectangle* (2016). Since then, her work has been published in *Prairie Schooner*, *HeArt (Human Equity Through Art)*, *Anti-Heroin Chic*, and *Writers Resist*. She is an avid student of kajukenbo and a founding member of the Trigger Warning

Writers Group. Johnson graduated with an MFA from the University of New Mexico's Creative Writing Program in Albuquerque, New Mexico, in 2020.

Interview

What do you hope readers learn from your writing?

Empathy. Art/writing's purpose is to humanize us. I want the reader to be open to understanding what it is to be an Indigenous person navigating life in a Western society, which is often at odds with a lot of our values. I want the reader to recognize herself in my work and I hope that resonance catalyzes their own art/writing.

When you are writing, how does the Navajo language influence your work?

When I'm writing about home/the reservation or about my family, I tend to incorporate Navajo to anchor the pieces, particularly in my poetry. It's important that I, as a Native American writer, consciously include Navajo in my writing. Use of Navajo then becomes an assertion of identity that has been historically suppressed; it's empowering.

Who or what inspires you?

I tend to write a lot about the complexities of mental health and social justice issues. Right now, I'm writing a novel about a young Navajo woman who's struggling to live in the aftermath of her mother's racially motivated murder, which takes place in the border town of Farmington, New Mexico. The book speaks to the disturbing and overlooked phenomenon of missing and murdered Indigenous women (MMIW).

What advice do you have for beginning writers?

Write as if you were going to die tomorrow. Write fiercely, unapologetically. The way to write originally is to write in your own voice. And that is simply honed by the act of writing. Make writing a habit, try to do it daily. Always keep a writer's journal at hand.

What was your favorite book in high school? What are you reading now?

My favorite books were Anne Rice's *Chronicles of the Mayfair Witches*, three books including *Lasher*, *Taltos*, and *The Witching Hour*. Right now, I'm reading Anne Sexton's collected poems, *The Art of Memoir* by Mary Karr, Kiese Laymon's *How to Slowly Kill Yourself and Others in America*, and *An Unquiet Mind* by Kay Redfield Jamison.

Who was the first Diné writer you read?

Laura Tohe. Her work is phenomenal, especially her poems and writings about the devastating impact Western educational systems have on Native American children.

Apple

In fourth grade Mr. Wilson
grabbed my cousin Terry by the sleeve
of his camouflage Salvation Army jacket and threw
him out of his desk, to the floor.
The desk tilted and then righted
itself. We, all Navajo students, learned then
not to laugh, not to say anything
at all.

When I was six, I watched my mother
wash apples in the sink. She held
the weight of each
one in the palm of her worn,
brown hand, and rolled each one so it shimmered,
glazed in water.

She handed them to me and I
stacked them in a wooden
fruit bowl. They were almost too large
for my hands—I had to use both to cradle

them. I imagined
that they were what hearts
looked like, felt like, tasted like—heavy,
heavy, too rich and too sweet, with a crisp
core that breaks too cleanly.

She found one with a brown spot that collapsed
under the pressure
of her finger. She scooped out the rotted
piece with her thumb and rinsed it
into the drain, afterwards sucking
the residue off her finger. *You have to take*
out the bad part, but the apple
is still good.

In ninth grade, Mr. Carter, the high
school coach, reached into
the core of me, corrupting
me. And, because I'd been taught
silence in fourth grade, it was a weapon,
razor-keen, which I cut
myself against.

During my college freshman
year, I tried my best
to fit in with the Native students,
many of whom could speak their native
languages. I couldn't get past good
morning—*Yaa'a'teeh abini.* They
rolled their eyes and called me
apple. Years later, a friend told me what
it meant—red on the outside,
white on the inside.

Nowhere Place

This poem responds to the gruesome, racially motivated killing of two Navajo homeless men, Allison Gorman (Cowboy) and Kee Thompson (Rabbit), who were brutally beaten and murdered by three teenage Hispanic boys, here in Albuquerque, New Mexico, in 2014. The poem also honors their lives/hózhó.

I

At first your lives were only a sheer, crisp
line between death and blessing, one

which you traced with fingers in red dirt. Gradually,
it changed—became a place,

a weight you carried in backpacks that bowed
your spines. You unpacked it, slept in it, that vacant lot, cut

off by tilting, rusted chain-link fences and walls
of corrugated steel panels, where you three, Rabbit, Cowboy,

Eskeets, slept on a mattress, drinking and putting yourselves
to sleep sharing jokes, laughing, rapping, and singing our Native

songs, and, yes, reciting poetry. Street
family. Put aside, discarded, disregarded. Did you dream

you were fancy-dancing along the nowhere
border between the asphalt and the vaulted blue

sky? Closer to beauty, closer to blessing—hózhó.

II

Three teenage boys, willful, with the hot surge of hate
and alcohol, found you sleeping. They began to beat

you—one of you escaped. Rabbit and Cowboy remained
in that suspended space as those boys raised

cinderblocks over their heads and flung
them down. There were tree branches, a metal

pole, and finally knives. When they were done they threw
dirt into your eyes, a part of our sacred Mother

Earth—ni'hi'ma nahasdzaan—and she reclaimed
you both. A flimsy wooden cross, with the words "Jesus

Saves" painted sloppily in white, leans against
the fence. Deflated party balloons, red

and yellow, tangle along the wall. White lilies
bow over the weed-crowded dirt—hózhó

nahaasdlii—you walk in beauty above,
beauty behind, beauty around, and beauty

before you, with the cool breeze
on your bodies—it has become beauty again

Hers Was a History of Grief

She'd lost four husbands / as if they'd been misplaced
by death / she'd borne eleven children and outlived half

of them / a pair of twins had died in infancy / alcohol had a tendency
to take the others / Daniel, a father of four, died drinking

a fatal cocktail of hairspray and household cleaning
products / Diabetes and cirrhosis claimed Arlene

in her forties / A drunk driver crumpled Willard
inside of his silver '69 Shelby at a Colorado

pass / And in her storage room she hoarded
memories tucked on shelves behind opaque

glass / along with folded squares of mold-stained
lace and ceramic effigies of a mournful,

bleeding Christ / Each afternoon she drew out the artifact loaded
with life's grief / a black metallic helmet whose chin

strap and inner lining were discolored a dull
ocher / her youngest Gabe had driven his motorcycle into

the highway construction company's unmarked
barb-wire fence / it had caught him just beneath his

chinstrap / and she murmured prayers into them

PAIGE BUFFINGTON

Credit: Paige Buffington

PAIGE BUFFINGTON (b. 1987) is Nashashí and born for bilagáana. Her maternal grandfather is 'Áshįįhí and her paternal grandfather is bilagáana. Her family is originally from Tohatchi, New Mexico, a small town sitting at the base of the Chuska Mountains, a mountain range running north into Colorado from Gallup, New Mexico, where she currently lives. Buffington graduated from Gallup High School in 2005 and began working toward a degree in elementary education before deciding to pursue creative writing—a passion that started in junior high, ran throughout high school, and never left. She received a BFA in creative writing from the Institute of American Indian Arts in 2013 and an MFA with a focus in poetry in the summer of 2015. She first published three poems as an undergraduate in IAIA's 2009–10 anthology series, *Voyeurs of War.* Buffington is a recipient of the Truman Capote Fellowship. Her work has appeared in *Literary Hub*, *Connotation Press*, *Taos Journal of International Poetry and Art*, and *Hinchas de Poesia*. Her poem "All American Poem," published by *Narrative*, was named best Western poem by Western Writers of America for 2016. She is at work on her first book of poetry.

Buffington is an elementary school teacher. Most of her students are from the Rock Springs, China Springs, and Yatahey communities. She feels that her students teach her as much as she teaches them. At the end of each day, Buffington says she "leaves school with full heart, acknowledges the Chuska Mountains who can be seen just north of the school, and is happy to be home."

Interview

What do you hope readers learn from your writing?

I hope to take readers on journeys with each prose piece—I'm very interested in big narratives living in a consolidated space, in finding the beautiful shards inside troubled places, in pairing simple language alongside elegant language. I hope they read that there can be both.

How does the Navajo language influence your work?

The Navajo language's richness inspires me to be more descriptive with my writing. I could say October, *or* I could describe it as the time the seasons separate, the month's translation in Navajo. Providing this description of a month makes me want to write! The language has run through my life and the stories I've heard. It's going to be a part of my writing and influencing my stories even when I'm unaware.

Who or what inspires you?

When I was young, I spent summers traveling to the homes of different relatives with my grandmothers. They spent hours visiting, and telling stories. I try to write some of these images into my prose poems. Sometimes, I'll hear a part of a story (like playing the game of telephone), hold on to an image, and try to build upon that single image.

The desert landscape and its animals, old country songs, love stories, song lyrics, and traditional Navajo stories and their images are other inspirations.

What advice do you have for beginning writers?

I have struggled, and still sometimes struggle, with facing the story I want to tell. Don't be afraid to hit hard—the best stories are the ones that build and break our hearts. After you have written it—defend it. Believe in your story. Take your time. Navigate with grace.

Who was the first Diné writer you read?

My mom, Deenise Becenti, began her career as a journalist. Her written portrayals of people living all around the Navajo Nation and their stories trickled onto me. Irvin Morris's *From the Glittering World* and Sherwin Bitsui's *Shapeshift* were the next.

What was your favorite book in high school? What are you reading now?

I did not read much in high school. Anthony Kiedis's *Scar Tissue* was one I remember reading, among just a few others. I've been reading more flash fiction and nonfiction than poetry lately. I'm currently reading Leslie Marmon Silko's *The Turquoise Ledge*.

Your work included here seems informed or inspired by people in your life. What sort of reception have these works received from those who know you and know those who are represented? How did you acquire the bravery to write/speak with honesty and truth?

I always try to write with honesty. I have to be confident with my narratives and images and know that all of it is coming from an honest and good place. My family has been supportive and believe in my stories as well. Although, as mentioned above, I still struggle with facing the stories I want to tell.

At Mention of Moab

Dad sleeps in a fish-tin trailer. Fifty miles inside Utah state lines, diesels hum, split his spring-filled canteens. The restless highway winds wake the pages of a bedside bible, tear worn maps taped across aluminum walls. His fingertips know the textures of those rising paper mountains, the mesas, the thin blue lines of rivers—but wading waist-deep in their shimmering worlds is something he has always struggled to understand.

The insides of his lightless apartment once held our favorite landscapes—the horizon of a mattress, the curve of a barrel, a coffee cup. We sat in a rust-ringed bathtub, wrapped our arms around legs, hands around flashlights, we stayed warm together. Dad pulled the knife from his pocket, cut parade glow sticks in two, splattered their contents on the walls, created neon constellations. We loved the night on nights like these—tracing the ghost tails of meteors, the telescopes, our hair unbraided and shining. *Girls, one day, I'll go on a trip alone.*

For years, we left prayers around his tire rims, inside the envelopes stacked in his glovebox. We took his words into fists, blew them to the North. *This is what I'll do, I will go to Arizona or Colorado. It will be late and I'll swerve into the other lane. My ashes should be placed on a mountain, or mixed with gunpowder be sure to hold the rifle like I taught you—*

and this is where we stopped listening.

No hot water this morning or yesterday morning. Small, cold mountains rose on our skins. Dad never touched our waist-long hair or the soap beside the washbasin. We remember how long we stood barefoot in dirty dish and coffee water.

The smartest ones leave this place, he said while grandma taught us that we would never be alone, to throw bees in the mouths of our dogs for protection, spit in their mouths so they'd never leave, she'd ask, *What burns longer, hotter? Cedar or pitch? One day, we won't be here when you don't know what to do* or say when dad asks if I remember holding her skirt, crying after her, if I want a beer when he talks about the man who fell asleep on the train tracks, lists where police found his leg and arms, beside a pine, beneath the hood of a broken down car I asked, *Where did you find his heart?* He said, *Like most men, I don't think he had one to lose.*

But I remember his beating heart when he ran behind me on that fourth morning. We ran with hungry dogs, struggled for miles in spring cold. I watched for sun, the quiet way it pulls the purple horizon from the dark, listened for the hooves separating snow, the envelopes full of prayers opening—

Be careful. But keep going.

Grandma asked him to bring a truckload of wood, to run, to yell to call everything holy to us. Every few steps he yelled into the dark and we may not have beat the sun, but we made it home, oh yes, we made it home.

Radio

Grandma sat in the back-most room.

The room caught the trailer's heat, the strongest signal. We unfolded chairs, stacked cardboard boxes, squeezed our smaller-selves into the blanket-draped places—used crochet needles as microphones, pretended to be country stars. At times, we opened our arms to fly—shirts lifted, us spinning, showing our white bellies just as the hawks did in our rectangle of the sky.

We loved the language spilling from AM radio, *All Navajo All The Time* and everything animal-shaped. We crawled on all fours, held our breath until we turned blue. We peeked through moth and mouse holes in the blankets, watched her stitch landscapes, palominos into pillowcases. We learned the mountain songs, her shuffle, traced the patterns her skirt left in floor-dust, hummed to the sound of plastic lids peeling off plastic boxes—crawled until she caught our legs, pulled us against her while she cleaned our ears, blew the dead skin off the bobby pins—held us until she was sure her girls were listening.

First, there was only a little static, a small snow. We were able to ignore it—collected restaurant suckers and made pictures with pushpins, listened to old country and trucks kick up dust on the road, waited for new seasons. Sweat crawled down our temples, broke apart on shoulders and knees, stirring her from sleep. She asked for the names of family places, Bitter Springs and Red Mesa, listened closely, brown paper eyelids opened behind yellowed lenses to make sure her girls were too.

She yelled at small storms, trains, blamed the static on lost satellites. She said that it was getting worse but we heard voices and words the same—Turn where white marks are carved into the edge. We rearranged furniture and dusted antennas, stood on the trailer's roof and raised our arms, mimicked telephone poles and radio towers, changed batteries, ran aluminum up corners, along the ceiling.

She made us take down the clubhouse, keep our bellies covered. I can't clean up after you girls anymore and we unbraided our hair.

We stopped searching for glass beads and buttons and started counting coughs, pink fingers just under her nose to make sure she was still breathing.

We clung to everything we knew through the static. Bingo. Room. Táláwosh. Star. Hospital and North. A deep-snow covered the satellites, and we thought of words we used to say.

MANNY LOLEY

Credit: Manny Loley

MANNY LOLEY (b. 1994) is 'Áshįįhí, born for Tó Baazhní'ázhí; his maternal grandfather is Tódích'íi'nii and his paternal grandfather is Kinyaa'áanii. Loley is from Casamero Lake, New Mexico, and is a PhD candidate in English and literary arts at the University of Denver. He received an MFA in creative writing-fiction from the Institute of American Indian Arts in 2018. His work has been featured in *HIKA*, *Pollentongue*, *RED INK*, and the *Santa Fe Literary Review.* Loley's short story, "Na' Nízhoozhí Dí," was nominated for a Pushcart Prize in fiction by Austin Eichelberger at the *Santa Fe Literary Review*. Loley is a member of Saad Bee Hózhǫ́: A Diné Writers' Collective, co-founder and director of the Emerging Diné Writers' Institute, and former chair of the advisory board to the Navajo Nation Poet Laureate.

In addition to a book of poems, Loley is at work on a novel titled *They Collect Rain in Their Palms*, which details the experience of an LGBT couple in the face of the Navajo Nation's ban on same-sex marriage. Throughout the novel, as in the following excerpt, "Niłtsą́ Biką'," prose interacts with poetry like ancestral, cultural narratives interact with the contemporary. Both inform each other. Loley notes, "A central premise in my novel is that Diné cultural narratives continue into the present and our stories are intertwined with the stories of Changing Woman, the Warrior Twins, natural elements, and more. The relationship between the protagonists, Naat'áanii and Anderson, is mirrored in the relationships between natural elements like Female and Male Rain. In this way, Naat'áanii and Anderson's relationship almost seems fated."

Interview

What do you hope readers learn from your writing?

Writing is more than a solitary act. Our writing stems from our upbringing, personal experiences, and, although we may not think about it often, from our ancestors. We carry their stories in our being. As Diné writers, we have a responsibility of representation and cultural legacy that non-Diné writers may not have to deal with.

How does the Navajo language and/or Navajo culture influence your work?

Writing using Diné language and cultural elements allows me to figure out more about myself. Through writing, I can explore questions I wouldn't feel comfortable sharing with other people. I feel more connected to my ancestral heritage in that way. Diné language unlocks worlds beneath my psyche where the ancestral stories and teachings dwell.

Who or what inspires you?

I am most inspired by my family and our home. My mother, who is a gifted storyteller herself, taught me the value of language and storytelling. My home is a central element in my forthcoming novel and inspires much of my writing.

What advice do you have for beginning writers?

Reading is fundamental and is what inspires many of us to become writers. When we read, we pick up the "tricks of the trade." We see how other writers craft engaging stories, beautiful novels, epic poems, and, above all, how they tell their own story. We learn how to give voice, energy to our words. We also may witness a lack of story and begin to create stories that we wish we could have read growing up.

Who was the first Navajo writer you read?

The first Diné writer I read was Luci Tapahonso. One weekend, my mother drove our family to Northern Arizona University to see Luci read. I was so enamored by her stories, which used familiar places to me and language that meant home, and the way she read them brought new life to writing. Luci's writing taught me that it was possible for a Diné to write and influence others. I will always be thankful to Luci for inspiring me to write.

What was your favorite book in high school? What are you reading now?

In high school, I gravitated toward books depicting a gay storyline. My family has always been accepting of me, but our communities, heavily influenced by colonization, adopted hatred toward LGBT identities. When I perused the books in my high school's library, I looked for books that reflected my experience as a gay Diné youth. The only books I found focused on white, gay characters like Garret Weyr's *My Heartbeat*, which was a favorite of mine at the time. This experience has been one of the impetuses for my novel in progress, *They Collect Rain in Their Palms*, and why I write about the Navajo Nation's ban on same-sex marriage and gender issues.

Most recently, I finished reading *Tin Man* by Sarah Winman and *Balzac and the Little Chinese Seamstress* by Dai Sijie. Currently, I am reading *A Little Life* by Hanya Yanagihara and *War of the Foxes* by Richard Siken, one of my favorite poets.

Tell us more about your work with Saad Bee Hózhǫ́: A Diné Writers' Collective and the role you imagine it playing for other up-and-coming writers.

Saad Bee Hózhǫ́ began as the Diné Writers' Association at an inaugural gathering of Diné writers in 2017. Irvin Morris and I organized a meeting between various Diné writers to discuss our respective works and possibilities of mentorship. It was our hope that we could mobilize Diné writers to impact literary culture on the Navajo Nation and to begin thinking about the future of Diné writing. Since then, we've had another meeting during the second Emerging Diné Writers' Institute (EDWI), a summer program geared toward growing the next generation of Diné writers. In the future, Saad Bee Hózhǫ́ would like to foster a mentorship program, workshops for aspiring Diné writers, conduct community teach-ins, and support writing programs like EDWI.

Niłtsą́ Biką'

Naat'áanii's home, with towering mesas all around, sat comfortable, pondering the day's torpor-inducing heat and listening to their woes. It sighed and hummed and opened its arms in that comforting way like a mother to her children. Naat'áanii stood atop the hill that ran down from the mouth of his grandparent's home like a familiar, dusty tongue. This place, his grandmother reminded him, was made for them and they were formed of this place, tied to it with their umbilical cords buried deep within the earth. You'll always return home, in this way. A smile creasing her eyes as she said it. *This is the center of the world,* Naat'áanii thought, *and there's nothing more that I could want farther out, where senseless noise pervades everything.* Here, each sound was meaningful and beautiful; birds sang as they darted back and forth down the road, his younger brothers and sisters imitating their swift movements in play; cattle bleated in the distance, bringing them closer to home on evenings when they explored arroyos, jumped from boulders, climbed squat trees, picked déèh from the sloping mesa; cars rattled along a dusty road that winded through their valley, connecting them to the outside world. The evening blue sky quilted with pink and orange streaked clouds fanned out overhead. His family seemed that way to him too; thoughtful and each complementing the other. Naat'áanii turned back and called his grandmother from her seat beneath the towering box elder.

"Shimásání!" He smiled. "Let's take a walk."

Together, they turned onto the road leading down to a makeshift intersection, connecting their land to his aunt's at the next hill over. She walked beside him saying nothing, but humming. Her eyes focused on a point ahead, perhaps not a physical location, but something only she could access, in the before time when his Christian aunt, Nanabah, was his grandmother's strong-willed daughter with a woman warrior's name.

"Naat'áanii."

He looked to his left.

"Don't ever lose yourself."

"Of course not," he said.

"I mean it." Her smile quivered.

Naat'áanii reached for his grandmother's hand. He could feel her pulse, a steady thrum in her palm. Ba-bum. Ba-bum. Ba-bum.

"You'll be there to remind me, won't you?"

She looked at him and smiled. Her eyes were misty. "Áshinee', shi yázhí, shi awéé'. My precious one. My sweet one. My dear one."

In the distance, coyotes' high-pitched song rose into the horizon; their howls seemed to rustle orange and yellow leaves, bristly purples, spiny greens, and thin stems.

"When coyotes sound like that," Naat'áanii looked at his grandmother, "what are they saying?"

She paused. "They're calling the rain."

There was loud beauty too, in their whispering valley; not man-made beauty like singers belting out Naat'áanii's favorite songs, but something beyond men. Wherever Niłtsą Bi'áád, Female Rain, traveled, Niłtsą Biką', Male Rain, was not far behind. He trailed her, the thundering of his horse's hooves near the hem of her flowing skirt, as if to say *I'll protect you always.* The flash of his lightning leaving his enemies stunned in his path.

They met on the mountain's crest

and he said:

For you, anything—my heart,
like a thousand horses
thundering from worlds below,
settles in that place
only we know.

His water hands travel
across her tributaries
and she pulses, mist rolling down the pinnacle.
Know my power
has sunk ships
though I may quiver
from your lips
there is still a storm
brewing within,
she said.

But his arms
thick with rain-thunder-lightning
his legs, all cyclone and surge,
pressed her tighter into atmosphere

his naked chest, his ribs spiraling like her
dreams,
licked up her
breath

Still wet, she lay next to him
Creation, she breathed, *creation extend from*
here.
Dew glistening
in the dawn.

As Naat'áanii and his mother sat in their warm living room, Naat'áanii's eyes closed while his mother waded in pensive silence. Muted light peeked from the kitchen.

He sighed. "Mom?"

"What is it, shiyáázh?"

"I just don't know."

"About what?"

"All of it." He sat up. "We left before the chapter meeting ended."

Rain thrummed against the window.

His mother's face surprised him. Tears glistened on her cheeks, a gentle stream pulled downward by gravity.

"I'm so sorry," she said. "I'm sorry about what Nanabah said."

Naat'áanii put his hand on her arm. He thought about the chapter meeting earlier in the day, about his grandmother's tears and her sunken face at witnessing his aunt's transformation from strong, Diné Àsdzáán with beautiful and careful words to a born-again, Christian woman with a forked tongue. He thought about his mother's stories of her older sister. *She was beautiful, your aunt, my sister. . . your grandmother's favorite . . . she broke your grandmother's heart. Just like Gallup and the alcohol claimed her, so did Jesus and his followers.* But most of all, Nanabah's looming presence in the chapter house, her pointed eyes resting on Naat'áanii's grandmother, and her words like bees in Naat'áanii's memory stung him over and over. *This is wrong,* Nanabah said while her hand hovered over him, *sinners. The only story that matters is His. God,* whispered from Nanabah's heretic smile. She supported the Navajo Nation's marriage ban.

"Naat'áanii," his mother said, calling him back to their living room. "I don't want you to ever feel like we don't love you."

"I know." His vision blurred. Bees continued to swarm in the background.

She wiped her eyes and nose with her shirt sleeve.

"How do you feel?"

Thunder rumbled nearby.

"Like running away," Naat'áanii said. "Maybe the reservation isn't home after all."

She reached for his hand and held it.

Always so warm, Naat'áanii thought and he began to cry. His mother pulled him into her arms until he could hear her heart pumping against his ear. It rushed from him. He cried thinking about his grandmother's face crumpled at seeing her long-lost daughter claimed by hatred, about how he didn't say anything, couldn't say anything because he was scared and angry. He cried until his shoulders shook and it was hard to breathe.

"They think their bilagáana god owns the whole world," Naat'áanii's mother said between clenched teeth.

Naat'áanii wiped his eyes. "Who?"

"The lost ones. Stuck-in-the-in-between ones. The flock."

"Nanabah?"

"Yes, her and others like her."

"But why?" Naat'áanii whispered.

His mother stroked his hair.

"My old grandma, Grandma Red Lady, Asdzą́ą́ Łichíí', used to say bilagáanas were cursed in their own homeland, so they came to ours."

Lightning flashed white, lighting up the living room. Thunder boomed in response.

They paused. Naat'áanii's mother turned off the light in the kitchen.

"Niłtsą́ Biką' is riding through," she said. "Best to sit in silence with the lights off until he passes."

In the distance, jagged white streaks enveloped the sky, casting gray shadows in all directions, and roaring thunder silenced everything. Lightning and thunder danced late into the night. As Niłtsą́ Biką' rode away, sometime after midnight, coyotes howled another song.

"I've always loved taking walks with my grandma and talking to her," Naat'áanii said. "The way she listens and nods, sometimes looking off somewhere like she's seeing into the future or seeking an answer from something greater. She teaches me patience."

"That's why you're so thoughtful," Anderson said. "You see beyond, into something deeper. You see into me."

Anderson was not of the land like Naat'áanii was. Anderson's umbilical cord was buried closer to town; his home skirted the city.

As they resumed walking beneath an arching turquoise sky, Naat'áanii told Anderson about the chapter meeting, about the white hate he could see emanating from his distant aunt, about the night he cried and the Male Rain that shook their valley, about lightning that flashed across the sky and into his dreams, and about coyotes' rain song.

Spots of light opened and closed, their fuzzy outlines shining on tufts of bottlebrush squirrel tail and blue grama. Dancing spiny leaves like bristly fingers reaching for summer sky provided shade.

Anderson and Naat'áanii ventured up the sloping mesas and down beside the river's edge, a place, among others, that had become their usual spot. Most others their age spent their summers driving an hour or two to Gallup or Albuquerque for movies or swimming and other capitalist distractions.

Over the next few weeks, Naat'áanii and Anderson explored arroyos, climbed trees to get a better view of the valley, picked dééh deeper in the mountains, plucked strands of orange moonlight broom and sucked on the bright orange petals (sweet like chocolate his grandmother said). Naat'áanii picked apart fescue and showed Anderson how to throw them like missiles until they stuck to each other's clothes. Coyotes, Naat'áanii told Anderson, weren't only messengers of bad luck to come, but also messengers of good fortune and things like rain. Horned toads were their cheiis and warranted an offering for protection. Catching a hummingbird, sprinkling it with corn pollen, and catching the discarded pollen was good luck. Anderson listened intently and surprised Naat'áanii by how much he remembered. It was Anderson who remembered to bring along water and get them back before the sun set. Naat'áanii thought he had never met someone so diligent.

One evening, they had lost track of time in the hills and light seemed to disappear in a few minutes rather than the hour it took for them to get home. They saw a dark shape moving in the moonlight; a fuzzy outline with a tail scurrying into the shadows. Naat'áanii grabbed Anderson's hand to steady his thumping chest and he did not let go until their porch light was within reach. *His hand, so large*, Naat'áanii thought, *how neatly we fit with each other.* When they were together, time did not matter, and Naat'áanii found himself saying things he never admitted to anyone, not even himself. The way Anderson's eyes bore into Naat'áanii's unlocked a hidden pool of realizations, thoughts, and desires and Anderson's eyes, his touch, was just enough to urge them forward.

Perhaps it was this comfort in telling someone his deepest yearnings and fears, to have someone to pour his secrets into and for them to validate his existence, his flawed humanity, that Naat'áanii craved. For Anderson to look at him with such admiration and desire, like only this moment mattered to each of them, that breathing each other's air was what kept them alive, was all that he could have hoped for.

There is a natural law in Diné cosmology that every action in the universe ripples into other actions and so no single action is static. Naat'áanii thought about this rule often, about how somewhere in his lineage, an ancestor said a prayer that extended this far to create his reality and perhaps his ancestors hoped for Naat'áanii to find Anderson here—tall gracefulness, tilted smile, earth tone skin, scent of hummingbird mint.

Somewhere, whispered into rocks and plants, the ancestors' prayer continued:

Let our prayers cross over
for love
for this, our language inherited
from holy people who know
the truth of this earth, our home,
for the first sound
uttered at creation, uttered at birth,
in muted darkness before
we wake to morning dew
in the middle of our glittering world
that carries just as much sadness
as a time when we were removed
from our mountains
ascending from worlds below
into the 21st century.
Let our words extend—náasjį' dóó nee'nijį'
rising from the first hooghan
to meet new homes
and keep us close,
we return with fog
in the cusp of early morning.

May our children be everlasting
    and beautiful living.
So it was
So it is
So it will be
    for all time
    for all time
    for all time
        for all time

The days Naat'áanii and Anderson spent roaming the valley, down winding dirt trails, hand in hand, skin on skin, were etched in the land, potent, just for them. *I want all of me, my arms, my legs, my abdomen, my neck, that delicate skin behind my earlobes, to belong only to him.* Naat'áanii mused. In his dreams, they became one person, enveloped in each other until they returned to dust.

Yours
Mine
It doesn't make a difference
Convergence
First Man and First Woman
Changing Woman and the Sun
The rain
The rain
The rain
    on the mountaintop
The rain

ERIK BITSUI

Credit: Jim Ruland

ERIK BITSUI (b. 1975) is Ta'neeszahnii and born for Tótsohnii. His maternal grandfather is Tó'aheedlíinii and his paternal grandfather is Kinyaa'áanii. Bitsui is from Blue Gap, Arizona; he admits he's frequently asked, "Where the hell is Blue Gap?" to which he answers, "It's the small town between Pinon and Chinle, Arizona." He also grew up in Many Farms and later graduated from Chinle High School. His family moved to Flagstaff in 1983, where he still lives today with his wife and two daughters.

Bitsui earned a BA in English from Northern Arizona University in 2004 and an MFA from the Jack Kerouac School of Disembodied Poetics at Naropa University in Boulder, Colorado, in 2013. In the late 1990s, Bitsui wrote a few articles for *Flag Live!*, a weekly newspaper in Flagstaff, but nearly twenty years later, in February 2019, four of his pieces were published in *Waxwing Literary Journal*, including the two published here. When pushed to define his work in terms of genre, Bitsui jokingly answers, "I don't know."

As Hostiin Bitsui, he deejays a weekly heavy metal radio show, the Metal Meltdown, on Flagstaff's KSZN 101.5 FM. At age five, Bitsui was blown away by the rock band KISS performing on television. Soon after, he found Iron Maiden, Judas Priest, AC/DC, and Ozzy Osbourne, thanks in large part to his cousins and uncle. He remembers buying his first heavy metal album at a flea market in Gallup, New Mexico, around 1985; he still owns that copy of Metallica's *Ride the Lightning*. Bitsui distinctly remembers seeing Metallica—his first heavy metal concert—in Phoenix, Arizona, on June 10, 1992. Although he has lost exact count, since then he has seen Metallica in-person at least thirteen to fourteen other times.

Interview

What do you hope readers learn from your writing?

My writing says a little something about humanity and the nature of self-awareness. Hopefully, readers in the distant future will learn something about heavy metal, Navajo culture, Navajo humor and/or consciousness at the beginning of the twenty-first century. I try to keep my reader engaged so I use humor to emphasize certain points. Also I would like for people to know I am way cooler than Sherwin Bitsui! (Dear Reader: please ask Sherwin if he is related to me! He owes me a beer every time someone asks him!)

How does the Navajo language and/or Navajo culture influence your work?

The culture is always there—it is inescapable. My own culture and language are my link to the universe itself. Through stories and storytellers, I am aware I am a sentient, five-fingered being within the cosmos. And I am still learning every day. I am not a fluent speaker of my own language but I am learning. Nevertheless, my culture and language are things I cannot take off like a coat or a mask. It is always within me.

Who or what inspires you?

My biggest inspiration are other fellow writers. I do like the reciprocal relationship between the storyteller and the listener. By sharing our minds we bridge our lives together. Then, not long ago, I became a father to two beautiful Navajo daughters. I try to share as many stories with them as well. I feel it is the duty of every sentient being on earth to share stories.

What advice do you have for beginning writers?

Read as much as you can. Write everything down. And research those storytellers who influence the writers you like. Just like with anything else, writing can be discouraging. It ain't easy! Is playing guitar easy? No Way! Is learning how to ride a bike easy? Hell No! Is learning a new language (or your own) a piece of cake? Yeah Right! Writing takes time. But first you gotta go through a lot of BAD WRITING. Your first stories will NOT be good—but keep writing. You may be scared to write down a lot of things—but keep writing. Others may say you are not good enough—but keep writing. Then edit edit edit edit. Read more. Write more. Then edit edit edit edit.

Who was the first Navajo writer you read?

I think the first Navajo writer I read was my second-grade Culture teacher, Mrs. Etsitty. She worked at Many Farms Elementary School and she wrote Navajo stories. She showed us we could record our own voices, our own stories, our own people, through writing—and I don't know if she ever knew how much that left an impact on me. SHE was the writer. SHE was Navajo. And SHE was a teacher to our own people.

What was your favorite book in high school? What are you reading now?

Quite a few books made a big impact on me in high school but above them all *A Clockwork Orange* by Anthony Burgess ranks the highest. I read the book around twenty-seven times within three years. The main character's creative use of language, love of music, and teenage experiences knocked me out. I just finished reading Gary Larson's *The Far Side Gallery* for the umpteenth time, and I'm now reading Charles Bukowski's *The Last Night of the Earth Poems* and Barbara Henning's *You, Me, and the Insects*. Next up is *The Gun* by C. J. Chivers.

≡

Marrying *Welcome to Hell*, a Hell-Made Match

Venom's 1981 debut album *Welcome to Hell* is so good, man. In fact, I'd marry *Welcome to Hell*—oh hell yeah, I'd do it! But the first problem I see is I'm already married! I'll have to ask my wife who'll probably tell me to get lost! But I think she'd understand, right? She knows how much I like *Welcome to Hell.*

Venom, an English black metal band, is pretty cool. I like their look, their style and their sound. And Venom doesn't care what other people think—*Welcome to Hell* makes an unmistakable point which I totally respect. Venom does their job which may not please everyone and may offend a lot of people but many of their enemies are my enemies too. Because of this, we, myself and *Welcome to Hell*, are a well-suited match because we have similar interests for a great marriage.

And what kind of spouse would *Welcome to Hell* be? We'd probably have fantastic times at HIGH volume and energy with booze and drugs flowing in and out of loud mouths. But in anger we'd fight epic battles as we would call upon all the supernatural powers and forces to punish our beloved spouse. But we'd make up somehow like all couples do because I couldn't live without *Welcome to Hell.*

But I'd still marry *Welcome to Hell*—I think.

I wish I could walk hand-in-hand with *Welcome to Hell* and tell everyone how much we loved each other but we probably wouldn't. I alone would talk privately of how much I loved *Welcome to Hell* and end up wishing things were a bit different. Hell, for all I know *Welcome to Hell* will go on without me and marry someone else—sheesh, that's a tough one. But I know myself enough to say I'd stick with *Welcome to Hell* as long as possible and make our marriage work.

So why marry *Welcome to Hell*? That album makes me feel great, dude. And it doesn't take much for the album to turn me on and get me loose for major moving and grooving. *Welcome to Hell* nourishes me every time I blast it. The dearly beloved album is always on my mind providing an internal soundtrack. I can't walk around or do much without *Welcome to Hell* at my side anyway. I have become *Welcome to Hell.*

So how would this marriage take place? I'd have to tell my in-laws as well as my own family, friends and colleagues—and they'd lose their minds! I'd have to quickly make an argument of why I needed to complete this union between Navajo man and seminal album. In the end, I would have to defend my new spouse as well as my own actions.

Nevertheless, as a traditional Navajo man, *Welcome to Hell* and I would have a traditional Navajo wedding ceremony inside a Navajo hogan. On our wedding day, seated on the north side of the hogan would be my family, SLAYER, Anthrax, Megadeth and Metallica. And seated on the south side of the hogan would be *Welcome to Hell* in all forms: the LP, the CD, the audio cassette, all imports, B-sides, re-issues, singles and an 8-track cassette.

In the ceremony, *Welcome to Hell* would have to pour water over my hands. And I would pour water over the hands of *Welcome to Hell.* This action performed to cleanse the other of their past. Then *Welcome to Hell* and I would feed each other blue corn mush—wait, where would *Welcome to Hell*'s hands and mouth be anyway?

Then we'd all feast on a Navajo meal of frybread and mutton stew.

However, I have a feeling *Welcome to Hell* would throw the food around the hogan which would offend all of our guests. Then *Welcome to Hell* in compact disc form would pull itself out of its jewel case and run around with only its bare disk self. I even bet the vinyl album would pull itself in and out, in and out of its sleeve and say to all of the guests, "Get a load of this!"

And that's how my family, guests and all the holy Navajo beings would be introduced to my new spouse, *Welcome to Hell.*

I don't know, maybe this isn't a good idea.

Maybe *Welcome to Hell* could be a great mistress instead, just like Metallica's *$5.98 EP* and Pantera's *Far Beyond Driven* and Black Sabbath's *Volume 4*.

Wait, could I just marry all of those albums?

I don't know—I better not ask my wife.

Eddie and Norman, Norman and Me, Me and Eddie

Although Eddie was always around, Norman and I never talked about him. Maybe I should ask Norman what he knows about Eddie.

Out on the Navajo rez, at my grandmother's house, my uncle Norman wore an Iron Maiden t-shirt. That white t-shirt with black long sleeves was plastered to Norman's young Navajo chest. Printed on the shirt was the cover photo of Maiden's 1983 *Piece of Mind* album which depicted the band's mascot, Eddie, in a straitjacket chained to a wall of a padded cell. I never did ask my uncle where he got it from.

All of Norman's nieces and nephews—me among them—knew Eddie was the Iron Maiden mascot, a half-dead character drawn by Derek Riggs. All the kids in the family examined every detail of that t-shirt, from Eddie's black eyes to Eddie's elbows ripping from the jacket—he was moments away from escaping. I too stared into Eddie's eyes: I awoke Eddie within me just by looking deep into his eyes. And for some reason, all the grownups looked away.

In late 1983, Norman walked around my grandmother's house and all around Blue Gap, AZ, with Eddie painted on his chest.

At shimasani's house, that t-shirt chopped wood, herded sheep, talked with the adults, and that shirt teased shimasani. That shirt hauled buckets of water into a house with no running water no matter how cold it was outside and never spilled a drop. That shirt drove shichei's truck to the Blue Gap Trading Post with a bunch of kids inside bundled up because the heater didn't work. And that shirt sat at tableful of kids laughing and joking. But at times, that shirt scolded the kids when they did wrong.

But that shirt was all about survival through hard work and laughter. That shirt shared funny jokes and stories with the elders and kids. And that shirt always ate heartily and cleaned up afterwards. Life itself was hard work and could often be cruel but that shirt made existence one long laugh despite all the pain and stretching to make the ends meet one more time.

What did Eddie's unmistakable attitude mean to my uncle?

And that shirt played Iron Maiden albums—it slapped cassette tapes into a broken stereo plastered with AIM and Free Leonard Peltier stickers. The speakers blasted harrowing vocals, twin distorted guitars, fingered bass lines and thundering drums all over the holy contours of Blue Gap.

In fact, at that time in my life, shimasani's house was the only place I ever heard Iron Maiden. I never knew what Iron Maiden sang about but whatever it was, their message must have been important because the music moved Norman and the landscape. Iron Maiden always made familiar Blue Gap into something different than before. As far as the kids cared, the music was able to bring Eddie back to life.

Although we never talked about it, Norman must have known Eddie's unmistakable attitude. When I actually sat down to listen to Iron Maiden lyrics, I had my epochal moment of Eddie for myself. As the years have gone by, I've memorized much of Iron Maiden's catalog. This band from England is a band that keeps me going and makes me feel ethnic pride, a pride in who I am, where I come from. When I listen, I appreciate my homeland, my voice and my genetic profile. When I listen to an Iron Maiden album, I feel my homeland coursing through chi meridian highways. I wonder if it has something to do with Iron Maiden's strong connection with the British Isle—their own homeland. I'll never know.

So what did Iron Maiden and Eddie mean to Norman?

Maybe Norman didn't need to tell us kids but instead as uncles do, Norman just showed us a way and we, his nation of nieces and nephews, had to walk through the door of knowledge by our own selves. Eddie was always there waiting and that shirt showed us we could still be Blue Gap kids, be metal heads, and walk confidently into any situation just like Norman did.

As an uncle and a semi-grown-up—pretty much an older kid—Norman must've known and kept that knowledge away or never found a moment to discuss Eddie's passion. Or maybe it never crossed his mind to share it with us as we looked in with something else looking back out.

TATUM BEGAY

Credit: Tatum Begay

TATUM BEGAY (b. 1990) is Naasht'ézhi Tábąąhí on her mother's side, Tábąąhá on her father's, bilagáana from her maternal grandfather, and 'Áshįįhí from her paternal grandfather. She grew up in Page, Arizona, and earned a BA in English with a minor in Asian studies and Japanese from Northern Arizona University in 2013 and an MA in English from Northern Arizona University in 2015. As a graduate assistant for Native American Student Services at NAU, Begay advised and mentored students, worked with action research teams on issues facing Indigenous peoples, and supported the work of first-year seminar instructors teaching Indigenous rights and Native humor. Today she works as a program adviser at Phoenix College.

In her spare time she draws comics, some of which appear as webcomics. In 2014 she started a successful webcomic series called *The Pretty Okay Adventures of Tatum*, which to date has had more than 304,800 views, with 2,200 subscribers (her work can be found at https://tapas.io/series/The-Pretty-Okay-Adventures-of-Tatum). Begay has self-published comics such as *Spiral* with Damon Begay (2017), *Nanaba's Summer* (2016), and print editions of *The Pretty Okay Adventures of Tatum.* She has been invited to Comic Cons, where she shares and sells her work. Begay's first official publication, as she calls it, is the story, "Aszdaa Changing," which was published in *Deer Woman Anthology* (2017), edited by Elizabeth LaPensée and Weshoyot Alvitre. "Stories of a Healing Way," which follows here, is an original work Begay composed for this anthology; while it may be autobiographical, it is also meant to reflect the tension experienced by many Diné writers and artists who strive to be true to their cultural knowledge and value systems but also yearn to be original.

Interview

What do you hope readers learn from your comics?

My hope is that young readers see themselves in my illustrations and that they can relate to the growth of other young writers who look like them. I didn't have a lot of exposure to seeing other writers/artists grow and succeed who looked like me, so I hope to give that to readers now. I also want readers, especially young readers, to learn that you can incorporate as many contemporary things as you like into your writing or drawing about your own culture. Manga, anime, comics, and literature, all make up who you are just as much as your culture does, so don't be afraid to write/draw about all of those things.

How does the Navajo language and/or Navajo culture influence your work?

I've always wanted to use Navajo creation stories and folklore in my illustrations, so I relied a lot on the teachings my father had learned when he was young. I remember learning creation stories as a child, and participated in many healing ceremonies that have shaped who I am today. Although I am not fluent in Navajo I try to incorporate as much as I can of the language into my stories in hopes that others learn a few words as well. Whenever I go back to the reservation and sit in ceremonies I think, "there's nothing like this," and am moved to my core at the familial healing bonds that come together to cook, eat, laugh, and pray. I want to capture these feelings in my work.

Who or what inspires you?

I actually read a lot of manga more than American comics, so I am inspired by the art of several manga artists, like Masashi Kishimoto, and Rumiko Takahashi. I am inspired by their ability to weave their Japanese folklore into their stories, and create elaborate worlds with beautiful art. I strive to create worlds as elaborate and full of meaning as these, but with the Navajo culture and my experiences growing up in it.

What advice do you have for beginning writers/illustrators?

Start small, challenge yourself to create three-panel comics first. Even if you aren't wanting to become a sequential storyteller, you can learn a lot about yourself and your writing/art style by learning how to illustrate your stories with sequential art. Comics are layered reading and creating experiences because they challenge the artist and reader to engage in written word, sequential illustration, onomatopoeia, and visual breakdown of the story on a page.

Who was the first Navajo writer you read?

The first book I ever read by a Navajo writer was by Lori Alvord and Elizabeth Cohen Van Pelt, titled *The Scalpel and the Silver Bear: The First Navajo Woman Surgeon Combines Western Medicine and Traditional Healing*. I think this was the first time I ever read about someone trying to work past the many taboos the Navajo culture has.

What was your favorite book in high school? What are you reading now?

My favorite book used to be *The Vampire Armand* by Anne Rice. Now I continue my love for the supernatural and horror by reading horror comics and manga. Right now I'm reading *Shiver* by Junji Ito. It has a lot of gore and great artist's notes on his process and inspirations.

÷

Stories of a Healing Way

Don't show the holy people like that! Sand paintings are prayers! Not kid stories!
But what about my own sto—
Not good!

CASTLE

Rumiko Takahashi
Shakespeare

Me

THE RAVEN
Storyboard #1

CHRONOLOGY OF IMPORTANT DATES IN DINÉ POLITICAL AND LITERARY HISTORY

JENNIFER NEZ DENETDALE

The beings who became the Diné emerged into this present world, the fifth, after traveling through four worlds where the creation of the world began in Dinétah, in the San Juan region of present-day northwestern New Mexico. The Diyin Dine'é (Holy People) established the boundaries of Diné bikéyah with mountains in the four directions.

900–1400 When the Holy People created the Diné and established laws and practices that the People will live by, they left to reside in the sacred mountains, four of which mark the four directions, and two within Dinétah. Dinétah is the original homeland and from this place they interacted with other Indigenous peoples, forging kinship ties with them through marriage and adoptions. They also created bonds of alliance that facilitated trade and, when the foreigners appeared from the south, became military allies.

1582 Spaniard Antonio de Espejo became the first European to encounter the Navajos (in northwestern New Mexico). Spaniards recognized the vastness of Diné bikéyah and labeled the land base as "Providence of the Navajo."

1626 Spanish Franciscan friar Zarate Salmeron recognized the Navajos as a distinct tribe.

1630s–1860s Spaniards and later Mexicans carried out slave raids against the Navajos; one of the major reasons for ongoing hostilities between Navajos and their neighbors was directly related to the slave trade, which targeted Navajo women and children; Americans turned a blind eye to the slave trade.

1680 Navajos participated in the Pueblo Revolt by allying with Pueblo warriors, which effectively began to drive the Spaniards from the Southwest.

1706 First peace treaty signed between Spaniards and Navajos.

1749 Spain established Catholic missions of Encinal and Cebolleta in Navajo country and Navajo warriors drove them out. Those Navajos closest to Hispanic settlements acquired material culture and practices of their neighbors. They also participated in enslavement of their own people. The Diné acquired livestock, sheep, goats, and horses that they value so much that they have songs and prayers for their stock.

1786 At this time, Navajos were recognized by the Spaniards, who categorized them into five groups, based on their location upon the land: Canyon de Chelly, Cebolleta, Chuska Mountain, Ojo del Oso, and San Mateo.

1821 Mexico declared independence from Spain.

1846 U.S. colonel Stephen Kearny claimed Santa Fe, New Mexico, as territorial capital for the United States; Navajos and U.S. officials met at Fort Wingate, New Mexico, to establish peace. In the treaties that Navajo leaders signed with the Americans, there were provisions that Navajos who had been captured for the slave trade be returned to their people.

1848 Treaty of Guadalupe Hidalgo ended war between United States and Mexico. Under its terms, more than 1.2 million square miles of territory were ceded by Mexico to the United States for $15 million; the U.S. government claimed jurisdiction over all tribal peoples, including Navajos, in the Southwest.

1849 Treaty signed between U.S. government and the Navajos; this treaty along with one signed in 1868 are the only two of nine signed between the federal government and the Navajos that were ratified by the U.S. Senate.

1855 Manuelito recognized as one of the leading chiefs of the Navajo tribe.

1860 Manuelito and Barboncito led more than a thousand warriors in an attack on Fort Defiance in New Mexico territory. They opposed American claims to Navajo land.

1863 Under the orders of the U.S. government, Kit Carson launched a "burn and scorch" campaign against the Navajo people in order to force their surrender and remove survivors of the war to the Bosque Redondo ("round grove," in Spanish) concentration camp, near Fort Sumner on the Pecos River in what is now east-central New Mexico.

1864 Many Navajos died during the Long Walk, which was actually a series of forced marches—at least fifty-three, between 350 and 450 miles—to the reservation at the Bosque Redondo.

1866 Manuelito surrendered, and many Navajo leaders, including Barboncito, quickly follow suit. Barboncito had surrendered and made the forced march to Hwéeldi, but had escaped and then returned to the Bosque Redondo to be with his people.

1868 Navajos and the U.S. government signed the treaty that establishes initial boundaries of Navajo reservation in northwestern New Mexico (about one-fourth of the tribe's traditional territory); Barboncito was the chief negotiator for the Navajo people.

1878–86 Navajo reservation was increased in size by five major land annexations; in the 1930s, additional lands were added to the Navajo land base.

1879 Carlisle Indian Industrial School was established, under U.S. authority by General Richard Henry Pratt, as the first federally funded boarding school. This off-reservation school became a model for twenty-six Bureau of Indian Affairs boarding schools and countless private boarding schools, many sponsored by religious organizations. In the Southwest, three federal boarding schools were opened: Santa Fe Indian School (1890), Albuquerque Indian School (1881), and Phoenix Indian School (1891).

1883 A Navajo boarding school at Fort Defiance, Arizona, was established in 1883. Later, others were opened in different locations: Tuba City, Arizona (1902); Shiprock, New Mexico (1903); Tohatchi, New Mexico (1904); Leupp, Arizona (1909); Crownpoint, New Mexico (1909); Chinle, Arizona (1910); Toadlena, New Mexico (1913); Fort Wingate, New Mexico (1925).

1884 Henry Chee Dodge was named head chief of the Navajos by Indian agent Dennis Riordan.

1929 Oliver La Farge's *Laughing Boy: A Navajo Love Story* was published and won the 1930 Pulitzer Prize. La Farge, who was not Navajo, set his story in 1915 in a fictional town, T'o Tlakai. In 1934, a movie adaptation premiered, directed by W. S. Van Dyke and starring non-Navajo actors in leading roles.

1934 Navajos rejected the Indian Reorganization Act; congressional legislation added 243,000 acres of land to reservation.

1934–1940s U.S. government carried out the livestock reduction program.

1937 *The Colored Land: A Navajo Indian Book, Written and Illustrated by Navajo Children*, edited by Rose K. Brandt, was published by Charles Scribner and Sons. Brandt was the supervisor for elementary education, Bureau of Indian Affairs, Washington, D.C. The poems were written by a group of Navajo students from Tohatchi, New Mexico, under the direction of their teacher, Evangeline Dethman, and the illustrations were created by sixth-grade students at the Santa Fe Indian School.

1940 The Navajo Tribal Council passed a resolution banning the use of peyote on tribal lands; the Native American Church, which uses the plant in its ceremonies, held that the resolution violates the First Amendment. In *Native American Church v. Navajo Tribal Council* (1959), a federal court held that the First Amendment does not apply to Indian nations.

1944–86 Private mining companies leased one thousand uranium mines on the Navajo Nation and employed between three thousand and five thousand Diné. No protection was available for miners against the high levels of radon, and they suffered from high rates of cancers and lung disease. In 2018, five hundred abandoned mines were still needing reclamation by the EPA. Meanwhile, people, animals, and the water continue to suffer the effects of this environmental disaster.

1956 The Indian Relocation Act dispersed American Indian people, including Diné, from their reservation homelands—often through coercion, and under the banner of "progress" or "assimilation"—and relocated them to larger cities such as Denver, Minneapolis, Oklahoma City, Phoenix, Seattle, San Francisco, and Los Angeles. By the 1980s, more than 750,000 American Indian people had relocated to cities.

1958 The Navajo Tribal Council created its own newspaper, today known as the *Navajo Times*.

1962 The organization that would become the Institute of American Indian Arts was founded in Santa Fe, New Mexico, first as a high school. In 1975, IAIA became a two-year college; then in 2000, it began offering a BFA and other BA degrees; finally, in 2013, it began offering a low-residency MFA program. Fourteen authors in this book have graduated from IAIA undergraduate or graduate programs; others have taught there.

1965 Seven Navajo student writers published their work in the IAIA and BIA-sponsored publication, *Anthology of Poetry and Verse Written by Students in Creative Writing Classes and Clubs During the First Three Years of Operation (1962–1965)*. The handmade book *Four: Collaboration of Printmaking and Creative Writing Students at IAIA* (100 limited-edition copies) was also published and included work by four Navajo student writers.

1966 Rough Rock Demonstration School opened and provided students with a bilingual education in English and Diné bizaad. This was the first Bureau of Indian Affairs (BIA) school to be operated by Diné personnel.

1967 Blackhorse Mitchell's *Miracle Hill: The Story of a Navaho Boy* was published by the University of Oklahoma Press. It is the first book published by a Diné writer.

1968 The Navajo Tribe officially kicked off a yearlong remembrance of the one-hundredth anniversary of the Navajos' return from Bosque Redondo in 1868. The Navajo Community College was founded—the first tribal college in the United States. In 1997 it was renamed Diné College.

1969 Navajo Council officially changes the name of the Navajo Tribe to the Navajo Nation. Grey Cohoe published the story "The Promised Visit" in the *South Dakota Review*.

1971 The *Indian Historian* published "The Poetry of Gloria Emerson." The Navajo Community College Press was established and served as the publisher of important early works in American Indian and Navajo studies: Ruth Roessel and Broderick Johnson edited and published *Navajo Stories of the Long Walk Period* (1973). Later well-known publications include Simon Ortiz's edited collection, *Earth Power Coming: Short Fiction in Native American Literature* (1983) and Della Frank and Roberta Joe's *Storm Patterns* (1993).

1972 Gloria Emerson published "Slayers of the Children" in the *Indian Historian.*

1975 The federal Indian Self-Determination and Education Assistance Act was passed, restoring rights to American Indian parents to control their children's placement in off-reservation schools.

1977 Nia Francisco edited and published—with Peggy Beck and Anna Lee Walters—*The Sacred: Ways of Knowledge, Sources of Life* (Navajo Community College Press). Her poem "Táchééh," one of the first poems published in Navajo, appeared in the journal *College English.*

1978 Luci Tapahonso published her first story, "The Snake Man."

1979 Navajo Skills Center was established. It later became Navajo Technical College, in 2006, and Navajo Technical University in 2013. Navajo Technical University's Bachelor of Fine Arts in Creative Writing and New Media Program houses the Navajo Nation Poet Laureate Program, under the guidance of the Navajo Nation Office of the President and Vice President.

1980 Irene Nakai (Hamilton), Agnes Tso, and Nia Francisco were included in *The South Corner of Time: Hopi, Navajo, Papago, Yaqui Tribal Literature*, a collection of prose and poetry by Native authors of the Southwest, edited by Larry Evers and published by the University of Arizona Press.

1981 Laura Tohe published her first work, "Willow Man's Children," in Rudolfo Anaya and Simon J. Ortiz's anthology, *Ceremony of Brotherhood.* Ruth Roessel published the first full-length book on Navajo women, *Women in Navajo Society*, with the Rough Rock Navajo Curriculum Center.

1982 Luci Tapahonso published her first book of poetry, *Seasonal Woman.*

1983 Alyse Neundorf published *Áłchíní Bi Naaltsoostsoh: A Navajo/English Bilingual Dictionary.*

1986 Laura Tohe published her first book of poetry, *Making Friends with Water*.

1988 Nia Francisco published her first book of poetry, *Blue Horses for Navajo Women*, and Irvin Morris published his first work, "The Homecoming," in *MAAZO Magazine*.

1989 Rex Lee Jim published his first book of poetry, *Áhí Ni' Nikisheegiizh*. A national journal, *Stone Soup: The Magazine by Children*, published a special "Navajo Issue" that featured stories and poems by eleven Diné writers and photographs and art by six others.

1990 Tiana Bighorse published *Bighorse the Warrior*.

1991 Esther Belin published her first poem, "surviving in this place called the united states."

1992 Shonto Begay's first authored and illustrated book, *Ma'ii and Cousin Horned Toad: A Traditional Navajo Story*, was published.

1993 Laura Tohe became the first Navajo person to earn a PhD in English; Tohe earned her PhD at the University of Nebraska, Lincoln. *Neon Pow-Wow: New Native American Voices of the Southwest*, edited by Anna Lee Walters, was published and included ten Diné writers.

1994 Salina Bookshelf, specializing in Navajo-language books, was founded in Flagstaff, Arizona, by Eric and Kenneth Lockard.

1995 Hershman John published his first poems in University of Pennsylvania's *Expedition Magazine*.

1997 Irvin Morris published *From the Glittering World: A Navajo Story*. Sherwin Bitsui published his first poems in *Not the Last Word*, edited by Pola Leonard.

1998–99 The original treaty of 1868 was displayed at Northern Arizona University in Flagstaff, Arizona, so that Navajos could view the precious document.

2005 The Bosque Redondo Memorial at Fort Sumner, New Mexico, was officially opened on June 4. The Navajo Sovereignty in Education Act was passed; it established the Navajo Nation Board of Education and the Navajo Nation Department of Diné Education and confirms the commitment of the Navajo Nation to the education of the Navajo People.

2008 Evangeline Parsons Yazzie (with Margaret Speas) published *Diné Bizaad Bínáhoóaah or Rediscovering the Navajo Language* (Salina Bookshelf).

2011 Rex Lee Jim was elected the eighth vice president of the Navajo Nation and served under President Ben Shelley from January 2011 to May 2015.

2013 Luci Tapahonso became the first poet laureate of the Navajo Nation.

2015 Laura Tohe was named the second poet laureate of the Navajo Nation.

2017 Saad Bee Hózhǫ́, the Diné Writers' Collective, was formed at a gathering at Navajo Technical University, Diné tséékos haz'ánigi: A Gathering of Diné Writers. Their name is inspired by the poetry of Rex Lee Jim. In 2017, the Navajo Women's Commission and Navajo Technical University partnered to create a summer creative writing program, the Emerging Diné Writers' Institute (EDWI). The EDWI, now an annual event, introduces Diné high school and college students to Diné authors and publishers to inspire and foster students' interests in writing.

2018 The Navajo Nation celebrated the 150th anniversary of the signing of the Navajo Treaty with events in Window Rock and throughout the Navajo Nation.

2020 More than 150 public, private, and BIA schools are serving Diné students on the reservation. In addition, there are community Head Start Programs and an increasing number of bilingual and Navajo immersion programs in the schools.

RESOURCES FOR TEACHERS AND READERS

MICHAEL THOMPSON

I. *ON WRITING*: ORDER AND LITERARY FORM

Order—including parallelism, repetition, structure, and balance—are essential, pervasive aspects of Diné culture and reflective of Navajo prayers, songs, stories, and philosophy. Many writers draw attention to this sense of order in their use of particular poetic and prose forms. Consider the conventional forms that some Diné writers employ—concrete prose-like narratives that express oral storytelling or lyric forms or highly patterned structures, such as haiku, sonnets, sestinas, or traditional stanzaic verse. Also examine the innovative ways that other writers depart from these familiar structures—in free verse, surrealism, minimalism, ellipsis, interiority, fragment, indeterminacy—each with its own intentional effect.

CONSIDERATIONS AND REFLECTIVE TASKS

- Locate places in a certain work where the writer appears committed to a particular form that emphasizes particular ideas. Consider how this structure might illustrate Diné values of order and/or how it might simply be used for its literary functionality.
- Some Diné writers routinely experiment with or subvert traditional literary forms (perhaps "reinventing the enemy's language" as Joy Harjo has termed

it) as a means to explore their own particular sense of "Navajo-ness." Identify particular passages in which certain writers seem to employ unique language, syntax, imagery, form, and the like to explore their personal Diné worldview.

SUGGESTED WORKS TO CONSIDER

Nia Francisco, "naabeeho women with blue horses"
Luci Tapahonso, "The Canyon Was Serene"
Rex Lee Jim, "Saad/Language/Voice" and "Na'azheeh/Hunting"
Irvin Morris, from *From the Glittering World*: "Shikéyah" and "T'áá shábik'ehgo"
Esther G. Belin, "Backbone," "male + female divided," and "X+X+X+X−X−X−X"
Hershman John, "Storm Patterns"
Sherwin Bitsui, from *Flood Song*, including "tó"
Dwayne Martine, "Parsing" and "Thought Knife"
Tacey Atsitty, "In Strips"
Orlando White, "Fill in the Blank" and "Sentence"
Jake Skeets, "Blue Edge Cord"
Bojan Louis, "Currents"
Manny Loley, "Niłtsą́ Biką'"
Tatum Begay, "Stories of a Healing Way"

II. *ON WRITING*: SOUND AND OTHER SENSORY DEVICES

One of the significant ways that writers move readers is by powerful sensory images. Sound effects—resulting from poetic meter (rhythm), rhyme, repetition, consonance, assonance, and onomatopoeia (among other techniques)—sometimes recall familiar aspects of Diné song/prayer. Visual imagery results both from vivid description and from figurative language; as employed by Navajo writers, metaphor and simile often express familiar aspects of Diné life in their comparisons. Less common but also important is synesthesia, the mixing of senses.

Consider how colors, symbols, sounds, comparisons, and various other forms of sensory images evoke specific meanings.

CONSIDERATIONS AND REFLECTIVE TASKS

- Select a specific work in which you recognize a clear pattern of sound devices (rhyme, rhythm, repetition, and so on). Read it aloud and try to understand the purpose behind this sound pattern within the overall intention of the poem—in other words, does it appear to emphasize a particular idea or emotion or cultural value or a specific moment in a narrative?
- Metaphor—saying one thing in terms of another—is the heart of all figurative language (including simile, personification, hyperbole, and the like), but writers vary widely in the ways they use it. Some apply it in a clear pattern or in an extended and repetitive way; others use it sparingly, waiting for just the right moment to unveil it. Still others flood their poems with an array of comparisons, creating a powerful cumulative effect. Select two writers who seem to differ in the ways they use figurative language. Analyze how they vary in their applications.
- Vivid descriptions of sights, sounds, smells, tastes, touch are integral to evoking emotion in readers of many poems, perhaps especially in the works of writers who are interested in telling stories from within a long tradition of oral narrative. Writers who work in lyric poetry also utilize description in very intentional ways. Select works that contain particularly effective descriptive imagery and analyze its effects.

SUGGESTED WORKS TO CONSIDER

Blackhorse Mitchell, "The Drifting Lonely Seed"
Nia Francisco, "táchééh"
Gloria Emerson, "Grace's Hairnet"
Luci Tapahonso, "Náneeskadí"
Elizabeth Woody, "Rosette"
Rex Lee Jim, "Na'azheeh/Hunting" and "Three Short Poems"
Esther G. Belin, "X+X+X+X−X−X−X"
Shonto Begay, "Drawing Life: Delineating My World"
Hershman John, "Storm Patterns"
Norla Chee, "Good-bye Honey, Hello Silver and Dust"
Sherwin Bitsui, from *Flood Song*, including "tó"
Tacey Atsitty, "Calico Prints"

Venaya Yazzie, "gathering early dawn"
Orlando White, "Sentence," "The i is a Cricket," "n," "Meditation," and "DISSOCIATE"
Tatum Begay, "Stories of a Healing Way"

III. HUMOR

Humor is a part of all life, but in Native life, it often feels pervasive, perhaps because it is a survivance strategy (as Gerald Vizenor might term it). Of course, people laughing together reinforces human connection. Comic situations and jokes also reveal difficult truths and teach us how to persevere in an often absurd or cruel world. Identify how specific writers create humor through jokes, irony, puns, and other forms of verbal play (in English or in Navajo). And consider how some instances of humor might be designed to empower those who employ it, how it might be a defense against one's oppressors or against settler colonialism in general.

CONSIDERATIONS AND REFLECTIVE TASKS

- Humor can be very subtle or in-your-face. Select a writer in this text who appears to tackle difficult issues of Diné life head-on through overt humor, often generated by hyperbole, comic characterization, understatement, satire, pun, and the like.
- Identify at least one text that makes you smile. Reread this text seeking to locate the source of that smile. Where in the text is the source of that gentle humor?

SUGGESTED WORKS TO CONSIDER

Tina Deschenie, "You Bring Out the Diné in Me"
Luci Tapahonso, "Hills Brothers Coffee" and "Raisin Eyes"
Irene Nakai Hamilton, "Summer Coup, 1973" and "Dishwasher"
Laura Tohe, "Joe Babes"
Venaya Yazzie, "grandma loves SOBE," "The Pine Nut Eaters"
Orlando White, "The i is a Cricket"
Erik Bitsui, "Marrying *Welcome to Hell*, a Hell-Made Match"

IV. RACISM, PREJUDICE, AND INTERGENERATIONAL TRAUMA

A number of Diné writers speak to the historic and ongoing traumatic social conditions suffered by Indigenous peoples including racism and prejudice. Other writers explore the realistic representation of the difficult, lived experiences of Diné people, including addiction, poverty, violence, and so on. Either directly or indirectly, these issues are often represented as the result of genocide or colonization and the persistence of colonialism. Likewise, many works explore the effects of cultural dislocation, domestic and gender violence, environmental degradation, and language loss. At times, these artists also incorporate critiques of settler colonialism and capitalism as essential elements of their imaginative art.

CONSIDERATIONS AND REFLECTIVE TASKS

- Identify works that address stereotyping of, or outright racism against, Native people. Analyze the text to understand how this prejudice is illustrated. Consider whether these attitudes are connected in any way to the cultural or physical dislocation or oppression of a Native character or Native people generally.
- If a work includes some reference to addiction or domestic abuse and violence, consider whether the work alludes to a source of the trauma. Is this examination of negative behavior treated matter-of-factly or tragically or angrily or some other way? What does the tone tell us about the writer's perspective on intergenerational trauma?
- The economic conditions of Navajo people have been historically circumscribed by tensions between settler capitalism and Indigenous values about land and kinship. Locate a work in which personal poverty is clearly present. Then consider whether the character or the author appears to consider this a deficit in the same way that mainstream society might view it. Or consider a work in which environmental degradation is significant. How does the writer seem to understand this kind of loss—as personal or spiritual or as economic or societal or as something else?
- Cultural loss—of language and spiritual wisdom, especially through the loss of elders, ceremony, sacred sites—is also a concern of Navajo writers. Examine a text in which the diminishment of language or teachings or sacred spaces is central to the meaning of the work and explain how.

SUGGESTED WORKS TO CONSIDER

Nia Francisco, "ode to a drunk woman" and "i hate elvis presley"
Tiana Bighorse, *Bighorse the Warrior*
Luci Tapahonso, "In 1864"
Laura Tohe, "Within Dinétah the People's Spirit Remains Strong"
Irvin Morris, from *From the Glittering World*
Esther G. Belin, "Ruby's Answer," "Emergence," and "X+X+X+X−X−X−X"
Della Frank, "I Hate to See . . ." and "The Summer I Was 13"
Sherwin Bitsui, "Asterisk" and "Chrysalis"
Dwayne Martine, "Hwéeldi"
Tacey Atsitty, "Ach'íí'"
Venaya Yazzie, "No Español"
Orlando White, "Sentence" and "DISSOCIATE"
Bojan Louis, "Currents" and "Nizhoní dóó 'a'ani' dóó até'él'í dóó ayoo'o'oni (Beauty & Memory & Abuse & Love)"
Rachel Heather Johnson, "Apple," "Nowhere Place," and "Hers Was a History of Grief"
Paige Buffington, "At Mention of Moab"

V. RESILIENCE AND CULTURAL IDENTITY

Navajo writers frequently celebrate the strength of the Diné people that is grounded in culture and history and the many ways that they continue to find balance and resilience: through humor and spirituality, through reverence for place and philosophy, through familial and romantic love, through pride in Native sovereignty and ethnicity. Consider the many ways the powerful, persevering identity of Navajo people is expressed in various works.

CONSIDERATIONS AND REFLECTIVE TASKS

- Consider the way writers emphasize how cultural traditions and values are significant to their identities (or their characters' identities) and serve as a resource for strength. What attitudes are expressed toward particular traditions, experiences, and knowledge? If writers explore the challenge of connecting or reconnecting to aspects of being Navajo, what forces stand in the way or must be overcome?

- Pride in Native sovereignty, as well as resistance to settler culture, is not at all common in mainstream literature but frequently embedded in Navajo writing. Locate instances in which a writer makes explicit assertions of Native rights or challenges to non-Native culture. Examine closely the strategies used to highlight the ability of Native people to survive more than five hundred years of colonialism with enthusiasm and hope.
- On occasion cultural strength is expressed artistically in explorations of romantic love. Identify works that explore romance or passion both as a personal experience and as a source of Diné strength and balance.

SUGGESTED WORKS TO CONSIDER

Blackhorse Mitchell, selections from *Miracle Hill*

Grey Cohoe, "The Promised Visit"

Gloria Emerson, "Iron Track City" and "Shapeshifting"

Nia Francisco, "táchééh/sweat house," "iridescent child," and "naabeeho women with blue horses"

Tiana Bighorse, *Bighorse the Warrior*

Tina Deschenie, "You Bring Out the Diné in Me," "We Are Corn," and "In the Best of Dreams"

Luci Tapahonso, "This Is How They Were Placed for Us" and "The Motion of Songs Rising"

Laura Tohe, "Within Dinétah the People's Spirits Remain Strong," "Easter Sunday," "Tsoodził, Mountain to the South," and "Deep in the Rock"

Rex Lee Jim, "Tó Háálį/Spring"

Irvin Morris, from *From the Glittering World*: "Tséhílí" and "Shichei bighandi"

Esther G. Belin, "Sustainability: A Romance in Four Scenes," "Morning Song," and "X+X+X+X−X−X−X"

Hershman John, "My Feminist Grandmother"

Sherwin Bitsui, from *Flood Song*

Venaya Yazzie, "gathering early dawn" and "No Español"

Orlando White, "Meditation"

Byron F. Aspaas, "Interstate Badlands"

Jake Skeets, "From Under His Cover" and "Thieving Ceremony"

Bojan Louis, "Nizhoní dóó 'a'ani'. . . "

Natanya Ann Pulley, "In This Dream of Waking, a Weaver"

Danielle Geller, "Blood; Quantum"

Manny Loley, "Niłtsą́ Biką'"
Tatum Begay, "Stories of a Healing Way"

VI. RELATIONAL IDENTITIES

Many Diné writers explore how all human beings, Bilá' Ashdla'ii (Five Fingered People), value our relations to one another, to land, and to plants and animals. They especially explore the importance of our immediate family and friends and how we learn from those who have come before us. And they use their writing talents to draw vivid portraits of favorite and familiar individuals in order to share specific lessons and the many colors of our human diversity. This overriding relational sense of identity helps us understand how we should value each other, all beings, and the earth.

CONSIDERATIONS AND REFLECTIVE TASKS

- Consider how certain works express regard for Diné clan kinships (K'é, kinship / ak'éí, family, relatives) or for the Navajo writer's immediate family. This may be expressed in different ways, and some writers might be engaged in a process of learning and discovery.
- Healing is essential to overcome trauma, and in Native life, family is one of the most powerful sources of healing power. Consider various works in which family bonds or family stories, especially elder stories, provide a way for someone to recover balance or to reconnect to Diné culture and values.
- As Navajo is a place-based culture, contrast how different writers portray experiences growing up on the Navajo Nation with the portrayal of experiences by those growing up away from the Navajo Nation.
- Animal beings and their ancient and ongoing relationships with humans are also explored in many highly descriptive and evocative works. Study how various writers represent animal beings as significant to Navajo life.

SUGGESTED WORKS TO CONSIDER

Grey Cohoe, "The Promised Visit"
Nia Francisco, "iridescent child," "ode to a drunk woman," and "naabeeho women with blue horses"

Tiana Bighorse, *Bighorse the Warrior*

Tina Deschenie, "Near Crystal"

Luci Tapahonso, "She Sits on the Bridge," "Hills Brothers Coffee," and "The Canyon Was Serene"

Elizabeth Woody, "Chinle Summer"

Irene Hamilton, "Story of a Cricket, Spring 1978"

Laura Tohe, "Easter Sunday"

Rex Lee Jim, "Saad/Language/Voice"

Irvin Morris, from *From the Glittering World*

Esther G. Belin, "Euro-American Womanhood Ceremony," "Ruby's Answer," and "I keep my language in my back pocket . . ."

Della Frank, "Shimasani My Grandmother"

Roberta D. Joe, "Sunset Woman's Ivy League Escape"

Sherwin Bitsui, "The Northern Sun" and from *Flood Song*

Venaya Yazzie, "gathering early dawn"

Orlando White, "PAPER MILK"

Byron F. Aspaas, "Interstate Badlands"

Natanya Ann Pulley, "In This Dream of Waking, a Weaver"

Danielle Geller, "Blood; Quantum"

Paige Buffington, "Radio"

Manny Loley, "Niłtsą́ Biką'"

Erik Bitsui, "Eddie and Norman, Norman and Me, Me and Eddie"

VII. EDUCATION

Diné writers explore both traditional pathways to learning and the challenges for Navajo peoples caused by various so-called assimilation policies that included the removal of children to boarding schools where Diné bizaad was forbidden. This overt suppression of the Navajo language, as well as the separation of children from their families, is frequently represented as destructive to cultural knowledge and community and family bonds. There are also Navajo writers who have had great success in mainstream education and who have applied that mastery to write effectively and expressively about the Navajo contemporary experience.

CONSIDERATIONS AND REFLECTIVE TASKS

- Consider how Navajo writers of various eras portray the cultural conflicts that are inherent in colonizer educational systems, especially the overt exclusion of Diné bizaad. How is the emotional impact of losing one's language shown? How are writers reclaiming the language in their own work?
- Locate instances of the boarding school experience and outline the various responses that are portrayed. Compare these forced educational experiences of an earlier time with the more recent experiences of Navajo artists or scholars in college or graduate school, who are also often far from home. Identify possible factors that shape personal responses to historic and contemporary Western educational practices.

SUGGESTED WORKS TO CONSIDER

Blackhorse Mitchell, "I Do Have a Name," from *Miracle Hill*
Tina Deschenie, "We Are Corn"
Laura Tohe, "Our Tongues Slapped into Silence" and "Joe Babes"
Irvin Morris, from *From the Glittering World*: "Tséhílí"
Esther G. Belin, "Euro-American Womanhood Ceremony"
Roberta D. Joe, "Sunset Woman's Ivy League Escape"
Venaya Yazzie, "No Español"
Orlando White, "Sentence" and "The i is a Cricket"
Byron F. Aspaas, "Interstate Badlands"
Rachel Heather Johnson, "Apple"

VIII. CULTURAL KNOWLEDGE AND CREATION STORIES

Navajo people possess extensive philosophical and spiritual knowledge through rich cultural narratives of how to live in the world and how humans and all of their relatives came to exist, preserved in both story and song. These traditional stories instruct people how to take care of one another and provide a specifically Diné worldview, which includes a deep knowledge of science, politics, governance, psychology, art, and history. Think of how different writers convey elements of creation stories and other traditional stories—sometimes literally, sometimes thematically.

CONSIDERATIONS AND REFLECTIVE TASKS

- Examine works that incorporate specific references to the Diné creation story or the Diyin Dine'é or Ma'ii or to other natural beings in traditional narratives. Explore what relevance these ancient cultural elements still hold for modern Diné society.
- Specific imaginings of well-known traditional figures are frequently characterizations essential to a narrative or act as literary embodiments of foundational Navajo values and cosmology. Select a work containing a familiar Diné cultural icon and explore its function within the overall work. Consider carefully whether such a figure must necessarily be considered a symbol or metaphor; perhaps it could rather simply be an essential member of a fully realized Navajo world.

SUGGESTED WORKS TO CONSIDER

Grey Cohoe, "The Promised Visit" and "Awaken Me Redhouse-borne Again"
Gloria Emerson, "Shapeshifting"
Nia Francisco, "táchééh/sweat house" and "naabeeho women with blue horses"
Tina Deschenie, "We Are Corn"
Luci Tapahonso, "She Sits on the Bridge," "This Is How They Were Placed for Us," "Náneeskaadí," and "The Motion of Songs Rising"
Irene Nakai Hamilton, "Story of a Cricket, Spring 1978"
Laura Tohe, "Niłtsą Bi'áád/Female Rain"
Rex Lee Jim, "Saad/Language/Voice"
Irvin Morris, from *From the Glittering World*: "Shikéyah," "T'áá shábik'ehgo," and "Kééhasht'ínígii"
Esther G. Belin, "Emergence" and "I keep my language in my back pocket . . . "
Shonto Begay, "Darkness at Noon" and "Navajo Power Plant"
Roberta D. Joe, "Storm Pattern" and "Coyote Shuffle Romance"
Hershman John, "Storm Patterns," "The Dark World," and "A Strong Male Rain"
Norla Chee, "Wagon Ride" and "Far Ahead in the Past"
Sherwin Bitsui, from *Flood Song*
Dwayne Martine, "Parsing"
Byron F. Aspaas, "Interstate Badlands"
Jake Skeets, "Let There Be Coal" and "Blue Edge Cord"
Natanya Ann Pulley, "In This Dream of Waking, a Weaver"
Manny Loley, "Niłtsą Biką'"

Tatum Begay, "Stories of a Healing Way"

IX. THE NAVAJO LONG WALK/HWÉELDI

A number of works consider the pivotal moment in Diné history (1864–68) when the U.S. government forcibly rounded up and removed Navajo people from their sacred homeland and imprisoned them, along with Apache people, at Fort Sumner/Bosque Redondo, New Mexico. Diné leaders eventually negotiated the 1868 treaty to secure the release of their people. However, the effects of this collective tragedy continue to influence Diné people and the way artists and writers recall the past.

CONSIDERATIONS AND REFLECTIVE TASKS

- Consider how different writers make the Long Walk experience—including the pain and trauma—palpable and understandable for a contemporary audience. What types of language are used? What scenarios are represented? What does the detailed attention to this history tell us about the importance of tribal memory?
- Are there personal stories of your own family's dislocations or struggles that have helped you to understand the past? Consider how literary works are sometimes able to assist us in understanding significant moments of an entire people's history.
- Hwéeldi was a time of terrible suffering and loss. In reminding readers of the strategies and strength and resilience of those who survived, how do these writers speak to those who follow in their path?

SUGGESTED WORKS TO CONSIDER

Tiana Bighorse, *Bighorse the Warrior*

Luci Tapahonso, "In 1864"

Laura Tohe, "Within Dinétah the People's Spirit Remains Strong"

Irvin Morris, from *From the Glittering World* (also consider selections beyond those included in this volume)

Norla Chee, "An Exhibit Tells the History of Diné Women Weaving"

Dwayne Martine, "Hwééldi"

X. SACRED MOUNTAINS AND THE HOMELAND

According to Diné origin accounts, four sacred mountains were placed as boundary markers within which Navajo people were instructed to live. A number of works explore the powerful relationship of Diné people to specific land and places and to what's known generally as Diné bikéyah.

CONSIDERATIONS AND REFLECTIVE TASKS

- Consider how specific places or landscapes are intimately connected to the very essence of various characters or authors in this anthology or to an understanding of Diné people in general: who they are, where they belong, and what their roles as human beings should be.
- Locate a work in which a very specific element (or elements) of the natural world are integral to the meaning of the work as a whole. Attempt to understand how this significance, perhaps even sacredness, is illustrated.

SUGGESTED WORKS TO CONSIDER

Blackhorse Mitchell, "Beauty of Navajoland"
Tiana Bighorse, *Bighorse the Warrior*
Tina Deschenie, "Near Crystal"
Luci Tapahonso, "This Is How They Were Placed for Us"
Irene Nakai Hamilton, "Sunrise Flight into Acid Rain/Cancelled"
Laura Tohe, "Within Dinétah the People's Spirit Remains Strong" and "Tsoodził, Mountain to the South"
Rex Lee Jim, "Tó Háálį́/Spring"
Irvin Morris, from *From the Glittering World*: "Shikéyah," "T'áá shábik'ehgo," "Kééhasht'ínígii," and "Tséhílí"
Sherwin Bitsui, "The Northern Sun" and selections from *Flood Song*
Manny Loley, "Níłtsą́ Biką'"

XI. GENDER AND SEXUALITY

All cultures develop particular roles for different genders and have different understandings about sexuality. But not all identities or roles are valued the same or fixed in an unchanging way. Cultures are naturally shaped over time by the sociocultural shifts that occur around and within them. Gender and sexuality for Native peoples is a question that exceeds the singular context of social roles and relationships, and necessitates an understanding of issues of sovereignty and self-determination coming from a particular location and history.

Some ways of thinking about gender roles for Navajo people have been shaped by colonization and other outside forces, including religion. Other traditional Navajo understandings of gender roles and behaviors have been passed down within cultural narratives; these include a recognition and understanding of a third gender as well as a respect for and honoring of a matriarchal perspective based on k'é.

CONSIDERATIONS AND REFLECTIVE TASKS

- Compare two different works about romantic relationships and/or sexual desire. What do these works tell us about the different forces, physiological or cultural, that shape physical attraction or the nature of romance?
- Choose different works that represent particular roles for gender nonconforming peoples, men, or women. What do these works teach you about the social values and expectations ascribed to different genders? How do the works illustrate how people learn and perform particular roles?
- How does a particular work provide a space to build on a "decolonial imaginary," one that imagines possibilities for empowerment and resistance in terms of gender? What can Diné love, care, and healing look like outside of western, heteropatriarchal norms?

SUGGESTED WORKS TO CONSIDER

Nia Francisco, "naabeeho women with blue horses"
Tina Deschenie, "You Bring Out the Diné in Me"
Luci Tapahonso, "Raisin Eyes"
Irene Hamilton, "Dishwasher"
Laura Tohe, "Joe Babes"
Esther G. Belin, "Euro-American Womanhood Ceremony," "Backbone," and "male + female divided"
Della Frank, "Shimasani My Grandmother"
Hershman John, "My Feminist Grandmother"

Byron F. Aspaas, "Interstate Badlands"
Jake Skeets, "From Under His Cover" and "Thieving Ceremony"
Manny Loley, "Niłtsą́ Biką'"

ADDITIONAL RESOURCES

Denetdale, Jennifer Nez. "Chairmen, Presidents, and Princesses: The Navajo Nation, Gender, and the Politics of Tradition." *Wíčazo Ša Review*, vol. 21, no. 1, 2006, pp. 9–28.

———. "Representing Changing Woman: A Review Essay on Navajo Women." *American Indian Culture and Research Journal*, vol. 25, no. 3, 2001, pp. 1–26.

———. "Return to 'The Uprising at Beautiful Mountain in 1913' Marriage and Sexuality in the Making of the Modern Navajo Nation" in *Critically Sovereign: Indigenous Gender, Sexuality, and Feminist Studies*. Ed. Joanne Barker. Duke University Press, 2017, pp. 69–98.

———. "Securing Navajo National Boundaries: War, Patriotism, Tradition, and the Diné Marriage Act of 2005." *Wíčazo Ša Review*, vol. 24, no. 2, 2009, pp. 131–48.

Estrada, Gabriel. "Two Spirits, Nádleeh, and LGBTQ2 Navajo Gaze." *American Indian Culture and Research Journal* 35 (4), 2011, pp. 167–90.

House, Carrie. "Blessed by the Holy People." *Journal of Lesbian Studies*, 20:3–4, 2016, pp. 324–41.

Lee, Lloyd L. *Dinę́ Masculinities: Conceptualizations and Reflections*. CreateSpace Independent Publishing Platform, 2013.

Roessel, Ruth. *Women in Navajo Society*. Navajo Curriculum Center, 1981.

Thomas, Wesley. "Navajo Cultural Constructions of Gender and Sexuality." *Two-Spirit People*, edited by Sue-Ellen Jacobs, Wesley Thomas, and Sabine Lang, University of Illinois Press, 1997, pp. 156–73.

ACKNOWLEDGMENTS

We want to thank all of the contributors for their continuing enthusiasm and for having faith in this project. We owe particular thanks to Diné matriarch Gloria Emerson, a steadfast leader of The People. Gloria assisted in forging paths to many of the early writers included in this book. She is a wealth of wisdom and humility. She is a master painter who remains evermore part of the resilience and empowerment of The People. We want to acknowledge Joy Harjo, Simon Ortiz, and Inés Hernández-Avila for their kind words and for their generous support for this book. We extend our thanks to the publishers who have helped facilitate the inclusion of many writers' works and who have helped support the publication of Diné writing. The University of Arizona Press deserves a special call-out for their ongoing commitment to Diné literature and scholarship. We'd like to thank the entire editorial team at the University of Arizona Press for working to make this project a reality: Kristen Buckles, Amanda Krause, Leigh McDonald, Abby Mogollón, Mari Herreras, and Susan Campbell. Thank you for trusting our vision. Thank you to the numerous educators who have supported Navajo poetry in the schools and who have invited writers into their classrooms. Thank you to Manny Loley and the Emerging Diné Writers' Institute for creating a space to inspire new generations of writers. And thank you, Manny, for helping us with a few author biographies! Thank you to Jessie Cohoe Russell and the

Cohoe family for allowing us to include Grey's work. Thank you also to Sallie Maloney, Tiana Bighorse's daughter, and to Noëll Bennett, for supporting the inclusion of Tiana's work. We hope this book honors the legacy of writers who are no longer with us as well as the supporters of Diné literary sovereignty who passed on during the creation of this book: Larry Emerson, LaFrenda Frank, and Susan Brill de Ramírez. Thank you to the student workers in the NAU Department of English who helped us transcribe and scan much of this work. Thank you to Aimee Hosemann for assistance in reviewing the final manuscript. And, finally, thank you to Sierra Edd for her illustrated map of the Navajo Nation, and to Shonto Begay for granting us permission to use his beautiful painting as our cover image.

The process of working on this book confirms that my writing was never my own—and it will always be a vehicle for healing from the intergenerational trauma I've inherited. My four daughters are always the inspiration to keep pursuing my work, whether in writing or visual art. I thank them for following me as a leader especially during the times I had no idea where we were going. I thank the Creator of the Universe who led me to the IAIA where I met Simon Ortiz, who assisted in the publication of my first book, and Joy Harjo, who recommended me for one of my first poetry jobs. To longtime IAIA poetry faculty Arthur Sze, he laid a good foundation. The myriad of urban Indians all over the planet have also contributed to my poetry genealogy. Special appreciation goes to the Diné writers who continue to be a resilient pillar on the reservation and support Diné poetics: Irvin Morris, Orlando White, Gloria Emerson, Manny Loley, Jake Skeets, and Rex Lee Jim. I am thankful for the friendships of Jeff Berglund, Connie Jacobs, and Anthony Webster—each one's insight has helped me to stay focused and to honor the purpose of this book.

—Esther G. Belin

Deep appreciation to all of the writers in this anthology who have befriended me over the years and supported my work as a teacher and researcher. Laura Tohe and Simon Ortiz, you extended me support and trust and friendship at a crucial point in my professional life. Sherwin Bitsui, how did I luck out that you're now my colleague? I especially want to thank Jennifer Denetdale for great conversations, lots of laughs, and for being my friend since way back when we were new assistant professors at NAU. Thank you to the K–12 teachers who are part of NAU's Diné Institute for Navajo Nation Educators (DINÉ); your dedication to your students inspires me. I'm so grateful for the probing, insightful, and game-changing conversations I had with Mary Frances Begaye and Michael Thompson at Greyhills Academy High School in Tuba City at the 2001 National Endowment Summer Institute on American Indian literature I ran for high school teachers. Thank you to my students at NAU over the last two decades, especially Debbie Eriacho, who challenged me to think critically and deeply, and to Bojan Louis and Tatum Begay, who continue to astound me with their creative genius. Thank you to Celeste Jackson, Alejandra Valadez, Baylee Nasbah Garcia, and the Interns-to-Scholars Program, who supported my research efforts on various parts of this project. Thank you to Chad Hamill, Kathleen Frank, Sharon Doctor, Ora Marek-Martinez, Octaviana Trujillo, Priscilla Sanderson, Karen Jarratt-Snider, and Ricardo Guthrie for your support and enthusiasm. Special thanks are due to Bronwyn Carlson, Michelle Harris, and Harvey Charles for expanding the world for me. To my dear editorial colleagues, I thank you for trusting me to work with you. Tony Webster, your knowledge is boundless, and I appreciate your encyclopedic and generous mind. Connie Jacobs, I'm so grateful for the serious and focused discussions we have had about literature we both love so much and our students whom we care for so deeply. You've been an important role model to me. Esther Belin, I'm so glad Monica invited you to NAU in 2000. Who knew we'd stay friends and watch our daughters stretch up and move out into the world to accomplish so much? I value your friendship and artistic vision. And, finally, thank you to my family, from whom all good flows. I reserve special gratitude to Monica, for always inspiring me and showing me how to see a world of possibilities, and for our daughters Isabella and Juliana, for becoming my teachers and always reminding me that the future is here now.

—*Jeff Berglund*

I want to thank all of my Diné students at San Juan College, especially Byron Aspaas, who were the inspiration for me wanting to see a book like this for them to read and to dream that they, too, could be writers. This book wanted to happen, and it was because of the dedication of my co-editors, Esther Belin, Jeff Berglund, and Anthony Webster, that our idea became a reality. Esther is the heart of this volume. Her friendships with many of the featured writers allowed us entrées that would have remained closed to us without her. She guided us on sensitive cultural issues and gently but firmly corrected any of our missteps. Jeff Berglund is a master administrator. Not only did he manage schedules and all things technical, he also brought his considerable experience of teaching Diné students and Diné educators to bear upon this book. Jeff made all things happen, especially this book. Anthony Webster's fieldwork in Navajo linguistics and his acquaintance with many of the featured writers enhanced this book. To understand the nuances of a language and how they reflect culture was his important contribution, as well as his historical and contemporary knowledge of Diné writers. My gratitude to all of my editors for their dedication to this book and my gratitude to all of the Diné writers who so willingly and graciously shared their work with us.

—Connie A. Jacobs

I'd like to thank Aimee Hosemann for useful advice over the years, Chris McNett for taking care of some of the financial issues, and, of course, all the Navajos that I've talked with over the years about Navajo poetry, language, and culture. Research on the Navajo Nation was done under permits from the Navajo Historic Preservation Office. I thank them.

—Anthony K. Webster

BIBLIOGRAPHY

PRIMARY SOURCES

Atsitty, Tacey. *amenorrhea.* Counting Coup Press, 2009.

———. *Rain Scald.* University of New Mexico Press, 2018.

Beck, Peggy, Anna Lee Walters, and Nia Francisco, editors. *Sacred Ways of Knowledge, Sources of Life*. Navajo Community College Press, 1977.

Begay, Shonto. *Ma'ii and Cousin Horned Toad: A Traditional Navajo Story*. Scholastic, 1992.

———. *Navajo Visions and Voices Across the Mesa.* Scholastic, 1995.

Belin, Esther G. *From the Belly of My Beauty*. University of Arizona Press, 1999.

———. *Of Cartography*. University of Arizona Press, 2017.

Bighorse, Tiana. *Bighorse the Warrior*. University of Arizona Press, 1990.

Bitsui, Sherwin. *Dissolve*. Copper Canyon Press, 2018.

———. *Flood Song*. Copper Canyon Press, 2009.

———. *Shapeshift*. University of Arizona Press, 2003.

Bruchac, Joseph, and Shonto Begay. *Navajo Long Walk: The Tragic Story of a Proud People's Forced March from Their Homeland.* National Geographic Society, 2002.

Chee, Norla. *Cedar Smoke on Abalone Mountain.* UCLA American Indian Studies Center, 2001.

Cohoe, Grey. "Awaken Me Redhouse-borne Again." *Wičazo Ša Review*, vol. 1, no. 2, 1985, pp. 11–22.

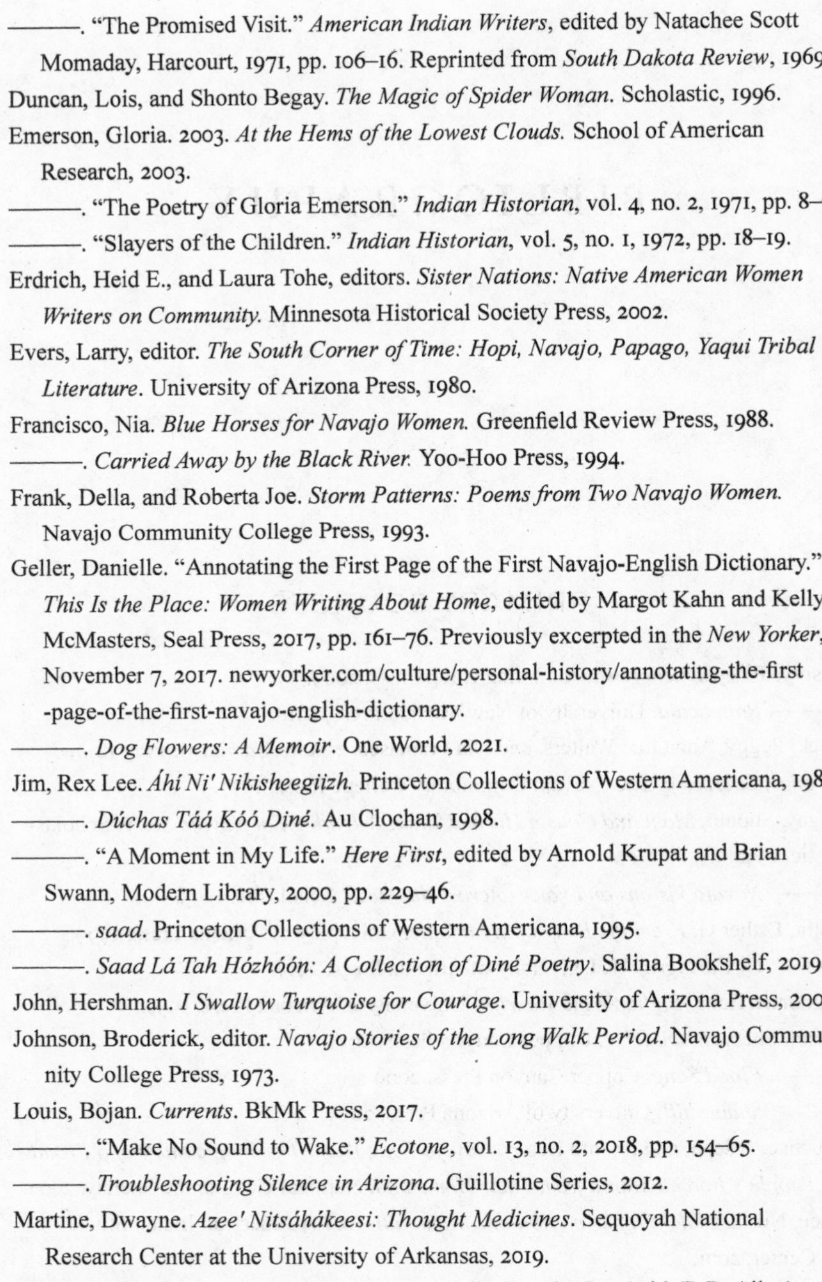

———. "The Promised Visit." *American Indian Writers*, edited by Natachee Scott Momaday, Harcourt, 1971, pp. 106–16. Reprinted from *South Dakota Review*, 1969.

Duncan, Lois, and Shonto Begay. *The Magic of Spider Woman*. Scholastic, 1996.

Emerson, Gloria. 2003. *At the Hems of the Lowest Clouds*. School of American Research, 2003.

———. "The Poetry of Gloria Emerson." *Indian Historian*, vol. 4, no. 2, 1971, pp. 8–9.

———. "Slayers of the Children." *Indian Historian*, vol. 5, no. 1, 1972, pp. 18–19.

Erdrich, Heid E., and Laura Tohe, editors. *Sister Nations: Native American Women Writers on Community*. Minnesota Historical Society Press, 2002.

Evers, Larry, editor. *The South Corner of Time: Hopi, Navajo, Papago, Yaqui Tribal Literature*. University of Arizona Press, 1980.

Francisco, Nia. *Blue Horses for Navajo Women*. Greenfield Review Press, 1988.

———. *Carried Away by the Black River*. Yoo-Hoo Press, 1994.

Frank, Della, and Roberta Joe. *Storm Patterns: Poems from Two Navajo Women*. Navajo Community College Press, 1993.

Geller, Danielle. "Annotating the First Page of the First Navajo-English Dictionary." *This Is the Place: Women Writing About Home*, edited by Margot Kahn and Kelly McMasters, Seal Press, 2017, pp. 161–76. Previously excerpted in the *New Yorker*, November 7, 2017. newyorker.com/culture/personal-history/annotating-the-first-page-of-the-first-navajo-english-dictionary.

———. *Dog Flowers: A Memoir*. One World, 2021.

Jim, Rex Lee. *Áhí Ni' Nikisheegiizh*. Princeton Collections of Western Americana, 1989.

———. *Dúchas Táá Kóó Diné*. Au Clochan, 1998.

———. "A Moment in My Life." *Here First*, edited by Arnold Krupat and Brian Swann, Modern Library, 2000, pp. 229–46.

———. *saad*. Princeton Collections of Western Americana, 1995.

———. *Saad Lá Tah Hózhóón: A Collection of Diné Poetry*. Salina Bookshelf, 2019.

John, Hershman. *I Swallow Turquoise for Courage*. University of Arizona Press, 2007.

Johnson, Broderick, editor. *Navajo Stories of the Long Walk Period*. Navajo Community College Press, 1973.

Louis, Bojan. *Currents*. BkMk Press, 2017.

———. "Make No Sound to Wake." *Ecotone*, vol. 13, no. 2, 2018, pp. 154–65.

———. *Troubleshooting Silence in Arizona*. Guillotine Series, 2012.

Martine, Dwayne. *Azee' Nitsáhákeesi: Thought Medicines*. Sequoyah National Research Center at the University of Arkansas, 2019.

Mitchell, Blackhorse. *Miracle Hill: The Story of a Navaho Boy* (with T. D. Allen). University of Oklahoma Press, 1967.

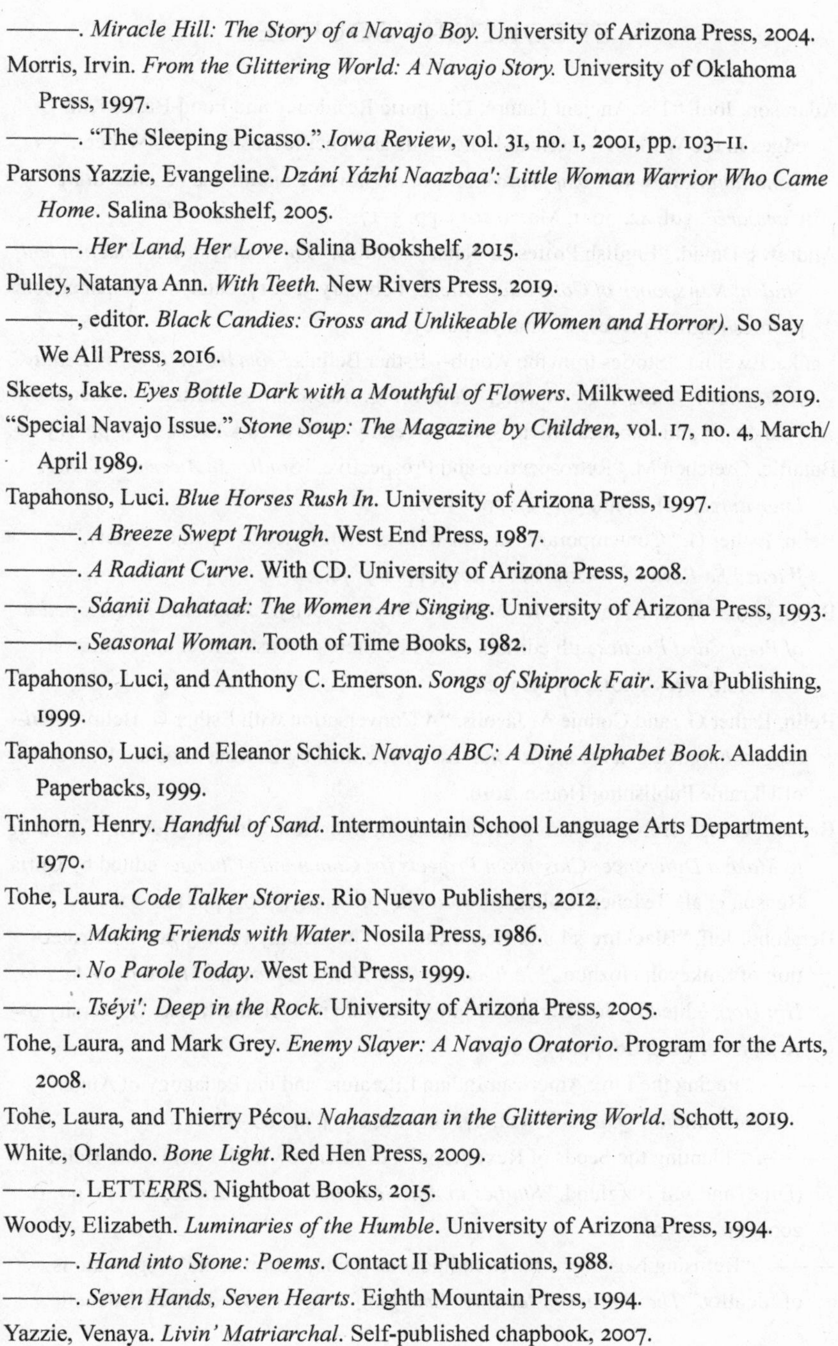

———. *Miracle Hill: The Story of a Navajo Boy*. University of Arizona Press, 2004.

Morris, Irvin. *From the Glittering World: A Navajo Story*. University of Oklahoma Press, 1997.

———. "The Sleeping Picasso." *Iowa Review*, vol. 31, no. 1, 2001, pp. 103–11.

Parsons Yazzie, Evangeline. *Dzání Yázhí Naazbaa': Little Woman Warrior Who Came Home*. Salina Bookshelf, 2005.

———. *Her Land, Her Love*. Salina Bookshelf, 2015.

Pulley, Natanya Ann. *With Teeth*. New Rivers Press, 2019.

———, editor. *Black Candies: Gross and Unlikeable (Women and Horror)*. So Say We All Press, 2016.

Skeets, Jake. *Eyes Bottle Dark with a Mouthful of Flowers*. Milkweed Editions, 2019.

"Special Navajo Issue." *Stone Soup: The Magazine by Children*, vol. 17, no. 4, March/April 1989.

Tapahonso, Luci. *Blue Horses Rush In*. University of Arizona Press, 1997.

———. *A Breeze Swept Through*. West End Press, 1987.

———. *A Radiant Curve*. With CD. University of Arizona Press, 2008.

———. *Sáanii Dahataał: The Women Are Singing*. University of Arizona Press, 1993.

———. *Seasonal Woman*. Tooth of Time Books, 1982.

Tapahonso, Luci, and Anthony C. Emerson. *Songs of Shiprock Fair*. Kiva Publishing, 1999.

Tapahonso, Luci, and Eleanor Schick. *Navajo ABC: A Diné Alphabet Book*. Aladdin Paperbacks, 1999.

Tinhorn, Henry. *Handful of Sand*. Intermountain School Language Arts Department, 1970.

Tohe, Laura. *Code Talker Stories*. Rio Nuevo Publishers, 2012.

———. *Making Friends with Water*. Nosila Press, 1986.

———. *No Parole Today*. West End Press, 1999.

———. *Tséyi': Deep in the Rock*. University of Arizona Press, 2005.

Tohe, Laura, and Mark Grey. *Enemy Slayer: A Navajo Oratorio*. Program for the Arts, 2008.

Tohe, Laura, and Thierry Pécou. *Nahasdzaan in the Glittering World*. Schott, 2019.

White, Orlando. *Bone Light*. Red Hen Press, 2009.

———. LETT*ERR*S. Nightboat Books, 2015.

Woody, Elizabeth. *Luminaries of the Humble*. University of Arizona Press, 1994.

———. *Hand into Stone: Poems*. Contact II Publications, 1988.

———. *Seven Hands, Seven Hearts*. Eighth Mountain Press, 1994.

Yazzie, Venaya. *Livin' Matriarchal*. Self-published chapbook, 2007.

SECONDARY SOURCES

Adamson, Joni. "The Ancient Future: Diasporic Residency and Food-Based Knowledges in the Work of American Indigenous and Pacific Austronesian Writers." *Canadian Review of Comparative Literature/Revue Canadienne de Littérature Comparée*, vol. 42, no. 1, March 2015, pp. 5–17.

Andrews, David. "English Professor Natanya Pulley." *The Catalyst, The Independent Student Newspaper of Colorado College*, February 3, 2017. catalystnewspaper.com/profiles/english-professor-natanya-pulley/.

Bańka, Ewelina. "Stories from the Womb—Esther Belin's *From the Belly of My Beauty*." *Indigenous Bodies: Reviewing, Relocating, Reclaiming*, edited by Jacqueline Fear-Segal and Rebecca Tillett, State University of New York Press, 2013, pp. 113–26.

Bataille, Gretchen M. "Retrospective and Prospective." *Studies in American Indian Literatures*, vol. 9, no. 3, 1997, pp. 25–30.

Belin, Esther G. "Contemporary Navajo Writers' Relevance to Navajo Society." *Wičazo Ša Review*, vol. 22, no. 1, 2007, pp. 69–76.

Belin, Esther G., and Anthony K. Webster. "Navajo Poetry." *Princeton Encyclopedia of Poetry and Poetics*, 4th edition, edited by Stephen Cushman et al., Princeton University Press, 2012, pp. 923–24.

Belin, Esther G., and Connie A. Jacobs. "A Conversation with Esther G. Belin." *Philological Measurements of National Identity*, edited by Oksana Shostak, University of Ukraine Publishing House, 2019.

Benson, Chris. "Between Sacred Mountains: An Interview with Rex Lee Jim." *Writing to Make a Difference: Classroom Projects for Community Change*, edited by Chris Benson et al., Teachers College, Columbia University, 2002, pp. 174–82.

Berglund, Jeff. "Blackfire's Land-Based Ethics: The Benally Family and the Protection of Shikéyah Hozhoni." *Indigenous Pop: Native American Music from Jazz to Hip Hop*, edited by Jeff Berglund, Janis Johnson, and Kimberli Lee, University of Arizona Press, 2016, pp. 179–200.

———. "Facing the Fire: American Indian Literature and the Pedagogy of Anger." *American Indian Quarterly*, vol. 27, nos. 1/2, 2003, pp. 80–90.

———. "'Planting the Seeds of Revolution': An Interview with Poet Esther Belin (Diné) and Jeff Berglund." *Studies in American Indian Literatures*, vol. 17, no. 1, 2005, pp. 62–72.

———. "Refusing Nostalgia: Three Indigenous [Diné] Filmmakers' Negotiations of Identity." *The Politics of Identity: Emerging Indigeneity*, edited by Michelle

Harris, Martin Nakata, and Bronwyn Carlson, University of Sydney e-press, 2013, pp. 185–208.

Brandt, Rose K., editor. *The Colored Land: A Navajo Indian Book Written and Illustrated by Navajo Children.* Charles Scribner and Sons, 1937.

Brill, Susan B. "Discovering the Order and Structure of Things: A Conversive Approach to Contemporary Navajo Poetry." *Studies in American Indian Literatures*, vol. 7, no. 3, 1995, pp. 51–70.

———. "Review *From the Glittering World: A Navajo Story* by Irvin Morris." *Studies in American Indian Literatures*, vol. 9, no. 4, 1997, pp. 80–89.

Brill de Ramírez, Susan. "Ałk'idáá' jiní . . . Luci Tapahonso, Irvin Morris, and Della Frank." *Cimarron Review*, vol. 121, 1997, pp. 135–53.

———. *Contemporary American Indian Literatures and the Oral Tradition.* University of Arizona Press, 1999.

———. "Literary Explorations into the Poetic Sonority of Contemporary Diné (Navajo) Poetry." *ANQ: A Quarterly Journal of Short Articles, Notes, and Reviews*, vol. 24, no. 3, 2011, pp. 181–92.

———. *Native American Life-History Narratives: Colonial and Postcolonial Navajo Ethnography.* Albuquerque: University of New Mexico Press, 2007.

Bruchac, Joseph. "A *MELUS* Interview: Luci Tapahonso." *MELUS*, vol. 11, no. 4, 1984, pp. 85–91.

Burkhart, Matthew, *"Travels in the Glittering World": Transcultural Representations of Navajo Country*. University of Arizona, PhD dissertation, 2010.

Clover, Faith. "Shonto Begay Talks About His Art." *School Arts*, vol. 97, no. 2, 1997.

Cruz, Margarita. "Lands Shift and So Should Poems: An Interview with Jake Skeets." *Thin Air Magazine*, October 17, 2018. thinairmagazine.org/2018/09/20/lands-shift-and-so-should-poems-an-interview-with-jake-skeets/.

DeLeon, Jennifer. "I Don't Stand Alone: Poets Orlando White and Sherwin Bitsui on the Importance of Mentors." *Ploughshares at Emerson College*. November 1, 2012. blog.pshares.org/index.php/i-dont-stand-alone-poets-orlando-white-and-sherwin-bitsui-on-the-importance-of-mentors/.

Denetdale, Jennifer Nez. "Chairmen, Presidents, and Princesses: The Navajo Nation, Gender, and the Politics of Tradition." *Wičazo Ša Review*, vol. 21, no. 1, 2006, pp. 9–28.

———. "Discontinuities, Remembrances, and Cultural Survival: History, Diné/Navajo Memory, and the Bosque Redondo Memorial." *New Mexico Historical Review*, vol. 82, no. 3, 2007, pp. 295–316.

———. *The Long Walk: The Forced Navajo Exile*. Chelsea House Publishers, 2008.

———. "'No Explanation, No Resolution, and No Answers': Border Town Violence and Navajo Resistance to Settler Colonialism." *Wičazo Ša Review*, vol. 31, no. 1, 2016, pp. 111–31.

———. *Reclaiming Diné History: The Legacies of Navajo Chief Manuelito and Juanita*. University of Arizona Press, 2007.

———. "Representing Changing Woman: A Review Essay on Navajo Women." *American Indian Culture and Research Journal*, vol. 25, no. 3, 2001, pp. 1–26.

———. "Securing Navajo National Boundaries: War, Patriotism, Tradition, and the Diné Marriage Act of 2005." *Wičazo Ša Review*, vol. 24, no. 2, 2009, pp. 131–48.

Fast, Robin Riley. *The Heart as a Drum: Continuance and Resistance in American Indian Poetry*. University of Michigan Press, 1999.

———. "The Land Is Full of Stories: Navajo Histories in the Work of Luci Tapahonso." *Women's Studies*, vol. 36, 2007, pp. 185–211.

Fugue Staff. "Bojan Louis Interview." *Fugue 54* Online Issue, 2018, fuguejournal.com/bojan-louis-interview.

Goeman, Mishuana. "(Re)routing Native Mobility, Uprooting Settler Spaces in the Poetry of Esther Belin." *Mark My Words: Native Women Mapping Our Nations*. University of Minnesota Press, 2013, pp. 87–118.

Hachard, Tomas. "Sherwin Bitsui: Sounds Like Water." *Guernica*, June 21, 2013. guernicamag.com/sherwin-bitsui-sounds-like-water/.

Hamilton, Amy T. "Remembering Migration and Removal in American Indian Women's Poetry." *Rocky Mountain Review of Language and Literature*, vol. 61, no. 2, 2007, pp. 54–62.

Harjo, Joy. "Sherwin Bitsui: Interview." *Bomb Magazine*, December 5, 2018. bombmagazine.org/articles/sherwin-bitsui.

Hoover, Jessica S. *(Re)claiming History and Visibility Through Rhetorical Sovereignty: The Power of Dine Rhetorics in the Works of Laura Tohe*. Illinois State University, PhD dissertation, 2017.

———. "Rhetorical Sovereignty in Written Poetry: Survivance Through Code Switching and Translation in Laura Tohe's *Tséyi'/Deep in the Rock: Reflections on Canyon de Chelly*." *Survivance, Sovereignty, and Story: Teaching American Indian Rhetorics*, edited by Lisa King, Rose Gubele, and Joyce R. Anderson, Utah State University Press, 2015, pp. 170–87.

"Intermountain Indian School." Utah State University Digital History Collections. https://digital.lib.usu.edu/digital/collection/IndSchool.

Jacobs, Connie A. "From California to the Four Corners: An Urban Navajo Returns Home: An Interview with Esther Belin." *Studies in American Indian Literatures*, vol. 12, no. 3, 2000, pp. 1–13.

———. "Mending the Broken Circle: The Power of Literature to Heal Racial Strife." *ADE Bulletin*, vol. 145, 2008, pp. 25–32.

Kahn, Margot. "A Conversation with Danielle Geller." *True: Proximity Magazine*, December 6, 2018. true.proximitymagazine.org/2018/12/06/a-conversation-with-danielle-geller/.

Katanski, Amelia V. *Learning to Write "Indian": The Boarding-School Experience and American Indian Literature*. University of Oklahoma Press, 2005.

Kelley, Klara, and Harris Francis. *A Diné History of Navajoland*. University of Arizona Press, 2019.

Killelea, Patricia. *Between These Songs: Contemporary Experimental Native American Poetry and Poetics*. University of California, Davis, PhD dissertation, 2015.

King, Farina. *The Earth Memory Compass: Diné Landscapes and Education in the Twentieth Century*. University of Kansas Press, 2018.

Kwasny, Melissa. "Ghost Dance: The Poetics of Loss." *American Poetry Review*, vol. 44, no. 2, 2015, pp. 11–19.

Lee, Lloyd, editor. *Diné Perspectives: Revitalizing and Reclaiming Navajo Thought*. University of Arizona Press, 2014.

———. "The Future of Navajo Nationalism." *Wičazo Ša Review*, vol. 22, no. 1, 2007, pp. 53–68.

———. "Navajo Cultural Identity: What Can the Navajo Nation Bring to the American Indian Identity Table?" *Wičazo Ša Review*, vol. 21, no. 2, 2006, pp. 79–103.

———, editor. *Navajo Sovereignty: Understandings and Visions of the Diné People*. University of Arizona Press, 2017.

———. "Reclaiming Indigenous Intellectual, Political, and Geographic Space." *American Indian Quarterly*, vol. 32, no. 1, 2008, pp. 96–110.

Lee, Tiffany. "'If They Want Navajo to Be Learned, Then They Should Require It in All Schools': Navajo Teenagers' Experiences, Choices, and Demands Regarding Navajo Language." *Wičazo Ša Review*, vol. 22, no. 1, 2007, pp. 7–33.

———. "Language, Identity, and Power: Navajo and Pueblo Young Adults' Perspectives and Experiences with Competing Language Ideologies." *Journal of Language, Identity, and Education*, vol. 8, 2009, pp. 307–20.

Lewis, Randolph. *Navajo Talking Picture: Cinema on Native Ground*. University of Nebraska Press, 2010.

———. "The New Navajo Cinema: Cinema and Nation in the Indigenous Southwest." *Velvet Light Trap*, vol. 66, 2010, pp. 50–61.

Lincoln, Kenneth. "Southwest Crossings: Luci Tapahonso and Leslie Silko." *Speak Like Singing: Classics of Native American Literature*, University of New Mexico Press, 2007, pp. 95–124.

———. "Diné Shapeshifter: Sherwin Bitsui." *Speak Like Singing: Classics of Native American Literature*, University of New Mexico Press, 2007, pp. 287–326.

Lockard, Louise. "New Paper Words: Historical Images of Navajo Language Literacy." *American Indian* Quarterly, vol. 19, no. 1, 1995, pp. 17–30.

Louis, Bojan. "Interview with Jake Skeets: On Negotiating Brutality and Beauty." *High Country News*, November 11, 2019. https://www.hcn.org/issues/51.19/interview-on-negotiating-brutality-and-beauty.

Low, Denise. "Boarding School Resistance Narratives: Haskell Runaway and Ghost Stories." *Studies in American Indian Literatures*, vol. 15, no. 2, 2003, pp. 106–18.

Magneson, Clare. "Writing the Diné Presence into Existence: An Interview with Laura Tohe." *Thin Air Magazine*, October 17, 2018. thinairmagazine.org/2018/10/17/writing-the-dine-presence-into-existence-an-interview-with-laura-tohe/.

Matt, Aretha. *Reclamation and Survivance: Diné Rhetorics and the Practice of Rhetorical Sovereignty*. University of Arizona, PhD dissertation, 2011.

McCullough-Brabson, Ellen, and Marilyn Help. *We'll Be in Your Mountains, We'll Be in Your Songs: A Navajo Woman Sings.* University of New Mexico Press, 2001. Print and CD.

Mitchell, Blackhorse, and Anthony K. Webster. "'We Don't Know What We Become': Navajo Ethnopoetics and an Expressive Feature in a Poem by Rex Lee Jim." *Anthropological Linguistics*, vol. 53, no. 3, 2011, pp. 259–86.

Moore, David L. "Rough Knowledge and Radical Understanding: Sacred Silence in American Indian Literatures." *American Indian Quarterly*, vol. 21, no. 4, 1997, pp. 633–62.

Parsons Yazzie, Evangeline, and Margaret Speas. *Diné Bizaad Bínáhoóaah or Rediscovering the Navajo Language*. Salina Bookshelf, 2008.

Penner, Andrea. "'The Moon Is So Far Away': An Interview with Luci Tapahonso." *Studies in American Indian Literatures*, vol. 8, no. 3, 1996, pp. 1–12.

Penner, Andrea Millenson. *At Once, Gentle and Powerful: Voices of the Landscape in the Poetry of Luci Tapahonso*. Northern Arizona University, MA thesis, 1993.

———. *"The Original in Ourselves": Native American Women Writers and the Construction of Indian Women's Identity.* University of New Mexico, PhD dissertation, 2001.

Peterson, Leighton C. "Reclaiming Diné Film: Visual Sovereignty and the Return of *Navajo Film Themselves*." *Visual Anthropology Review*, vol. 29, no. 1, 2013, pp. 29–41.

———. "'Reel Navajo': The Linguistic Creation of Indigenous Screen Memories." *American Indian Culture and Research Journal*, vol. 35, no. 2, 2011, pp. 111–34.

———. "Tuning in to Navajo: The Role of Radio in Native Language Maintenance." *Teaching Indigenous Languages*, edited by Jon Reyhner, Northern Arizona University Press, 1997, pp. 214–21.

Prampolini, Gaetano. "About the Genre(s) of Irvin Morris' *From the Glittering World: A Navajo Story*." *The Shade of the Saguaro/La sombra del saguaro: Essays on the Literary Cultures of the American Southwest/Ensayos sobre las culturas literarias del suroeste norteamericano*, edited by Gaetano Prampolini and Annamaria Pinazzi, Firenze University Press, 2013, pp. 139–50.

———. "The Growth of Luci Tapahonso's Poetic Voice." *The Shade of the Saguaro/La sombra del saguaro: Essays on the Literary Cultures of the American Southwest/Ensayos sobre las culturas literarias del suroeste norteamericano*, edited by Gaetano Prampolini and Annamaria Pinazzi, Firenze University Press, 2013, pp. 111–21.

Radar, Dean. "I Don't Speak Navajo: Esther G. Belin's *In the Belly of My Beauty*." *Studies in American Indian Literatures*, vol. 12, no. 3, 2000, pp. 14–34.

———. "Luci Tapahonso and Simon Ortiz: Allegory, Symbol, Language, Poetry." *Southwestern American Literature*, vol. 22, no. 2, 1997, pp. 75–92.

Roberts, Cody, and Gavin Healey. "Oral History Interview with Hershman John." March 2009. Video recording with transcript. cdm16748.contentdm.oclc.org/cdm/ref/collection/cpa/id/65009.

Roemer, Kenneth M. "It's Not a Poem. It's My Life: Navajo Singing Identities." *Studies in American Indian Literatures*, vol. 24, no. 2, 2012, pp. 84–103.

———. "The Nightway Questions American Literature." *American Literature*, vol. 66, 1994, pp. 817–29.

Schmidt, Anna. "'Fragmentary Holiness': Spirituality and Environmental Justice in the Poetry of Elizabeth Woody and Melissa Kwasny." *Isle: Interdisciplinary Studies in Literature and Environment*, vol. 25, no. 3, 2018, pp. 468–89.

Smith, Matthew Ryan. "Orlando White: Diné Poet and Educator." *First American Art Magazine*, 2016, pp. 100–103.

Tapahonso, Luci, and David K. Dunaway. Interview. *Writing the Southwest*. By Hand Productions, 1990. Sound recording.

Taylor, Michael P., and Terence Wride. "'Indian Kids Can't Write Sonnets": Re-membering the Poetry of Henry Tinhorn from the Intermountain Indian School." *American Quarterly*, vol. 72, no. 1, 2020, pp. 25–53.

Thomas, Wesley. "Navajo Cultural Constructions of Gender and Sexuality." *Two-Spirit People,* edited by Sue-Ellen Jacobs, Wesley Thomas, and Sabine Lang, University of Illinois Press, 1997, pp. 156–73.

Tillett, Rebecca. "Seeing with a 'New and Different Eye': Interactions of Culture and Nature in Contemporary Navajo Writing." *European Review of Native American Studies*, vol. 20, no. 1, 2006, pp. 17–22.

Tohe, Laura. "*Hwéeldi Béého̜niih*: Remembering the Long Walk." *Wičazo Ša Review*, vol. 22, no. 1, 2007, pp. 77–82.

———. "There Is No Word for Feminism in My Language." *Wičazo Ša Review*, vol. 15, no. 2, 2000, pp. 103–7.

Webster, Anthony K. "The Art of Failure in Translating a Navajo Poem." *Journal de la Société des Américanistes*, vol. 102, no. 1, 2016, pp. 9–41.

———. "Coyote Poems: Navajo Poetry, Intertextuality, and Language Choice." *American Indian Culture and Research Journal*, vol. 28, no. 4, 2004, pp. 69–91.

———. "'Don't Talk About It': Navajo Poets and Their Ordeals of Language." *Journal of Anthropological Research*, vol. 68, no. 3, 2012, pp. 399–414.

———. *Explorations in Navajo Poetry and Poetics*. University of New Mexico Press, 2009.

———. "'I Don't Write Navajo Poetry, I Just Speak the Poetry in Navajo': Ethical Listeners, Poetic Communion, and the Imagined Future Publics of Navajo Poetry." *Engaging Native American Publics: Linguistic Anthropology in a New Key*, edited by Paul V. Kroskrity and Barbra A. Meek, Routledge, 2017, pp. 149–68.

———. *Intimate Grammars: An Ethnography of Navajo Poetry*. University of Arizona Press, 2015.

———. "The Mouse That Sucked: On 'Translating' a Navajo Poem." *Studies in American Indian Literatures*, vol. 18, no. 1, 2006, pp. 37–49.

———. "A Note on Navajo Interlingual Puns." *International Journal of American Linguistics*, vol. 76, no. 2, 2010, pp. 289–98.

———. *The Sounds of Navajo Poetry: A Humanities of Speaking*. Peter Lang, 2018.

———. "'To Give an Imagination to the Listener': Replicating Proper Ways of Speaking in and through Contemporary Navajo Poetry." *Telling Stories in the Face of Danger: Language Renewal in Native American Communities*, edited by Paul V. Kroskrity, University of Oklahoma Press, 2012, pp. 205–27.

Wheeler, Jennifer L. *"Saad Bee Hahóózhǫǫd Jini": It Began Harmoniously with Language It Is Said: Navajo Women's Literature Analysis, Personal Short Fiction, and an Introduction to an Oral Narrative*. Arizona State University, PhD dissertation, 2011.

Witherspoon, Gary. *Language and Art in the Navajo Universe*. University of Michigan Press, 1977.

Yazzie, Ethelou. *Navajo History*. Navajo Community College Press, 1971.

Zolbrod, Paul G. "Navajo Poetry in a Changing World: What the Diné Can Teach Us." *Studies in American Indian Literatures*, vol. 6, no. 4, 1994, pp. 77–93.

CREDITS

Grateful acknowledgment is made for permission to reprint previously published material by the following authors. Unless noted below, all other work is original to this volume. The role played by these other publishers and editors of journals and books cannot be stressed strongly enough. We recognize and commend their role in sustaining and fostering the publication of Diné literature.

Blackhorse Mitchell: "I Do Have a Name" and "The Drifting Lonely Seed" were originally published in Mitchell's *Miracle Hill: The Story of a Navajo Boy* (University of Arizona Press, 2004), a revised version of *Miracle Hill: The Story of a Navaho Boy* (University of Oklahoma Press, 1967). "Beauty of Navajoland" was originally published in Anthony K. Webster's *Intimate Grammars: An Ethnography of Navajo Poetry* (University of Arizona Press, 2015).

Grey Cohoe: "The Promised Visit" was first published in the *South Dakota Review* in 1969 and "Awaken Me Redhouse-borne Again" was first published in *Wičazo Ša Review*, vol. 1, no. 2, 1985, pp. 11–14+.

Nia Francisco: "táchééh/sweat house" and "ode to a drunk woman" were originally published in *College English*, vol. 39, no. 3, 1977; "iridescent child" was originally published in *American Indian Quarterly*, vol. 6, nos. 1/2, 1982; "naabeeho women with blue horses" was originally published in Francisco's *Blue Horses for Navajo Women* (Greenfield Review Press, 1988); and, "i hate elvis presley" was originally published in Francisco's *Carried Away by the Black River* (Yoo-Hoo Press, 1994).

Tiana Bighorse: Selections from *Bighorse the Warrior* were originally published in *Bighorse the Warrior*, edited by Nöel Bennett (University of Arizona Press, 1990).

Luci Tapahonso: "She Sits on the Bridge" was originally published in *Earth Power Coming* (Navajo Community College Press, 1983); "Hills Brothers Coffee" and "Raisin Eyes" were originally published in Tapahonso's *A Breeze Swept Through* (West End Press, 1987) and in Tapahonso's *Sáanii Dahataał / The Women Are Singing* (University of Arizona Press, 1993); "In 1864" and "The Motion of Songs Rising" were originally published in Tapahonso's *Sáanii Dahataał / The Women Are Singing* (University of Arizona Press, 1993); "This Is How They Were Placed for Us" was originally published in Tapahonso's *Blue Horses Rush In* (University of Arizona Press, 1997); and, "Náneeskaadí" and "The Canyon Was Serene" were originally published in Tapahonso's *A Radiant Curve* (University of Arizona Press, 2008).

Elizabeth Woody: "Chinle Summer" was originally published in Woody's *Seven Hands, Seven Hearts: Prose and Poems* (Eighth Mountain Press, 1995); "Rosette" and "Wind's Movement" were originally published in *Luminaries of the Humble* by Elizabeth Woody. © 1994 The Arizona Board of Regents. Reprinted by permission of the University of Arizona Press.

Irene Nakai Hamilton: "Story of a Cricket, Spring 1978" and "Sunrise Flight into Acid Rain/ Cancelled" first appeared in the *South Corner of Time*, edited by Larry Evers (1980). "Dishwasher" appeared in the January 2019 issue of *Canyon Echo: A Journal of Southeastern Utah*.

Laura Tohe: "Our Tongues Slapped into Silence," "Joe Babes," and "Easter Sunday" from *No Parole Today*. Copyright © 1999 by Laura Tohe. Reprinted with the permission of The Permissions Company, LLC on behalf of West End Press, Albuquerque, New Mexico. "In Dinétah" and "Tsoodził, Mountain to the South" were originally published in *Sister Nations: Native American Women Writers on Community*, edited by Heid E. Erdrich and Laura Tohe (Minnesota Historical Society, 2002); "Deep in the Rock" and "Niłtsą́ Bi'áád/Female Rain" were originally published in Tohe's *Tséyi' Deep in the Rock: Reflections on Canyon de Chelly* (University of Arizona Press, 2005).

Rex Lee Jim: Versions of "Saad/Language/Voice," "Tó Háálį/Spring," and "Na'azheeh/Hunting" were originally published in Jim's *Dúchas Táá Kóó Diné: A Trilingual Poetry Collection in Navajo, Irish, and English* (Béal Feirste, 1998). Versions of these, including a revision of "Saad/Voice," were also previously published in Jim's *Saad Lá Tah Hózhóón: A Collection of Diné Poetry* (Salina Bookshelf, 2019). "Three Short Poems" was published in the November 3, 2010, issue of *Princeton Alumni Weekly* (paw.princeton.edu/article/video-poems-rex-lee-jim-86).

Irvin Morris: Selections from *From the Glittering World* were originally published in Morris's *From the Glittering World* (University of Oklahoma Press, 1997, revised edition, 2000).

Esther G. Belin: "Euro-American Womanhood Ceremony" and "Ruby's Answer" were originally published in Belin's *From the Belly of My Beauty* (University of Arizona Press, 1999); "Sustainability: A Romance in Four Scenes" was originally published in *Prairie Schooner*, vol. 86, no. 4, 2012; "Backbone" was originally published in Erv Schroeder's book of photographs, *The Memory of Stone: Meditations on the Canyons of the West* (University of New Mexico Press, 2014); "Emergence" was originally published in *Sister Nations: Native American Women Writers on Community*, edited by Heid E. Erdrich and Laura Tohe (Minnesota Historical Society, 2002); "Morning Song," "male + female divided," and "I keep my language in my back pocket like a special handkerchief that I only display when I want to show my manners in a respectful way" were originally published in Belin's *Of Cartography* (University of Arizona Press, 2017); "X+X+X+X−X−X−X" was originally published in *International Writing Program Collections: Narrative Witness 2: Indigenous Peoples, Australia-United States*, 2016 (http://www.iwpcollections.org/nw2-esther-belin).

Shonto Begay: "Darkness at Noon" and "Navajo Power Plant" were originally published in Begay's *Navajo Visions and Voices Across the Mesa* (Scholastic, 1995); "Drawing Life: Delineating My World" was originally published in *Flag Live!*'s "Letters from Home," March 12, 2015.

Della Frank: "Shimasani My Grandmother," "The Summer I Was 13," and "I Hate to See . . . " were originally published in Frank and Roberta D. Joe's *Storm Pattern: Poems from Two Navajo Women* (Navajo Community College Press, 1993).

Roberta D. Joe: "Emotional Illness," "Storm Pattern," "Sunset Woman's Ivy League Escape," and "Coyote Shuffle Romance" were originally published in Joe and Della Frank's *Storm Pattern: Poems from Two Navajo Women* (Navajo Community College Press, 1993).

Hershman John: "My Feminist Grandmother," "Storm Patterns," "The Dark World," and "A Strong Male Rain" were originally published in John's *I Swallow Turquoise for Courage* (University of Arizona Press, 2007).

Norla Chee: "Good-bye Honey, Hello Silver and Dust," "Wagon Ride," "Far Ahead in the Past," and "An Exhibit Tells the History of Diné Women Weaving" were originally published in Chee's *Cedar Smoke on Abalone Mountain* (UCLA American Indian Studies Center, 2001).

Sherwin Bitsui: "Asterisk," "The Northern Sun," and "Chrysalis" were originally published in Bitsui's *Shapeshift* (University of Arizona Press, 2003); excerpts from *Flood Song.* Copyright © 2009 by Sherwin Bitsui. Reprinted with the permission of The Permissions Company, Inc. on behalf of Copper Canyon Press, www.coppercanyonpress.org.

Dwayne Martine: "Parsing" and "Thought Knife" were originally published in *American Indian Culture and Research Journal*, vol. 38, no. 4, 2014; and "Hwéeldi" was originally published in *About Place*, vol. 3, no. 2, 2014.

Tacey Atsitty: Versions of "Ach'íí'," "In Strips," and "Calico Prints" were previously published in *Rain Scald* (University of New Mexico Press, 2018).

Venaya Yazzie: Earlier versions of "No Español" and "grandma loves SOBE" were published in Yazzie's *Livin' Matriarchal: Chapbook I* (2006); "The Pine Nut Eaters" was originally published in Lowell Jaeger's edited collection, *New Poets of the American West* (Many Voices Press, 2010).

Orlando White: the versions of "Sentence," "The i is a Cricket," "Fill in the Blank," and "Meditation" included here were originally published in *Bone Light* (Red Hen Press, 2009); the versions of "PAPER MILK," "n," and "DISSOCIATE" included here were originally published in LETT*ERRS* (Nightboat Books, 2015). © 2015 by Orlando White. Reprinted with permission of Nightboat Books.

Byron F. Aspaas: An earlier version of "Interstate Badlands," titled "Goodbye Once Upon a Time," was published in *Shapes of Native Nonfiction: Collected Essays by Contemporary Writers* (University of Washington Press, 2019).

Jake Skeets: "From Under His Cover" was originally published in the *James Franco Review* (January 2016). The versions of "Thieving Ceremony" and "Let There Be Coal" were published in *Eyes Bottle Dark with a Mouthful of Flowers*. Copyright © 2019 by Jake Skeets. Reprinted with the permission of The Permission Company, LLC on behalf of Milkweed Editions, Minneapolis, Minnesota.

Bojan Louis: "Currents" was originally published in Louis's *Currents* (BkMk Press, 2017) and "Nizhoní dóó 'a'ani' dóó até'él'í dóó ayoo'o'oni (Beauty & Memory & Abuse & Love)" was originally published in *As/Us* 4 (2014); the version included here was also published in *Shapes of Native Nonfiction*, edited by Elissa Washuta and Theresa Warburton (University of Washington Press, 2019).

Natanya Ann Pulley: "In This Dream of Waking, a Weaver" was originally published in *As/Us* 3 (2014); the version included here was also published in Pulley's *With Teeth* (New Rivers Press, 2019).

Danielle Geller: "Blood; Quantum" was originally published in *Brevity*, September 12, 2016.

Rachel Heather Johnson: "Apple" was originally published in *HEART: Human Equity Through Art* (September 2018).

Paige Buffington: "Radio" was originally published in "New Poetry by Indigenous Women," *LitHub*, curated by Natalie Diaz, 2018, lithub.com.

Erik Bitsui: "Marrying *Welcome to Hell*, a Hell-Made Match" and "Eddie and Norman, Norman and Me, Me and Eddie," were originally published in *Waxwing*, Winter 2019.

ABOUT THE EDITORS AND CONTRIBUTORS

ESTHER G. BELIN is a writer and multimedia artist. She is a Navajo Nation citizen and has lived in southwest Colorado for more than twenty years. A second-generation off-reservation Native American, she is a by-product of the U.S. federal Indian policies of termination and relocation. Her art and writing reflects the historical trauma from those policies as well as the philosophy of Saah Naagháí Bik'eh Hózho, the worldview of the Navajo people. Her writing is widely anthologized, and her latest volume of poetry, *Of Cartography*, examines identity politics, checkerboard land status, and the interplay of words (abstraction) and image (realism). In 2000, she won the American Book Award for her first book of poetry, *From the Belly of My Beauty*. She holds degrees from Antioch University, the Institute of American Indian Arts, and the University of California at Berkeley. Belin is currently a faculty mentor in the Low Rez MFA program at the Institute for American Indian Arts. www.estherbelin.com.

JEFF BERGLUND is a professor of English and a president's distinguished teaching fellow at Northern Arizona University. Berglund's research and teaching focuses on Native American literature, comparative Indigenous film, and U.S. multi-ethnic literature. His books include *Cannibal Fictions: American Explorations of Colonialism, Race, Gender, and Sexuality* (University of Wisconsin Press, 2006); *Sherman Alexie: a Collection of Critical Essays* (co-editor, University of Utah Press, 2010); *Indigenous Pop: Native American Music from Jazz to Hip Hop* (co-editor, University of Arizona Press, 2016); as well as *Indigenous Peoples Rise Up: The Global Ascendancy of Social Media Activism* (co-editor, Rutgers University Press, 2021). He is the author of articles on Native film, poetry, global Indigenous terminologies, and the pedagogy of American Indian literature. His other publications focus on Esther Belin; the Diné band, Blackfire; Diné filmmakers; Simon Ortiz; and The 1491s.

JENNIFER NEZ DENETDALE is Diné of the Navajo Nation and of the Tłógi and 'Áshįįhí clans. Originally from Tohatchi, New Mexico, she earned her PhD in history from Northern Arizona University in 1999 and is a professor of American studies at the University of New Mexico. As the first Diné to earn a PhD in history, Dr. Jennifer Denetdale is a strong advocate for Native people and strives to foster academic excellence in the next generation of students pursuing Native studies. She specializes in Navajo history and culture; Native American women, gender, and feminisms; and Indigenous nations, colonialism, and decolonization. Her book, *Reclaiming Diné History: The Legacies of Navajo Chief Manuelito and Juanita*, was published by the University of Arizona Press. She has published articles in *American Indian Culture and Research Journal, Journal of Social Archeology*, *New Mexico Historical Review*, and *Wíčazo Ša Review.* Dr. Denetdale also serves as the chair of the Navajo Nation Human Rights Commission.

CONNIE A. JACOBS is the author of *The Novels of Louise Erdrich: Stories of Her People* (Peter Lang, 2001) and co-editor of *Approaches to Teaching the Works of Louise Erdrich* (MLA, 2004). She has published an Oxford Bibliography Online entry on Erdrich, three book chapters, and various articles on Luci Tapahonso and Esther Belin. Her forthcoming publications include *Literary Sovereignty: Essays on a Continuing Indigenous Literary Aesthetic*, co-editor (University of Arizona Press, 2021); *Louise Erdrich's Justice Trilogy: Cultural and Critical Contexts*, co-edited (Michigan State University Press, 2021); and a conversation with Esther Belin for a Ukrainian collection of American Indian literary criticism edited by Oksana Shostak. She is professor emerita at San Juan College.

MICHAEL THOMPSON (Mvskoke Creek) was born in Holdenville, Oklahoma, and raised in south Georgia near the Flint River among pine trees, oaks, and swamp. He has a BA in English/journalism and an MEd and EdS from

Georgia Southern University. He has been a teacher for more than forty years in Georgia, Kansas, California, and New Mexico (primarily of English composition and literature). He recently retired from his position as the coordinator of alternative licensure at San Juan College and the site director of the Bisti Writing Project. He is married to Tina Deschenie (Diné), and between them, they have four children and several grandchildren.

ANTHONY K. WEBSTER is a linguistic anthropologist and professor of anthropology at the University of Texas at Austin. He also has affiliations with the Native American and Indigenous Studies Program and the Department of Linguistics. His work focuses primarily on verbal artistry, especially among Navajos. He's been doing this since 1997. He is the author of *Explorations in Navajo Poetry and Poetics* (2009), *Intimate Grammars: An Ethnography of Navajo Poetry* (2015), and *The Sounds of Navajo Poetry: A Humanities of Speaking* (2018). With Paul V. Kroskrity, he is co-editor of *The Legacy of Dell Hymes: Ethnopoetics, Narrative Inequality, and Voice* (2015). He lives in southern Illinois.